Media and Society

Media and Society: An Introduction, offers an interdisciplinary approach to media as means of social connection in everyday life and beyond.

Integrating theory and concrete analysis in case studies, exercises, and illustrative examples from around the world, *Media and Society: An Introduction* delivers a go-to reference work for learning about one of the essential social infrastructures of the twenty-first century. Standing on the shoulders of classic communication models, and covering legacies of research about media institutions, media texts, and media users, the chapters include both how-to sections on methods addressing current digital media forms and reflective segments that place TikTok, ChatGPT, and the emerging Internet of Things in the longer history of human communication.

As a comprehensive and up-to-date textbook on key conceptual, analytical, and normative issues facing students of media and communication today, this book is a practically applicable resource for teaching and learning about media, in the classroom, in self-study, and in different world regions. As such, it is a key resource for undergraduate students and professors in the fields of media, communication, and cultural studies.

Klaus Bruhn Jensen is Professor in the Department of Communication, University of Copenhagen, Denmark. His research and teaching emphasize communication theory, empirical research methodologies, and the history of media and communication. Recent publications include *A Handbook of Media and Communication Research: Qualitative and Quantitative Methodologies* (Routledge, 3rd edition, 2021), *A Theory of Communication of Justice* (Routledge, 2021), and *Comparing Communication Systems: The Internets of China, Europe, and the United States* (Routledge, 2023, coedited with Rasmus Helles).

Signe Sophus Lai is a tenure-track assistant professor at the Center for Tracking and Society, University of Copenhagen, Denmark. Her research and teaching are situated at the intersection between infrastructure studies, political economy of communication, and critical data studies, and are particularly focused on advancing new methods for empirical research on digital communication systems and infrastructural power. Recent publications include the monograph *Gateways: Comparing Digital Communication Systems in Nordic Welfare States* (2023, coauthored with Sofie Flensburg) as well as articles in *New Media & Society*, *Mobile Media & Communication*, *Big Data & Society*, and *Feminist Media Studies*.

Media and Society

An Introduction

Klaus Bruhn Jensen and Signe Sophus Lai

Routledge
Taylor & Francis Group

LONDON AND NEW YORK

Designed cover image: © naqiewei/ Getty Images

First published 2025
by Routledge
4 Park Square, Milton Park, Abingdon, Oxon OX14 4RN

and by Routledge
605 Third Avenue, New York, NY 10158

Routledge is an imprint of the Taylor & Francis Group, an informa business

British Library Cataloguing-in-Publication Data
A catalogue record for this book is available from the British Library

Library of Congress Cataloging-in-Publication Data
Names: Jensen, Klaus Bruhn, author. | Lai, Signe Sophus, author.
Title: Media and society : an introduction / Klaus Bruhn Jensen and Signe Sophus Lai.
Description: Abingdon, Oxon ; New York, NY : Routledge, 2025.|
Includes bibliographical references and index.
Identifiers: LCCN 2024018947 (print) | LCCN 2024018948 (ebook) |
ISBN 9781032655086 (hardback) | ISBN 9781032655048 (paperback) |
ISBN 9781032655109 (ebook)
Subjects: LCSH: Mass media–Social aspects.
Classification: LCC HM1206 .J46 2025 (print) | LCC HM1206 (ebook) |
DDC 302.23–dc23/eng/20240729
LC record available at https://lccn.loc.gov/2024018947
LC ebook record available at https://lccn.loc.gov/2024018948

ISBN: 9781032655086 (hbk)
ISBN: 9781032655048 (pbk)
ISBN: 9781032655109 (ebk)

DOI: 10.4324/9781032655109

Typeset in Times New Roman
by Newgen Publishing UK

Contents

Figures

Images

Tables

Boxes

Analysis

Notes on the authors

Klaus Bruhn Jensen is Professor in the Department of Communication, University of Copenhagen, Denmark. His research and teaching emphasize communication theory, empirical research methodologies, and the history of media and communication. Recent publications include the *International Encyclopedia of Communication Theory and Philosophy* (Wiley-Blackwell, 2016, 4 vols. and online, coedited with Robert T. Craig), *A Handbook of Media and Communication Research: Qualitative and Quantitative Methodologies* (Routledge, 3rd edition, 2021), *A Theory of Communication of Justice* (Routledge, 2021), *Media Convergence: The Three Degrees of Network, Mass, and Interpersonal Communication* (Routledge, 2nd edition, 2022), and *Comparing Communication Systems: The Internets of China, Europe, and the United States* (Routledge, 2023, coedited with Rasmus Helles). He is a Fellow of the International Communication Association, Life Member for Service of the Association of Internet Researchers, an Affiliate of the International Panel on the Information Environment, an elected member of Academia Europaea, and a recipient of the Royal Danish Order of Dannebrog.

Signe Sophus Lai is a tenure-track assistant professor at the University of Copenhagen, in its Center for Tracking and Society, Department of Communication. Her research and teaching are situated at the intersection between infrastructure studies, political economy of communication, and critical data studies. She is particularly engaged in advancing new methods for empirical research on digital communication systems and in raising a critical research agenda on digital infrastructural power. Her latest book, *Gateways: Comparing Digital Communication Systems in Nordic Welfare States* (2023, coauthored with Sofie Flensburg), investigates the political economy of digital infrastructures in the Nordics. Recent publications also include articles on digital communication systems and infrastructures in the *International Journal of Communication* and *Media, Culture & Society*, on datafication and tracking in *New Media & Society* and *Mobile Media & Communication*, and on digital methods and digital inequalities in *Big Data & Society* and *Feminist Media Studies*.

1   Media, communication, and society

The meaning of media

We ascribe **meaning** to the countless events – private and public – that we encounter in daily life and throughout our lives. But we experience a significant portion of both distant and close events secondhand, in and by media and communication. Especially the modern **media** of the last 500 years – from printed books to the internet – have enabled people to place themselves in wider social, historical, and existential perspectives. Media produce and circulate meaning in society, and as media users we each reflect on, communicate about, and go on to act on these meanings.

Certain news stories will attract intense public interest, but may nevertheless be forgotten within a day or two. Other news resonates with common frames of reference, and may turn into symbols with a long life in the media and in their users' experience and memory (Images 1.1 and 1.2). Fictional texts, too – television series and YouTube videos as well as theater performances and art exhibits – are forms of **communication** that enter into a common **culture**, slowly and incrementally, as they are interpreted and processed over time by audiences and publics. Culture constitutes sediments of meaning – when excavated, layers of meaning feed a better understanding of past and present. Here and now, it is the concrete contents and forms of communication that relate media, users, and society. But, over time, communication accumulates as culture – which delivers the background to ever more communication, about society as it is, but also how it could and, perhaps, ought to develop in the future. And, from time to time, communication centers on the media themselves – what they are, could be, and ought to be – in public debate, through research, and with textbooks such as this.

It takes a fair amount of digging into the long run of history to gain a broader and deeper understanding of the relationship between media and society. The brief of media and communication research is to describe, interpret, and explain how different media support various forms of communication and other social interaction, as they unfold in multiple steps, flows, and contexts throughout local and global settings. The focus of this book is the media of the 2020s. But we make

DOI: 10.4324/9781032655109-1

Image 1.1a Climate change around the world. Photo by Marcus Kauffman on Unsplash.

Image 1.1b Climate change around the world. Photo by Chamika Jayasri on Unsplash.

Media coverage of events such as droughts (here, in Sri Lanka) and forest fires (in California) invites audiences to participate in the production and circulation of meaning in society, locally and globally: about the vulnerability and impo-tence of humanity vis-à-vis nature, and about the human (ab)uses of Earth's resources driving climate change and extreme weather events.

a special point of relating contemporary media to the much longer history in which humans have navigated their natural and social circumstances through the media available to them, in order to make sense of, engage with, and act in and on the world around them. Today's media literally constitute an environment – a **media environment** – that has emerged across decades and centuries, and which conditions human existence and social coexistence into the future.

Two questions sum up distinctive approaches to analysis of the production and circulation of meaning in society (Jensen, 1991):

- *Where* is meaning? – Meaning can be understood as the contents of delimited containers or carriers such as news articles, feature films, or apps. Meaning is a **product** located 'inside' media; which was placed there by journalists, film directors, or app developers; and which audiences subsequently extract and interpret. In this perspective, communication amounts to a **transmission** of information from sender to receiver. News media continuously document the casualties and economic costs of droughts and forest fires; the feature film *Don't Look Up* (Adam McKay, 2021) offered a satirical treatment of the low interest scientists encounter when delivering urgent messages about the climate crisis to policymakers; and a variety of apps enable internet users to measure their personal carbon footprints and limit their emissions through suggested lifestyle changes.
- *When* is meaning? – Meaning can also be understood as a **process** with complicated trajectories and variable outcomes, depending on the participation of a wide variety of social agents. News articles, feature films, and apps are not one-take productions by journalists, directors, and developers; they emerge as mean-ingful narratives and services from the collaboration of multiple individuals and professions in a particular historical time and cultural place. The users of news, films, and apps, equally, ascribe meaning to media, interpreting contents and approaching functionalities in light of their personal background as well as wider social settings and cultural circumstances. In doing so, media users participate in a **ritual** generating a shared cultural experience (Carey, 1989b/1975), which over time contributes to building diverse **imagined communities** (Anderson, 1991) relating people from the local to the global level of social organization.

The two theoretical perspectives – communication as transmission or ritual, and culture as product or process – have traditionally been understood as conflicted and opposed. Recent media and communication research, however, has come to emphasize their complementarity and potential integration. Communication is both transmission and ritual. Meaning is a product as well as a process. And society is, at once, a relatively stable structure and a contingent configuration, subject to change, as the senders and receivers of media communicate in and about the society they share and, to a degree, shape.

NEW VISION

Japan appreciates Uganda's efforts to end Russia-Ukraine war

◷ Aug 03, 2023

It is important to achieve a just and lasting peace in Ukraine as soon as possible, Japan's foreign affairs minister, Hayashi Yoshimasa said this on Wednesday in Kampala.

Image 1.2 War in Europe, as observed from the Global South. Courtesy of New Vision/
        Vision Group – Uganda.

Russia's invasion of Ukraine on February 24, 2022, marked the outbreak of war in Europe for the first time since the end of World War II in 1945. Both the initial invasion and subsequent fighting gave rise to massive news coverage and public debate in the media of Europe and other parts of the Global North. Media in the Global South, such as The New Vision *daily in Uganda, carried regionally inflected perspectives on the conflict, reflecting a world divided both on the heroes and villains of the war, and on potential allies and adversaries in a present and future of renewed geopolitical tensions.*

The rest of this introductory chapter provides a framework for the presentation, in subsequent chapters, of theories and methods for analyzing, interpreting, and explaining the interrelations between media and society. The framework is premised on three key concepts:

- **Media of three degrees** – We distinguish three types or 'degrees' of media: human beings, classic mass media, and digital media.
- **Communication in three steps** – The common practice of communication intersects the three degrees of media, in three and often further steps.
- **Social action** – Communication constitutes a distinctive form of human action and social interaction, negotiating what to think and do, as communities, societies, and species. Media and communication, further, lend orientation to the many individual and collective actions that we perform every day, and which maintain and, to an extent, modify the political, economic, and cultural institutions that are the basic building blocks of society.

Media of three degrees

We begin with an invitation to the typical, youngish reader of this book: Ask your parents, or grandparents, what was meant by **mass media** and **mass communication** when *they* were about your age. Beginning in the 1990s, it became common to speak simply of 'media.' The altered terminology reflected the introduction of more and different types of media, and these several media, further, seemed to be merging in a so-called **convergence** of media (see Chapter 3, p. 117). For much of the twentieth century, it had been commonsensical to contrast, on the one hand, conversations between two or a few individuals and, on the other hand, communication by one (mass) medium to a large number of dispersed individuals – **interpersonal communication** as compared to mass communication. With the diffusion of the internet and mobile media throughout the world, it was becoming almost self-evident that media are, in fact, several different things – 'legacy' print and broadcast media as well as websites and social media such as Facebook, LinkedIn, and TikTok. In the process, communicative practices came to include much more than traditional one-to-one and one-to-many interactions: On social media, the many were now in a position to communicate to and with many others, too. And communication was crossing and blurring once familiar boundaries between work, education, and leisure, and between private and public areas of social life.

The historical shift sketched briefly here, presented research with the challenge of devising a conception of media that would be sufficiently broad and, at the same time, precise enough for analytical purposes. In fact, the very ideas of 'communication' and 'media' are surprisingly recent, given the long histories of humans speaking, writing, and printing their experience of and engagement with reality. It was only toward the end of the 1800s that **communication** came to be used as a common denominator for conversation and technologically mediated communication – in response to the breakthrough of the 'new' media of the time: the telegraph and telephone, and later film and radio (Peters, 1999). Similarly, it was not until the period after 1945 that **media** came to be thought of as one, general, inclusive category. By then, mass media had become thoroughly ingrained in social life, and different mass media could be seen to offer different perspectives on society and reality as such. A primary distinction was made between print and electronic media (radio and television). The Canadian media theorist Marshall McLuhan (1964) pinpointed the different implications of different types of media in his famous saying: "The medium is the message." Each medium could be said to carry an 'extra' message, above and beyond the information 'in itself.' Even if a television news story and a newspaper article – or a feature film and a novel – in a sense deliver the 'same' facts and fictions, they nevertheless give rise to distinctive experiences of the narratives they relay to readers, listeners, and viewers.

Definitions of media and communication, thus, have evolved in response to the introduction of new technologies and their embedding in society. Media and communication research, in its turn, has been at work specifying and differentiating conceptions of media and communication in several rounds. Human beings, first of all, constitute a form of media in their own right, communicating in the flesh. Only a relatively few people will witness particular instances of drought, forest fires, or death and destruction in Ukraine; many more come to see and hear about what happened through the internet and other communication technologies; and perhaps most people will learn about events from others they already know – and who have received word from established media organizations. It is these several intersecting flows of information and communication that motivate our reference to media of three 'degrees,' rather than to separate 'types.' 'New' media have emerged historically from, and have embedded 'old' media within them (Jensen, 2022). Today, the three degrees of media are interlaced to a remarkable extent, each passing on what had first been presented in and by another degree of media.

Media of the first degree are human beings – formally defined as biologically based and socially shaped resources with the distinctive capability of articulating an understanding of reality in signs and symbols, and subsequently communicating with others about this understanding. Less formally expressed, human beings – body and mind – are the point of reference for all other media. Although the human species has extended itself in remarkable ways across time and space through technologies, the intentions behind and interpretations of technologically mediated communication remain centered in humans. One of the philosophers of Greek antiquity, Protagoras, declared that humans are the measure of all things. The long history and much longer natural evolution of communication by embodied human beings (Lull, 2020) serve as a reminder and corrective whenever contemporary commentators may be tempted to conclude that new media are about to fundamentally change the human condition.

Sense impressions become communications when we receive and process diverse inputs through a great variety of perceptual, cognitive, and cultural competences, translating and sharing them in signs and symbols for others to receive and process. The human body constitutes the material platform (comparable to **technologies**) for different **modalities** of expression and representation. The primary example, for media of the first degree, is speech or verbal language. Other modalities include song, dance, drama, and visual arts, as associated with aesthetic forms of expression, supported by pens, brushes, musical instruments, and other tools. In all of these instances, communication depends on the simultaneous presence of sender and receiver in local time and space.

Media of the second degree comprise what, until recently, was referred to as (mass) media: technically reproduced and supported means of communication that do not require the physical presence of audiences, ranging from printed books, newspapers, and magazines to film, radio, and television. Their distinctive features are, first, the 1:1 reproduction, storage, and dissemination of a particular content, and, second, a radically enhanced potential for disseminating this content across time and space. One famous characterization of the social uses and consequences of such media was offered by the German philosopher Walter Benjamin, who spoke of "the age of technical reproduction" (Benjamin, 1977/1936), with special reference to the spread of photography, film, and radio in the late nineteenth and early twentieth centuries. In a longer historical perspective, the printed book occupies a special place among media of the second degree. Books enabled the wider dissemination and greater standardization (and hence practical applicability) of scientific ideas and political ideologies (Eisenstein, 1979). The printing press, therefore, became a key condition in pivotal social and cultural changes such as the European Renaissance, the Christian Reformation, and the gradual breakthrough and consolidation of political democracy as a form of governance in different nation-states and world regions.

Because **handwriting** and drawings record speech, music, and other modalities in relatively fixed formats (manuscripts and sheet music as well as other artworks), it is debatable whether it ought to be treated as a separate degree of media. Manuscripts replaced oral transmission as the infrastructure passing on a cultural heritage from generation to generation, and for millennia (see Table 1.1), manuscripts supported large and complex systems of governance, trade, and science in different parts of the world. The printing press, however, offered a vastly more efficient means of reproducing and distributing any and all kinds of information (Meyrowitz, 1994: 54). In this book – and in the contemporary perspective of media and communication research – we consider handwriting a medium of the first degree: Historically, it was reproduced locally and with great human effort (through laborious copying with a considerable margin for errors, some intentional, some not), and it was distributed in a highly selective fashion, within established social hierarchies, typically accompanied by oral commentaries from political or religious authorities on how the message should (not) be understood.

Media of the second degree reproduced modalities that were entirely familiar from media of the first degree – speech, song, sketches, and more – but in altered shapes. Early printed books, for example, would 'mime' the layout of handwritten manuscripts, including elaborate drawings and other visual effects. Media of the second degree, in a sense, translated the *contents* of media of the first degree to new *forms* of expression and dissemination. Speaking on the radio turned out as a quite different practice from giving a lecture face-to-face with an audience; performing on film or television required considerable adaptation of the techniques that actors had mastered on the theater stage. This transfer, adjustment, and **remediation** (Bolter & Grusin, 1999) of cultural conventions and traditions has been a continuous process throughout the history of human communication, and reached a new degree with the digitalization of communication and other social practices.

Media of the third degree refer to digital media. On the one hand, digital media reproduce and recombine all previous media in one medium; on the other hand, digital technologies afford additional ways of representing reality and interacting socially. Digital media, then, can be understood as **metamedia** (Kay & Goldberg, 1999 [1977]), that is, media providing access to several other kinds of media. Their foundation is the digital, programmable computer. The principles of computing enable the simulation *both* of good old-fashioned conversation *and* of mass communication, *as well as* entirely new forms of many-to-many communication as associated with social media.

In the 2020s, the key examples of media of the third degree remain various kinds of 'personal' computers and 'mobile' media – smartphones, tablets, and notebooks – linked and networked through the internet. These 'platforms' and 'interfaces,' however, are likely to change as digital technologies are embedded in physical reality at more granular levels and further adapted to the human senses. Such developments help explain why computers of the future have been referred to as *ubiquitous* (present everywhere) and *pervasive* (present in everything). One prospect is an *Internet of Things* (IoT): Already, cars, refrigerators, heat pumps, and other consumer items amount to computers that can be programmed by users, and which are subject to surveillance by public authorities as part of the regulation of traffic and the planning of energy systems. In several additional steps, both natural and built environments may become part of globalized networks of information and interaction. We return, in the last chapter of the book, to these future perspectives, asking whether ongoing developments may entail a transition to media of a **fourth degree**.

Media history so far indicates that the three degrees of media recycle each other to a great extent and in distinctive ways, not in a one-way process of 'the new' replacing 'the old,' but as part of an extended interchange in which new media both inherit and redevelop the formats of old media. The graphic user interfaces (GUI) of personal computers and smartphones have taken inspiration from the long legacy of conventions developed for book and newspaper layout as well as for flow television. Correspondingly, current affairs and sports programming on television has imported the overlapping 'windows' of computer screens to offer viewers several flows of information simultaneously. And the forms of communication associated particularly with social media can be seen to simulate media of the first degree: The informality of everyday conversation reappears in messaging systems and posts to social media, for instance (what was formerly known as) tweets (still awaiting the consolidation of a new terminology at the time of writing, after Twitter in 2023 became the service known today as X).

Figure 1.1 lays out the interrelations between media of the first, second, and third degrees. The model may be taken as the great wheel of human culture turning, circulating diverse contents and forms of expression, between media and across society, through the historically available technologies and institutions. The model

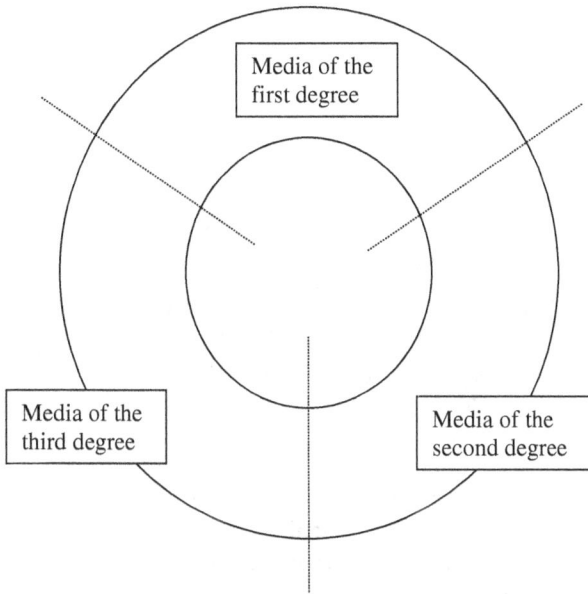

Figure 1.1 Media of three degrees.

recognizes aspects of historical continuity as well as discontinuity: Whereas media of the third degree followed media of the second degree, just as media of the second degree had departed from media of the first degree, in certain respects media of the third degree represent a return to forms of communication characteristic of media of the first degree. Digital media provide new resources of informal interaction, across time and space, but also right now, right here.

These brief introductory descriptions together suggest that, for each degree of medium, three sets of features must be considered to begin analyses of their potential uses and place in larger social structures:

- *Materials.* From the human body as a biologically based medium to the latest digital technology, physical matter – for instance, paper and metal, too – has been processed to make certain forms of communication possible, while others have remained *impossible* (so far). It was only from the late 1800s that sound recordings enabled the preservation of a significant part of the cultural heritage, which until then had literally disappeared into thin air. From the 1910s, portable gramophones made recorded sound mobile. From 1979, the Walkman allowed its individual users to create so-called *soundscapes*, at once mobile and private. And since around 2000, mobiles and smartphones have brought deeply private interactions into public spaces.
- *Modalities.* Communication depends on diverse materials, but also on immaterial forms of experience and expression – modalities. On the one hand, the human

senses – primarily sight and hearing – are conditions and common denominators for all human communication. It is through language, music, and still and moving images (including the configuration of letters on book pages, web pages, and in apps) that others (perhaps) are able to understand what we mean. On the other hand, these means of expression have been subject to a great range and depth of cultivation throughout human history. And **multimodality** – the combination of several modalities such as music and moving images in one message – became a distinctive feature, first of cinema and television, later of digital media. (And, importantly, also face-to-face interaction has evident multimodal features, as spoken verbal language is joined by nonverbal or so-called body language.)

· *Institutions.* Speech, manuscripts, printed books, newspapers, magazines, film, radio, television, the internet – all of these media took shape as social institutions in particular historical periods and cultural settings. Each medium was modeled, in part, on one or more familiar media, and each subsequently developed in response to the introduction of additional media and the resulting reconfiguration of the full media environment. Television was understood from the outset, like radio, as a medium for use in and by private households, even if it might equally well have been organized and institutionalized along the lines of cinemas or community centers. Today, television viewing also takes place en route to and from the cinema – on smartphones and laptops.

Box 1.1 Exercise

Old media and new media environments

Go through Table 1.1 about the changing forms of media and communication throughout history – then ask yourself:

1. Which developments (minimum of two, maximum of five) have had the greatest impact on how people communicate in the present day?
2. Argue for your choices to your fellow students. Discuss arguments for and against the choice of particular developments as the most important, and as a group produce a top-three list of developments.

Table 1.1 ends in 2015. But media and communicative practices keep changing. In 2023, for instance, Twitter was rebranded as X under the leadership of Elon Musk, the richest man in the world. With fellow students, describe what could be considered the most important developments since 2015 in the domain of media and communication, and choose a minimum of one, maximum of two.

3. Discuss whether one or both of these developments belong among the top three ever.

Table 1.1 The long history of human communication

Media of the first degree

c. 50–150,000 BCE	spoken language
c. 40,000 BCE	cave paintings
c. 3,000 BCE	hieroglyphics and cuneiform writing
c. 2,500 BCE	Linear A writing system
c. 1,450 BCE	Linear B writing system
c. 1,200 BCE	logographic writing (China)
c. 800 BCE	phonetic alphabet (Greece)

Media of the second degree

1040	printing with loose type (China)
1377	printing with metal type (Korea)
1450s	printing with loose metal type and hand press (Johannes Gutenberg, Germany)
1605	newspaper (Germany)
1839	photography
1844	telegraph
1867	typewriter
1876	telephone
1888	gramophone
1895	public film exhibition
1895	radio transmission
1911	television transmission
1920	scheduled radio broadcasts
1936	scheduled television broadcasts
1948	long-playing records (LP) for gramophone
1956	videotape
1957	satellite (Sputnik)
1962	television transmission via satellite
1963	cassette tape
1976	VHS videotape
1978	telefax (with international standard)
1979	Walkman
1982	audio CD

Media of the third degree

1936	theoretical basis for the digital computer (Alan M. Turing)
1938	*the World Brain*, prediction of an archive covering all human knowledge (H.G. Wells)
1945	first draft for a programmable computer (John von Neumann); the idea of links between documents (Vannevar Bush)
1946	first electronic programmable computer, ENIAC
1965	the concept of "hypertext" (Theodore H. Nelson)
1969	ARPANET, under ARPA (Advanced Research Projects Agency) of the U.S. Department of Defense
1971	first email program; first microprocessor

(Continued)

Table 1.1 (Continued)

1972	File Transfer Protocol (FTP) for upload and download of digital files; the @ sign in email program on ARPANET
1973	first international ARPANET connection (from the U.S. to the U.K. via Norway)
1974	TelNet, first public data service as commercial version of ARPANET
1975	first personal computer (MITS Altair 8800); first ARPANET mailing list
1976	first Apple computer
1977	first gaming console (Atari 2600)
1978	first MUD (Multi-User Dungeon)
1979	news groups on USENET; first emoticons in emails
1981	IBM's Personal Computer (PC); first portable computer (Adam Osborne I, weighing 12 kg)
1982	digital CD audio format (Philips or Sony); Simple Mail Transfer Protocol (SMTP), standard for email; Commodore 64 computer
1983	TCP/IP (Transmission Control Protocol/Internet Protocol) as internet standard
1984	Apple MacIntosh: first computer with "mouse," graphic user interface, and WYSIWYG ("what-you-see-is-what-you-get"); Domain Name System (DNS) of internet; first reference to cyberspace (William Gibson's novel *Neuromancer*)
1985	Microsoft Windows 1.0; Commodore Amiga computer
1986	LISTSERV, first mailing-list software
1988	Internet Relay Chat (IRC)
1989	Tim Berners-Lee's proposal for an internet-based hypertext system, later the World Wide Web; Game Boy console
1990	National Science Foundation Net (NSFNET) replaces ARPANET
1991	U.S. Department of Defense leaves internet collaboration; end of restrictions on commercial use of the internet; World Wide Web (www) published by CERN; Gopher, first point-and-click hypertext navigation
1992	Moving Picture Expert Group approval of MPEG-1 as standard for compression of video or audio, including Audio Layer 3 (MP3); reference to "surfing" the internet
1993	first graphic web browser (Mosaic)
1994	Netscape Navigator 1.0 browser; PlayStation console; first online store; first cyberbank; first banner advertising; first radio stations on internet; Amazon.com; Yahoo!

Table 1.1 (Continued)

1995	NSFNET leaves internet collaboration; Microsoft Internet Explorer browser; Java software; eBay auction site; Wiki software
1996	Hotmail; Nintendo 64 computer; Ultima Online role-playing game
1997	Netflix DVD-by-mail service; IBM's Deep Blue computer beats incumbent world chess champion
1998	Google Inc.; PayPal payments system
1999	Rich Site Summary or Really Simple Syndication (RSS); Napster music sharing system; blogger.com
2000	beginning of dot-com crisis; Tripadvisor comparison website
2001	Apple iPod; Xbox gaming console; *Wikipedia*; Napster declared illegal and relaunched as subscription service
2002	Last.fm music website; first flash mobs in New York City, organized via the internet
2003	MySpace and LinkedIn social media platforms; WordPress web content management system; Skype internet phone system; iTunes; Second Life online virtual world
2004	Facebook; Google Gmail; World of Warcraft online role-playing game
2005	YouTube; Google Earth
2006	Twitter; YouTube bought by Google; WikiLeaks, publisher of leaked, secret documents
2007	iPhone 1.0; Netflix video-on-demand platform; Google Street View
2008	App Store; Spotify; Dropbox
2009	Google Docs; WhatsApp; Bitcoin currency
2010	iPad; Instagram; Pinterest
2011	WeChat social media platform (China); Snapchat
2012	Tinder dating app; Facebook exceeds 1 billion users; *Gangnam Style* first YouTube video with 1 billion viewers
2013	Netflix and YouTube together account for 50% of internet traffic
2015	Google searches from mobile devices exceed desktop searches; 1 billion Facebook users on a single day

Sources: Dansk mediehistorie [Danish media history], vol. 4 (Jensen, 2016); *A Handbook of Media and Communication Research* (Jensen, 2021).

Communication in three steps

The study of media and communication emerged as a separate academic field, with university departments, journals, and international conferences, around the middle of the twentieth century (Park & Pooley, 2008; Simonson et al., 2013). The background was the growing importance of print and electronic media in society, not least as carriers of advertising and in political life. As media became part of the economic, political, and cultural infrastructures of society, both analyses of their operations and graduates that were competent in the study as well as the practical administration of media were in increasing demand. At the same time, it had become a common public perception that media could have strong effects on people's attitudes and actions, affecting anything from political opinions and shifting fashions to everyday shopping. But several early studies found that, in fact, the media did not have the sort of massive or direct effects on their audiences that different stakeholders variously feared and hoped for (Katz & Lazarsfeld, 1955; Lazarsfeld et al., 1944). The findings, instead, suggested that media (of the second degree) enter into **two-step flows**: Media make information available, which so-called **opinion leaders** (media of the first degree) next refer to in conversations with family, friends, acquaintances, and colleagues, either incidentally or in an attempt to have them adopt specific viewpoints and positions: Buy this commodity! Vote for this politician! A two-step flow, then, served to couple **mass communication** and **interpersonal communication**.

Although the two-step-flow model has been contested (Gitlin, 1978), it delivered an important contribution to a more nuanced understanding of human communication, including mass communication, as a process unfolding in several stages and with a wide range of potential effects, strong and weak, at different levels of society. The coming of digital media has lent renewed relevance to the understanding of communication as a multistep process. When people share a news item, a joke, or an everyday occurrence, either broadly on their preferred social media or to a small number of contacts in closed groups, they engage in **many-to-many** communication: The stream of information and subsequent posts, likes, and shares may continue across people, platforms, and contexts in unpredictable numbers of steps and evolving patterns. And many-to-many communication is coupled to **one-to-many** as well as **one-to-one** communication: News and jokes frequently originate from established media organizations or famous influencers (one category of opinion leaders in today's media environment), who communicate **one-to-many**, just as news items or fun facts are staples of **one-to-one** communication, face-to-face and through technological mediation. Digital media, in short, have facilitated new steps and streams of communication that amount to what has come to be referred to, today, as **networks**. While two-step flows connected local networks, digital media in general and the internet in particular support much larger and more complex networks. Analyses of digital media and communication are well advised to consider **three-step flows**, comprising one-to-one, one-to-many, as well as many-to-many interactions (Jensen, 2009) to account for the media–society juncture.

It is essential to note, further, that the different *steps* of two-step and three-step communication commonly represent different *types* of communication and involve different *categories* of communicators. The earliest study identifying the role of two-step flows, examining a presidential election campaign in the United States in 1940 (Lazarsfeld et al., 1944), recognized a basic difference between, on the one hand, radio newscasters, newspaper journalists, and columnists addressing listeners and readers and, on the other hand, these listeners and readers engaging in conversation about the candidates for office and their political programs. In the twenty-first century, equally, political debates on television or online assessing the policies and performances of candidates, evidently differ from the interactions among ordinary voters on social media or the platforms made available by news media and party organizations.

Three-step flows, then, do not entail information simply flowing from point A to point B and on to point C – say, from a national or international news organization via local opinion leaders and into their networks. In some cases, information flows in the opposite direction, for example, when heated debates on social media are picked up by journalists and other attentive users, carrying over to traditional news media, which may in turn feed into policy debates, legislative initiatives, and other political processes. The concept of a three-step flow points to the more or less likely combination in concrete instances of certain basic forms of communication, whose trajectories and outcomes must be examined in empirical and contextual detail. According to the United Nations' Universal Declaration of Human Rights, adopted in 1948, all humans have the same right to express themselves in political and other matters. In practice, however, the opportunities to gain a voice, to be heard, and to achieve influence differ in fundamental ways. Not all media or steps of communication are created equal.

Figure 1.2 joins communication in three steps with media of three degrees (Jensen & Helles, 2011). Along the vertical axis are listed the three forms of communication that unfold one-to-one, one-to-many, and many-to-many, highlighting that all three occur in all three degrees of media, even if each form constitutes the prototype of one degree of medium. One-to-one communication is associated, on historical and evolutionary timescales, with humans as media; one-to-many communication with mass media of the modern period; and many-to-many communication with digital media of the past few decades. These three configurations of technologies and institutions – the media of three degrees – are laid out on the horizontal axis of the figure.

The figure suggests both a historical point and a systematic point. In historical perspective, different media have facilitated distinctive forms of communication – communicating with many others is so much easier via messenger apps than it would have been standing in a marketplace or town square. In a systematic perspective, the figure reiterates the insight that new media do not replace or displace old media; instead, they inherit and redevelop forms of communication thoroughly familiar from old media. Different degrees of media, moreover, complement each other in the present: Maintaining contact with friends

Communication	Media		
	Media **of the first degree**	Media **of the second degree**	Media **of the third degree**
One-to-one	PROTOTYPE Face-to-face conversation, hand-written letter	Telegraph, telephone, fax	Email, text message, instant messaging, IP telephony
One-to-many	Manuscript, theater, painting, sculpture, architecture, musical composition	PROTOTYPE Book, newspaper, magazine, broadcasting, audio and video recording	Web 1.0 / webpage, download, streaming (mass) media
Many-to-many	Cave painting, gaming, graffiti, notice board, agora, marketplace, stadium	Community media, public-access radio and television, telephone chat services	PROTOTYPE Web 2.0 / wiki, file- sharing site, online chat, massively multiplayer online gaming, social network site, blog, auction site

Figure 1.2 Communication in three steps.

and family on social media has not led people to abandon frequent interactions face-to-face with the same people. On the contrary, conversations particularly with one's strong ties and close networks continue across media and contexts. Communication is a fundamental way of being social – and when we communicate, we act in and on society.

Communication and action

Thinking before speaking – and before acting – is sound proverbial advice. These figures of speech normally refer to individuals. However, collectives and communities are also well advised to communicate before they act. Families, organizations, corporations, and entire societies communicate as they move toward and finally arrive at decisions with implications for all their members, a majority, or even a small minority. Communication is a distinctive kind of social action that anticipates and evaluates a wide variety of other actions: What can and ought we (not) to do? In theory as well as in practice, human communication and social action are intertwined in three different respects.

First, whether they were intended as such or not, actions constitute communications in and of themselves. **Action is communication**. There was a clear intention behind Russia's invasion of Ukraine on February 24, 2022 (Image 1.2). Many lives have been lost, and material resources destroyed, in the pursuit of a manifest purpose, at once military and symbolic, namely, the reassertion of Russian power and influence both regionally and geopolitically. At the opposite end of a scale of intention, we find body language or nonverbal communication, which commonly does not carry such a specific or explicit message. And yet, anyone watching the television coverage of frightened people on the run in the streets of Ukrainian cities could understand their body language. Even physical objects, chance events, and nature can be considered meaningful. Depending on political or religious persuasion, droughts and forest fires (Image 1.1a and 1.1b) may be interpreted as nature's response to human (ab)uses across decades and centuries, or as a message from a deity punishing humanity for its sins against the rest of nature.

Second, communications carry out actions, with a purpose and in a context. Saying something means doing something – **communication is action**. This understanding has been elaborated in philosophy and other academic disciplines under the heading of speech-act theory (Austin, 1962; Searle, 1969). When speaking to and with others about local or global events, about mutual friends, or about the weather, we engage in the maintenance of our social relations. The insight was originally formulated by the philosopher Ludwig Wittgenstein (1953), who concluded that language, rather than providing a representation of an already existing reality, is a medium in which we collectively construct versions of reality. Through the use of verbal language and, indeed, all our communications, we engage in what Wittgenstein termed **language games**. And these games, importantly, are not played for fun: The game of communication is serious business, because we live our lives *within* language, *within* communication, and, thus, *within* society. In media and communication research, the speech-act perspective aligns with the understanding of communication, already noted, as ritual: Reality is continuously "produced, maintained, repaired, and transformed" (Carey, 1989b/1975: 23) through diverse media and in multiple communicative steps.

Third, communication anticipates action – in view of what has happened in the past, the present state of things, and what could and should (not) be done in the future. **Communication is a reflective form of action** – in and by communication, we reflect on ourselves, on others, and on society. Communication establishes moments and spaces for people to reflect and deliberate in common, consider and resolve disagreements, doubt one's own initial position, and change one's mind. Such moments and spaces have been referred to as 'possible worlds' (Divers, 2002). Another philosopher, Karl R. Popper, distinguished three categories of worlds. World 1 is the world of physical objects and states – the world 'out there.' The corresponding World 2 'in here' – in my mind – is the world of consciousness, mental states, and the readiness to act in relation to objects, humans, and social contexts. World 3, lastly, relates the first two worlds, and may take a variety of forms, from scientific accounts to fictional narratives – this is "the world of the objective contents of thought" (Popper, 1972: 106). In this last world of communication, people are in a position to express themselves, to engage with material as well as imagined realities, and to articulate their biggest dreams and worst fears in words and images.

The concept of communication as action is key to understanding the relationship between media and society, and has been elaborated in several disciplines and interdisciplinary fields feeding into media and communication research. 'Actions' are carried out by humans, but also by technologies, and increasingly by humans and technologies in concert. This is the case especially for digital media that afford **interactivity**: Humans act together *with* – and *through* – digital media in distinctive ways (Jensen, 1999; Kiousis, 2002; McMillan, 2002), as most recently illustrated by chatbots and other artificial intelligence (AI) technologies. Interactivity is sometimes associated narrowly with the technical design of the 'human-machine' interface to facilitate user-friendliness or usability and a good user experience (UX). But the very idea of interactivity raises basic questions of how media enter into interactions between individuals, and between the individuals and larger social entities and structures.

To address these questions, we first return to **sociology** – the science of society – which for more than a century has relied on **interaction** as one its key analytical concepts. One premise of sociology is that it is inter-action – coordination and collaboration among persons, but also among social institutions such as parliaments and stock exchanges – which makes society, of any kind and size, possible. Even when controversies or conflicts occur, for instance, between social classes, political parties, or ethnic groups, these entities can nevertheless be seen to interact with each other: Although the parties direct their actions *against* one another, they inevitably relate to and interact *with* each other.

The concept of interaction has subsequently been transferred from sociology to **computer science** and translated as 'interactivity,' highlighting the features that distinguish human–machine interaction from human–human interaction. Since the 1960s, the subfield of computer science known as **human–computer interaction** (HCI) has explored the nature of this general process, and has contributed to practical improvements of the interfaces and exchanges relating digital devices and their human users (Jacko, 2012).

In a third and final step, **media and communication research**, since the 1980s, has been seeking to combine and integrate the perspectives of sociology and computer science. As digital technologies have become part of everyday life, 'interaction' and 'interactivity' represent complementary phenomena and concepts. Interactions between and among individuals, and interactions within and between social institutions, commonly involve interactivity with media. This state of affairs has motivated terms such as 'the information society' (Porat, 1977) and 'the network society' (Castells, 1996): Technologies of information and communication have become critical components of social infrastructures. Theories and models of media and society, in turn, must be designed to cover all media and all of society.

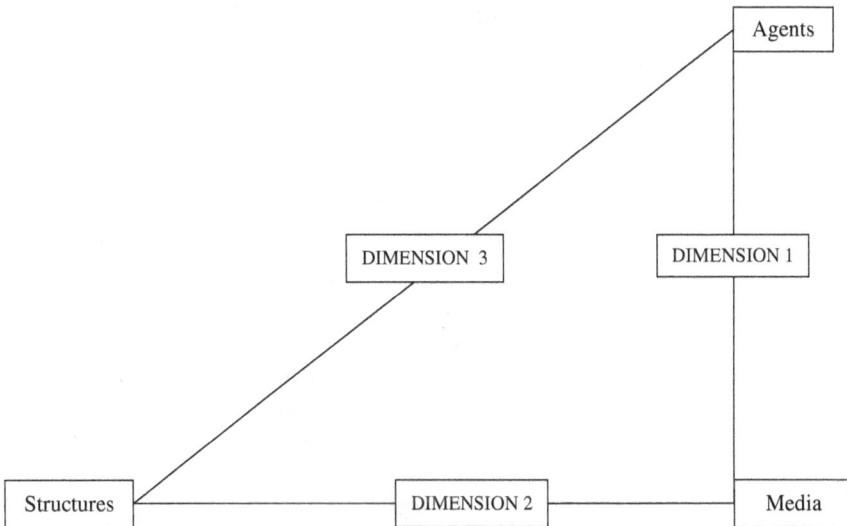

Figure 1.3 Media, agents, and structures of society.

Figure 1.3 reviews the full configuration of media, society, and agency. The model is grounded in contemporary social theory, which emphasizes the continuous interaction between the **structure** of society as a whole and its many constituents – individuals as well as institutions – that all exercise **agency** (Giddens, 1984). The premise of the model, on the one hand, is that people act in particular circumstances and within particular structures; they do not exercise 'free will' as traditionally understood. On the other hand, the model recognizes that the structure of society is not a straitjacket keeping people in their place; structure is a necessary and, indeed, welcome condition for them to be able to act, express themselves, and live their lives. Structure both enables and constrains agency. The upshot is that the innumerable actions which persons, social groups, private companies, and public institutions constantly perform, serve to maintain – but also, to a degree, to adjust and alter – the structure of society, from the local to the national and global levels of social organization. In the process, all these agents also do things with words and with media – they communicate. Media and communication researchers have reminded social theorists that media and communicative practices serve to orient the ongoing interactions of individuals and institutions and, hence, the extended, gradual evolution of social structures (Jensen, 1995; Silverstone, 1999; Thompson, 1995). Both before and after the introduction of the internet, technologies have significantly enhanced human capabilities of communicating and acting across social space and time.

The three corners of Figure 1.3 – **agent, structure, media** – stake out the field in which human actions and social interactions unfold. The sides of the triangle capture three dimensions of the agent–structure dynamic, which is given meaning through media use and communicative practices:

- *Dimension 1* covers what computer scientists, but also many ordinary media users will refer to as 'interactivity,' namely, the selections and interventions that are routine (and necessary) elements of the use particularly of digital media: clicking on a link in an app or at a website, commenting on a post on social media, or 'shooting at the enemy' in an online computer game. For other media, the scope of interactivity is certainly more limited, for instance, when choosing a radio channel, checking results for one's favorite team in the sports section of a newspaper, or finding out whodunit with a sneak preview into the last few pages of a crime novel. But, for all media, users are interactive along this first dimension: They navigate, turn their attention toward, and interpret a particular content. And, along the same dimension, media organizations are not just senders, but also recipients of information, when they register users' presence and behavior. In digital communication systems, users leave behind traces – including so-called **metadata** (see Chapter 2, p. 54) – which media collect, process, and repurpose, as part of their own planning and product development, and as a valuable commodity that can be sold to advertisers and other stakeholders in the online world.
- *Dimension 2* addresses the special relationship that exists between media and the institutions of political governance. Communication, as noted, is a specific form of human action; media constitute a distinctive kind of organizations and, together, make up a unique institution in modern societies. Whereas the state regulates the media, the media keep tabs on the state. Long before the coming of digital and interactive media, this relationship was described with reference to the press as a fourth branch of governance – the press plays the role of a watchdog observing the other three branches (the legislative, executive, and judicial powers of governance). Other social institutions, as well – from businesses to cultural institutions – are subject to scrutiny by the media. With the emergence of an ever more tightly spun network of media, questions have suggested themselves regarding the power of the media: Is this power stronger or weaker than that of the other branches of governance, or perhaps a different type of power? The internet has extended the capability of both media and their users to observe and communicate about states, including what states do to citizens and with their data, which offer additional means for states to exercise authority and control over peoples.
- *Dimension 3*, finally, returns to the interchange between society as a comprehensive structure and the many social agents contributing to its ongoing structuration – who, importantly, include individual citizens as well as powerful political interests and economic entities such as tech giants and other multinational corporations. The actions of each of these agents literally make a difference over time for the structure of society, albeit in different ways and to very different extent. In each case, communication via media of the first, second, or third degrees lends orientation and meaning to agents' concrete actions. One

example of technologically mediated action at a distance is *crowdsourcing*, that is, the practice of using websites and apps to collect many small donations in the service of different causes, for example, aiding the victims of climate change (Image 1.1) or of war (Image 1.2). Another example is communication involving patients, general practitioners, and other agents of healthcare, which complements face-to-face consultations, and anticipates further actions by each agent – taking blood samples and writing referrals, being hospitalized and undergoing surgery, exercising and changing lifestyles. In the widest sense, citizens participate in the maintenance of political democracy when they access information, communicate about current issues, and perhaps become actively involved in political parties and nongovernmental organizations (NGOs). Media and communication are necessary, if far from sufficient, conditions for the practice of democracy.

Box 1.2 Exercise

If there were no media

Think first of the diverse media of the first, second, and third degree that have developed over the course of history – now imagine a situation in which media do not exist. Discuss which personal and social activities would be difficult or impossible to uphold if the following media and communicative practices were to disappear – one by one:

- Smartphones
- Apps
- Basic mobile phones (for speaking and texting)
- World Wide Web
- Email
- Television
- Radio
- Film
- Magazines
- Newspapers
- Books
- Writing
- Speech

In a variant of the exercise, you remove just one or a few media from the list and then discuss, first, which activities would be difficult or impossible to engage in, and, next, how the media that are still available might stand in and compensate for the ones missing.

The chapters of the book

Media and society are related in and by communication, which constitutes, at once, actions undertaken by individuals and collective reflections on what could and ought to be done going forward – by these same individuals as well as by larger social groups, companies, public institutions, civil-society organizations, and entire societies. It is that complex set of interrelations which are laid out in the following chapters, from six different perspectives:

- *Chapter 2 – Texts in the media.* Our first encounter with media is through **texts** that are made up of **signs** – words, sounds, and images – and which, in innumerable combinations, become sources of meaning. The chapter explains how signs communicate, how they enter into human actions and social interactions, and how the communicating texts and communicating actions relate to their origins and settings – their **con-texts** – a term referring both to other texts and to social situations. The relations between texts and contexts are articulated in **genres** – different ways of addressing others in and by communication. And texts and genres typically assume different shapes in different media. Media carry a great variety of **discourses** – meaningful signs and texts that are communicated as part of particular contexts, with distinctive intentions and social consequences. Digital media have introduced additional varieties of signs, which are analyzed and discussed in further detail in later chapters.
- *Chapter 3 – Society in the media.* Texts, in a sense, are to be found 'inside' the media. Social forces, similarly, manifest themselves 'inside' the media, in their organization and modes of operation. Media are **technologies** that allow humans to transcend time and space: Through media, we receive news from the other side of the globe as well as fact and fiction about past historical periods. Media represent a wider **economy** – they are sources of income and increasingly critical components of social infrastructures that enable the production and distribution of other commodities, locally and globally. And media are **organizations** – large, complex entities that depend on the collaboration among employees and departments for communication to succeed, internally within the organization and externally with clients and other stakeholders.
- *Chapter 4 – Media as institutions.* Two aspects of the interrelations between media and society have traditionally been at the top of agendas both for media and communication research, and for public and political debate about media, and we devote a full chapter to each aspect: the **senders** and the **recipients** of communication. As senders, the media together make up a social institution in its own right, affording means of insight and agency to persons and publics, and contributing to the incremental structuration of society. This process may be hard to detect in particular programs or messages, but is nevertheless an important aspect of the interchange between media and society over time. Elaborating on Dimension 2 in Figure 1.3, Chapter 4 situates the media institution within society as a whole – as a source of meaning, power, and profit.

To account for the media as a social institution, we relate it to other institutions across the public and private sectors of society, tracing its role in the local and global chains of the production and distribution of meaning. We specify, further, how media of different degrees, with different historical legacies, enter into the media institution as currently configured. And we emphasize how senders and recipients – media professionals and media users – come together in multistep and multidirectional flows of communication within and beyond the media institution itself.

- *Chapter 5 – Media users.* The following chapter turns to Dimension 3 of Figure 1.3, elaborating on the recipients or audiences of media as, simultaneously, active **users** of media in different social contexts. Users constitute the first point of contact between media and society – a pivot around which many 'effects' of the media can be seen to turn. Academic media and communication research, from the outset, had worried that the modern media could have adverse or 'unwanted' effects on audiences, for instance, through representations of violence leading to real-life violence; the premise of commercial traditions of research, in comparison, has been attempts to identify and document 'wanted' effects such as public attention for and purchase of particular goods and services. The implications of these two sets of questions for citizens' lives as well as for the structure of society have made audience and effects studies a central and, at times, contested area of research. The breakthrough of digital media and communication over the past few decades has stimulated further scientific and public interest in what media *do to* users, but also what users can and will *do with* media (Katz, 1959).

- *Chapter 6 – Methods on media.* To account for the complex interrelations between media and society, more than basic descriptions and theoretical interpretations are needed – **empirical methods** are required to collect and analyze different kinds of qualitative and quantitative **data** to support inferences and conclusions. This requirement applies both to *basic* research, which seeks to better understand the interdependencies of communicative processes and other social processes, and to *administrative* and *critical* research proposing to either administer or reform, even revolutionize, the media in their present form. The chapter reviews and illustrates the uses of six standard methods of empirical media and communication research: interview and survey, observation and experiment, discourse analysis and content analysis. Each method has its strengths and limitations, depending on the object and purpose of inquiry; in many instances, it is advantageous to combine several methods for concrete studies and projects. One portion of the chapter singles out a particular category of data – **metadata** – that have special relevance for the study of digital media, and that have prompted the development of specifically digital methods: As users of digital communication systems, we all leave behind traces that are collected, analyzed, monetized, and applied by commercial operators as well as by public authorities – for better and for worse. The account of that ground rule of digital communication concludes one of the long lines running through the book, reaching back, through Chapter 2 on signs and data, to the present introductory chapter: Beyond one-to-one, one-to-many, and many-to-many communication, media users engage in **many-to-one** communication, 'into the system' (Jensen & Helles, 2017). This digital condition presents the study of media and society with fundamental ethical and political questions regarding the implications of human communication for issues of meaning and power – which we address several times throughout the book and elaborate in the concluding chapter.

• *Chapter 7 – Media in society.* Where Chapter 3 traces the impact of social forces 'within' the media, the last chapter of the book reverses the perspective and provides an overview of media 'within' society. This concluding perspective returns to the 'big issues' that commonly motivate not just students and researchers, but most people to take an interest in and have an opinion about media and communication. Media potentially empower their users to observe society 'from the outside,' at a distance, so that they may reflect on and communicate about the present state of society and the world. It is this potential of media and communication not just to describe and understand, but to criticize and change society that has motivated censorship, in some societies and some historical periods, and which has inspired diverse and sometimes conflicting philosophies concerning the politically legitimate and ethically appropriate uses of media. For centuries, one category of theories – **normative** theories – have explored not so much what media *are*, but what they *could* be and *ought* to be. Chapter 4 on media as a social institution anticipates the values at stake, including universal human rights, and associated debates; Chapter 7 extends the analyses and discussions with particular reference to digital media, which have variously reiterated and reformulated classic agendas. The chapter and the book close with an account of the practical relevances and uses of media and communication research in contemporary society. When the findings and insights of research are communicated back into society, they contribute to and participate – like the media – in producing, maintaining, repairing, and transforming society (Carey, 1989b/1975: 23).

All textbooks are products of premises and priorities – they are media communicating in particular ways, with particular purposes, in particular historical times, and in particular cultural settings. This textbook seeks to strike a balance between a continuous narrative and a number of more detailed analyses of central instances of contemporary media and communicative practices as well as reviews of key theoretical traditions in dedicated boxes. Our aim is to make accessible the sort of scientific concepts and models that, at first sight, may appear forbiddingly abstract or complex, but which represent helpful handles in coming to grips with the complex interdependencies of media and society. In addition to boxes providing in-depth treatment of selected theories, methods, and analytical themes, we have included a broad range of references to both classic and recent studies as an invitation for readers to select their own further reading, depending on their interests and focus of study. Along the way, we outline a number of the disagreements, sometimes fundamental, that are part and parcel of doing research (in boxes on 'theories at issue'). Like other forms of inquiry, media and communication studies regularly question received wisdom, within scholarly communities and among publics. This is one way in which theories translate into practical relevance and concrete applications – for the media, their users, and society at large. As suggested by one of the founders of media and communication research in the United States, Kurt Lewin (1945: 129), "nothing is as practical as a good theory."

2 Texts in the media

Ways and means of communicating

The term of 'ways and means' has a long history, referring to taxes and other charges that the public has been required to pay in order to cover government expenses. In the United Kingdom, the collection of these funds was administered, between 1641 and 1967, by a Committee of Ways and Means (UK Parliament, 2023). In the United States, the House of Representatives still has a Committee on Ways and Means, which oversees taxation and various public services such as Social Security (Ways & Means, 2023). In other countries, too, these funds are the concrete 'means' of making the wheels of government turn, and of ensuring citizens' livelihood. The 'ways' of collecting and disbursing these means – according to legislative principles and administrative procedures – are further indicators of how the society in question proposes to regulate the relationship between the individual and the collective, through a generic 'means' of getting things done: money.

Media, equally, provide generic ways and means of getting things done, and of regulating the relationship between individuals, collectives, and the institutions they share, by circulating information in public and supporting communication about the ends and means of individual existence and social coexistence. The 'means' are the concrete signs and symbols, words and images, that carry information and communication; the 'ways' are the diverse configurations of these discursive means – texts – according to received conventions and traditions of representing and engaging with society and other aspects of reality. Texts invite each of us to be and do certain kinds of things, and we associate meaning both with the texts and with the social practices and personal identities that texts contribute to building over time, in and by communication. The first comprehensive and formalized approach to texts and communication in different degrees of media – the first theory of communication – was rhetoric.

Rhetoric

Today, rhetoric is often referred to in pejorative terms: 'That's just rhetoric,' people will say, form without substance, likely designed to persuade someone

DOI: 10.4324/9781032655109-2

about something through dubious ways and means. However, the tradition of rhetoric that originated in classical Greece has, in fact, explored the interrelation of form and content in detailed and nuanced fashion, for analytical as well as practical purposes, departing from spoken language (for overview, see Schiappa, 2016).

The attention devoted to the close relationship between the forms and the contents of communication within the rhetorical tradition is suggested by the five stages of preparing a speech:

- *inventio* (selecting and combining the materials or topics for the speech)
- *dispositio* (outlining or structuring the speech)
- *elocutio* (choosing particular phrases and formulations for the speech)
- *memoria* (remembering the form and content of the speech)
- *actio* (performing the speech)

Inventio, to begin, highlights the interdependence of form and content – between knowing *something* and knowing *how* to communicate with others about that something. As suggested by the term *inventio*, something is to be invented or constructed, not in the sense of making things up, but of selecting specific items of information, and then combining and configuring the information into meaningful patterns. If you were to explain to someone who had not read this book what, then, is the interrelation between media and society, you would necessarily select and synthesize certain points and then share your understanding in your own choice of words. In this way, the general message of the book would (probably, hopefully) come across to your conversational partner. And, on top of *their* understanding, articulating something to someone else typically enhances one's *own* understanding: When communicating with others, we simultaneously communicate with ourselves.

Rhetoric, then, approaches communication literally as a process of production. A speech – whether a public address by a president or royalty, a political statement on the campaign trail, or a personal appreciation of a family member at a private party – constructs a relationship between speaker and addressees, and a world for them to consider and engage with. The addressees may, in turn, join the construction, perhaps to question either the world being built before their ears and eyes, the speaker's manner of articulating that world, or the role being assigned to themselves as recipients and potential partners (or not) in conversation. And, depending on the conventions of the particular context, for instance, in a court of law or a parliament, they will react silently, inwardly, or they may stand up and speak out to challenge the speaker's construction.

The openness, variability, and unpredictability of the full process of construction are suggested by further set of classical rhetorical concepts:

- *ethos*
- *logos*
- *pathos*

Image 2.1a Protesting in a medium of the first degree. Michael Campanella/Getty Images News.

Image 2.1b Protesting in a medium of the second degree (television). Stephanie Keith/ Stringer/Getty Images News.

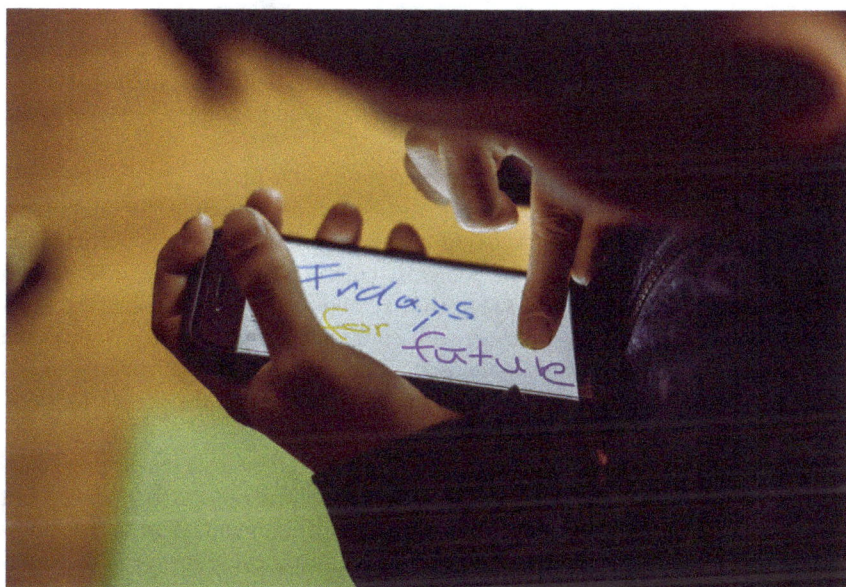

Image 2.1c Protesting in a medium of the third degree. Photo by Markus Spiske on Unsplash.

The Swedish climate activist Greta Thunberg has communicated her message in media of all three degrees (Chapter 1, p. 5). Originally seated outside the Swedish parliament, she expressed herself through a handwritten sign that read, in Swedish: "school strike for the climate" (media of the first degree). When appearing at meetings at the United Nations, her speeches accusing the Secretary-General and other powerful people in the world for failing coming generations were covered by classic news media around the world (media of the second degree). And, through digital platforms and smartphones (media of the third degree), Greta Thunberg's initiative attracted several million followers to a youth-led global climate strike movement, Fridays For Future.

The three concepts cover different strategies that people pursue in seeking to persuade someone of something. First, speakers are likely to foreground their own good character and trustworthiness – their ethics, broadly speaking (*ethos*). Second, they will suggest the quality of the arguments and evidence they are presenting – a speech ideally follows an internal logic (*logos*). Third, speakers commonly seek to generate positive feelings or attitudes among their audience – you need not become pathetic, or overly emotional, in order express and evoke relevant emotions (*pathos*).

A concrete speech combines *ethos*, *logos*, and *pathos*. Conversations, too – indeed, any communication – typically involve all three strategies to different degrees and in variable combinations. The choices depend on the purpose and the context of communication. To illustrate, all scientific lectures (hopefully) build on solid arguments (*logos*), but will be more or less persuasive depending on whether the lecturer is a recent graduate in the field or a Nobel Prize winner (*ethos*). And any lecture must be attuned – in its examples and vocabularies – to the particular audience (*pathos*), taking into account whether one is addressing experts or a group of interested laypeople.

In a contemporary perspective, the various media of the first, second, and third degrees (Chapter 1, p. 5) afford distinctive opportunities for mobilizing *ethos*, *logos*, and *pathos*. With moving images at one's disposal, the articulation of an argument (*elocutio*) may include cross-cutting between different levels and domains of reality to produce a suggestive, symbolic universe, enabling the presentation of a personal vision (*ethos*) with emotional depth (*pathos*). And, in the case of digital, interactive media, the performance (*actio*), more than a speaker's statements, consists in the participation and involvement of the people formerly known as addressees and audiences.

The five phases of preparing and performing a speech indicate the origin of classical rhetoric – in the terminology of this book – in media of the first degree. Cut loose from humans as media, the common practice of communication has been fundamentally redefined and differentiated through a historical sequence of technologies. Once written down, printed, or saved in a database, there is much less reason to memorize (*memoria*) the contents of texts, as previously passed on through oral tradition. Instead, texts can serve as manuscripts for speeches. Most important, texts have come to communicate in and of themselves, and to lend themselves to comparative studies of what they have to say about their original senders and social settings: By retracing statements by and images of Greta Thunberg (Image 2.1), we begin to understand both aspects of her personal and political development, and her position in the development of local and global awareness of climate change and its human and social repercussions.

It is with hindsight that we recognize rhetoric as the very first theory of communication, departing from media of the first degree. Subsequent technologies stimulated the development of further theories and models of communication, which came to variously complement and compete with rhetoric. One of the most significant and durable contributions to the study of written and printed texts has been delivered by hermeneutics.

Hermeneutics

Hermeneutics is the theory and practice of interpreting texts, whether fact or fiction (for overview, see Zimmermann, 2015). The original focus of hermeneutics was scriptures associated with religion and law, laying down rules and regulations of how people could and ought to act as members of communities and societies. Applied as definitive measures to concrete human and social actions, the interpretation of such texts could have existential consequences, pronouncing a death sentence in a court of law or the eternal damnation of the souls of sinners.

Interpretations of religious and legal texts have served, time and again, in societies around the world, to legitimate unequal opportunities in life for rich and poor, Black and White, men and women, and to motivate wars and atrocities against other peoples and religious persuasions. Anyone not subscribing to received and authoritative interpretations of more or less 'holy' texts, has been subject to exclusion from communities centered in such texts. **Excommunication**, a term associated especially with the Catholic church, meant (and still means) that the individual in question cannot remain part of a range of rituals and religious events: That person is literally communicated 'out of' (*ex*) the church, and subsequently does not have access to sharing their faith – communicating – with others 'inside' the church, understood both as a specific location and a spiritual, **imagined community** (Anderson, 1991) seeking salvation through God.

From the beginning of the 1800s, hermeneutics was gradually applied to many more categories of texts – arts and culture, broadly speaking. Indeed, hermeneutics has increasingly come to include among its objects of analysis and interpretation not only signs on paper, but the thoughts in people's heads as well – human consciousness as such, including everyday experience of society and the world. Even social structures and human interactions may be conceived as texts carrying meaning and inviting interpretation (on this extended conception of texts, see further p. 43).

In contemporary philosophy and scholarship, the **hermeneutics of suspicion** (Ricoeur, 1981: 46) refers to a strategy of probing the multiple and partially hidden or secret layers of consciousness, communication, and culture. Associated, in particular, with the works of three modern thinkers – Karl Marx, Friedrich Nietzsche, and Sigmund Freud – the hermeneutics of suspicion questions whether and how humans are, in fact, in a position to understand themselves, their own thoughts and actions, as well as those of others. We know from common experience that people do not always say what they mean, or mean what they say. There is good reason, therefore, to be suspicious – in the specific sense of asking critical questions before drawing conclusions and accepting commitments – regarding the many different things that we think, say, and write, to others and to ourselves (Image 2.2).

You should always read the fine print, people will warn each other, and be sure to also take note of what is being said between the lines. But how to do so in practice? Hermeneutics offers a variety of analytical resources, which lend themselves to the study of contemporary media, too. Several insights are summed up in the idea of a **hermeneutic circle** (Figure 2.1) (Alvesson & Sköldberg, 2009: 106). The figure, first of all, refers to the commonsensical but essential principle that the individual **parts** of a text can only be understood with reference to the **whole**, just as an understanding of the whole requires attention to the details. The parts and the whole presuppose one another: The whole is more than the sum of the parts, and all the individual parts must be joined for the whole to fall into place.

The **analysis** of texts, accordingly, involves their parsing into smaller elements, but also a recombination of the elements in relevant patterns: Analyses lead

'I made Steve Bannon's psychological warfare tool': meet the data war whistleblower

Image 2.2 Suspicious texts. Copyright Guardian News & Media Ltd 2024.

The interpretation of important events in the world frequently depends on the interpretation of texts. Some texts are, at first, secret or hidden from the public eye. In 2018, a former employee of Cambridge Analytica, Christopher Wylie, revealed that, through its collaboration with Facebook, this company had wrongfully gained access to data about millions of internet users. As a result, the company was able to create detailed user profiles, which allowed their clients to target voters in online political campaigns. Especially Cambridge Analytica's role in U.S. President Donald Trump's successful 2016 presidential election campaign led to public debate about the need for national and international regulation of the collecting, processing, and reselling of user data (see further Chapter 5, p. 153). The news coverage of Christopher Wylie's whistleblowing and the scandal that followed, here by the online version of the British The Guardian *newspaper, served as a reminder that readers are well advised – as citizens and voters – to engage in a hermeneutics of suspicion regarding the selective political information presented to them (p. 31).*

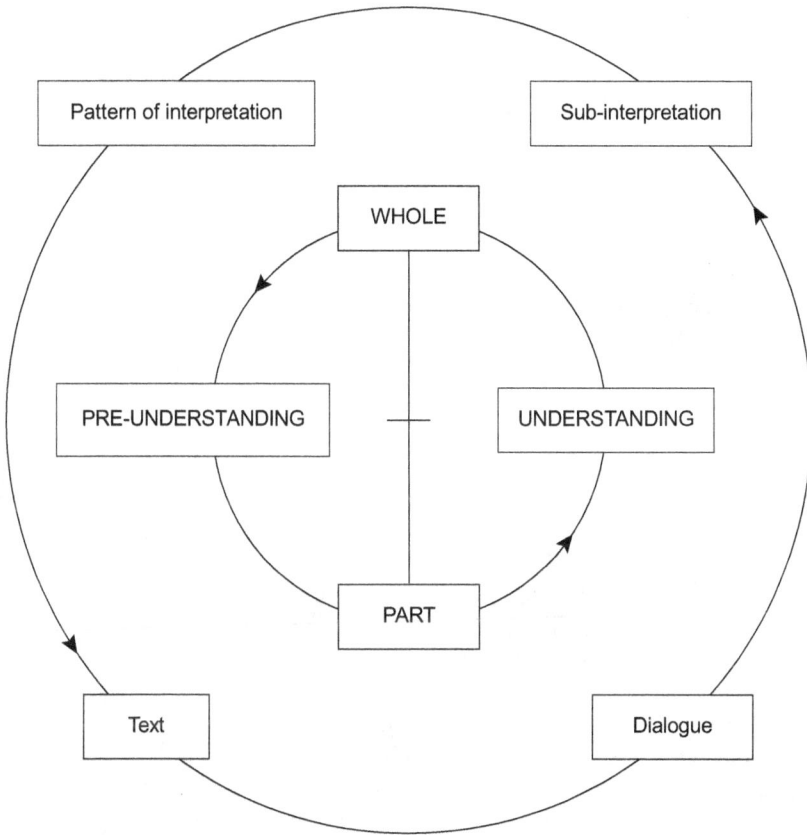

Figure 2.1 The hermeneutic circle.

Source: Alvesson & Sköldberg, 2009: 104.

on to new **syntheses**. In Figure 2.1, the inner circle refers to the basic part–whole dynamic of texts. The outer circle, further, suggests the point that readers enter into 'dialogue' with texts, which can be said to offer answers to the interpretive questions readers raise. The outcome is, first, a set of partial interpretations, next one or more patterns of interpretation, and finally (ideally) a full and rounded interpretation.

The part–whole dynamic, moreover, extends beyond the boundaries of the particular texts in front of readers. Consider this message sent via texting or a messaging app: 'How r u?' The initial challenge is how to make sense of two minimal elements – the letters 'r' and 'u.' Most people know from common experience, however, that single letters acquire additional meanings when spoken aloud (or thought about). How r u – how are you? If you are a native speaker of English (or if you are one of the roughly one billion other individuals around the world who are able to speak English), you get the point. Most likely, you already know the person addressing you in this manner. It might be a mother or father texting a child when school is out; two persons in a relationship checking in with each other during a workday; or a married individual contacting a secret lover to plan a rendezvous. In each case, the interpretation of the message is facilitated by familiar social roles.

Wider interpretations of the example are aided by the history that the people communicating typically share. If the child is not in primary school, but has, instead, just moved away from home, or has recently given birth herself, the implication of a message from her parents, 'how r u,' may be the cautious opening to an offer of (more) care and assistance. In the case of the couple, if the two are in the early stages of a relationship, the background to the message might be a physical separation that has lasted days, even weeks, just as one lover might be reaching out to restart the affair following months of silence by the other. Recent history matters, too: If the lovers, the couple, or parents and children just had a fight, a message in writing begins to make up for words spoken in the heat of the moment.

Small parts come together in large wholes, also for signs and symbols other than verbal language. Emojis would be common in our example – 'how r u' – so common, in fact, that they have become standard elements of the interfaces of smartphones and other digital devices. A **smiley** at the end of a message takes the sting out of controversial or difficult communications; the term 'smiley' recalls the body language of face-to-face interactions. And, of course, several emojis may be inserted in longer messages. And each emoji itself constitutes a whole with variable parts, including the shape of eyes and mouth ☺; color to indicate a state of mind ☺; a face turned upside down to express light-headed confusion ☺; and additional effects to suggest that someone is having a party ☺ or, perhaps, being bored and falling asleep ☺.

The interpretation of textual parts and wholes is shaped, moreover, by the communicative context and the background knowledge of the participants, who may share some or most of their past, present, and future. While Chapter 5 returns to the diverse roles of audiences and users in communication, the hermeneutic approach can be summarized from the perspective of the individuals reading texts. As laid out in the hermeneutic circle, making sense of a text is a gradual process. But, already from the outset, readers have some form of preliminary or **pre-understanding** of the nature of the communication underway (Gadamer, 1975/1960): They hold **pre-judices** – judgments in the sense of premises framing interpretation – which, paradoxically, is a good thing. Human understanding – whether of texts, events, or other people – never starts from scratch. Each person brings to communication past experiences and present interests that inevitably orient how they interact, and how they interpret what others bring to the conversation. Prejudices or pre-understandings are a strength to the extent that they enable each participant to place both the message and the entire interaction in perspective. It is not only our general capability of using language and other symbols, but also our specific history with a few significant others that bring home the meaning of the message on our smart-phone: 'How r u 😊.'

In parallel with rhetoric and hermeneutics, a third tradition has contributed theoretical concepts and analytical categories for the understanding and study of texts: Semiotics – the study of signs – stands out because of the specific attention this tradition has devoted to modern media and communication. Over the last century, the development of semiotics represents one of the most sustained attempts at accounting for the many different categories of signs that are produced and circulated in society, not least, through the media of mass and networked communication.

Semiotics

The most widely cited definition, offered by one of the two founders of the trad-ition, namely, the Swiss linguist Ferdinand de Saussure (1959/1916: 16), is that semiotics is the science of **the life of signs in society**. Saussure proposed to transfer the principles and procedures of linguistics from the study of verbal language to the full range of human and social means of expression, representation, and commu-nication – semiotics has taken up artifacts and practices as diverse as photographs, films, music, and computer programs. The other founder of semiotics was the American philosopher Charles Sanders Peirce, who addressed classic philosoph-ical problems in terms of the concept of signs: How do human beings come into contact with reality (through signs), how do they produce more or less adequate and relevant descriptions of reality (through additional signs), and how do they communicate with others about reality so that, as communities and societies, they will be in a position to variously adapt to and adjust reality as they find it (through ever more signs)? Coming out of different fields of inquiry, Peirce and Saussure were unfamiliar with each other's work during their lifetimes, but together they delivered the building blocks for an interdisciplinary study of signs that, today, is being applied to new media as well as old communicative practices.

In the philosophical perspective that Peirce advanced, the concept of signs serves to specify three aspects of the perennial question of how humans – as indi-viduals and groups – can know anything about the world in which they find them-selves. Signs refer to something 'out there' in reality; 'inside' my consciousness signs allow me to engage with particular features of reality; so that the signs consti-tute mediating links – media – between consciousness and reality. One of Peirce's key points was that all three aspects must be incorporated into models of how signs enable human cognition and social interaction. A sign, thus, has three elements:

- *representamen*, which is the mediating component (as suggested by the related term 'representation' – something is literally re-presented or presented once again and to someone else);
- the *object* being referred to and represented (which may be either material or immaterial, factual or fictional, a hamster or a hobbit); and

- the *interpretant*, which relates object and representamen through an act of interpretation.

In a first step, Peirce focused on how individuals become aware of something or other. In a further step, signs relate not only individuals to reality – signs relate individuals, specifically when they seek to arrive at a common understanding of objects and events in the world, so that they may agree on how to go on and act in and on the world. Without signs, there can be no communication, no community, no human survival or social coexistence.

In the terminology of contemporary digital media, signs can be thought of as *interfaces* – between human beings and the world around them, and between humans as they engage with the world they share. Signs are more than the result or **product** of human cognition and communication; signs are also constitutive elements of the **process** in which persons and communities gradually arrive at interpretations and explanations of what is the case. We think through signs, and we communicate with others through signs.

This stepwise process is illustrated in Figure 2.2. At the first or lower level, someone arrives at an understanding (interpretant) through reference to a sign (representamen) establishing contact with particular phenomena (objects). Visual and auditory sense impressions register, for instance, a smartphone: 'that's my smartphone.' At subsequent levels of interpretation, the opening recognition – 'that's my smartphone' – may produce a sense of relief: 'I thought I had lost it,' and subsequent self-awareness: 'I gotta stop leaving my smartphone lying around.'

Perhaps the person in question recognizes a message on the screen of the smartphone – 'how r u' – with or without emojis. Through additional steps of interpretation, it gradually becomes clear who sent the message, and what the response should be, how soon. The smartphone represents a point of access to a wider social world – a medium – so that its owner can relate to absent others (in the earlier example, mother, father, boyfriend/girlfriend, or lover). Peirce referred to this extended process of interpretation and engagement as **semiosis**. The rest of this section elaborates on how simple signs enter into more complex signs – meaningful texts – which, in turn, give rise to interpretation in multiple steps, followed by ever more cognitions and communications.

Where Peirce centered on processes of mediation, Saussure emphasized the study of signs as **structures**. The point of departure for his **semiology** was verbal language. Languages such as English, Spanish, and Chinese have been subject to substantial and continuous transformations across the centuries. Here and now, however, each language can be described as a **system** (Saussure referred to *langue*, or language system). It is these general systems that can be seen to operate below or behind, and generate endless streams of, concrete statements (*parole*, or language use).

In a structural perspective, language is organized along two axes. On the **syntagmatic** axis, single letters, words, and expressions combine to make up meaningful wholes (syntagms): a full sentence, a conversation, a narrative, and so on.

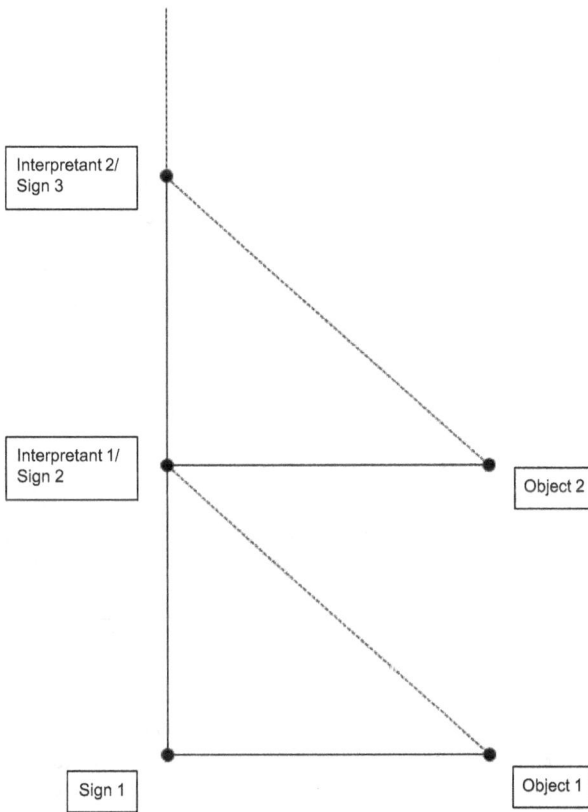

Figure 2.2 The process of semiosis.

On the **paradigmatic** axis, for each element of the syntagmatic whole, a language user will choose from a number of options (a paradigm), mostly without giving each choice much thought. Spelling provides an example: A spelling error is the 'wrong' paradigmatic choice. If you enter 'medio and society' into the database of your local library or a search engine, you'll likely be able to identify and order or reserve this book, but the correct title is 'media and society.' A few sentences ago, we wrote that, on the paradigmatic axis, speakers will 'choose' one word rather than another – we might instead have written 'select.' The paradigmatic choices for particular elements are accumulated and together contribute to the generation of particular meanings, including the style of the whole (the syntagm). In the present example, 'select' sounds slightly more formal or academic than 'choose.'

Languages, in short, are extraordinarily flexible systems of selecting and combining signs for communicating about practically anything and in seemingly endless variations, in a literal as well as a figurative sense. In fact, figurative senses are the product of particular intersections of the paradigmatic and syntagmatic axes. When news media report that 'the White House' issued a statement about a national or international issue, that is a distinctive kind of syntagm. Houses cannot speak, of course, but it is well known to readers, listeners, and viewers that the expression refers to the president of the United States and the things that he (so far, not she) says and does. The part – the house – stands for the whole, which is the office of U.S. president. Operating along the syntagmatic axis, this principle is referred to as **metonymy**: 'the White House' is a metonym for the current president and his ways and means of performing the office.

On the paradigmatic axis, a similarly creative or unusual choice results in **metaphor**. As with metonyms, some metaphors are thoroughly familiar or 'dead': Chairs have legs, but not in the same sense as humans. In other instances, metaphors may contribute novel perspectives, for instance, on political movements and issues. Historically, the United States has often been described through the metaphor of 'a melting pot,' in which immigrants from all over the world came together to emerge as a new category of people – the differences presumably have been dissolved. In response, critics of this notion have noted not only that great divides, in fact, persist in American society between groups of different national and ethnic backgrounds, but also that distinctive practices of cultural expression and social interaction represent unique values to be preserved and nourished. During the 1980s, the value of difference was foregrounded by a 'rainbow coalition' with the politician and activist Jesse Jackson as its spokesperson. In speeches and other communications, the movement held up differences of color as a source of community and its renewal in the United States. The beauty of the rainbow is inherent in the multiple colors of the whole (Drotner et al., 1996: 195). Many years later, the slogans of Barack Obama's first presidential campaign in 2008 – 'change' and 'yes, we can' – could be taken as updates of the rainbow message through other linguistic means. Obama used the personal pronoun 'we' to signal a strategy of inclusion (rather than homogenization) to support social transformation – 'change.' Donald Trump's 2016, 2020, and 2024 campaigns, in turn, challenged both of these historical precedents with the slogan 'make America great again': 'We are not the sum of our differences, but a unified "America," which can become "great" not by looking ahead, but by returning to some past golden age ("again").'

One final contribution of semiotics is the insight that the very relationship between signs and the reality they capture remains open to change. Saussure underscored that a sign has two sides – a conceptual content (*signifié*) and a physical expression (*signifiant*) – and that these have an **arbitrary** relation. This is evident from the fact that different languages use different expressions for the same conceptual content: 'change' in English, *cambio* in Spanish, 变革 in Chinese. Also more complex signs – narratives, artworks, and entire cultures and worldviews – are, to an extent, arbitrary representations of the world. Signs have been selected and combined in what constitutes, at once, a **representation** and a **construction** of reality. It is equally evident, however, that individual language users cannot simply use particular expressions and choose the contents to go with them as they prefer.

The point is that whereas languages (and cultures) are arbitrary in principle, in practice they make up social conventions binding anyone communicating to and with others. Languages and cultures change slowly and incrementally, through ever more communications.

Box 2.1 Analysis

The meanings of images

Signs typically carry multiple layers of meaning. One source of such layering is the many possible combinations of letters, words, and sentences in the messages sent. The subsequent process of reception and interpretation only adds to the complexity of the messages received. It is essential to be able to detect 'undertones' in conversations and to 'read between the lines' of social media posts (as highlighted by hermeneutics as well as semiotics). And the layering applies to images and other nonverbal signs, too: We look more closely at news photos to go beyond the surface, and we make inferences from the shots and scenes of feature films to their moral lessons. Most people have remarkable skills of intuitively navigating the layers of meaning. Semiotics offers a set of analytical tools for systematizing intuitions and enabling further reflection and deliberation on semiosis in society.

One widely applied tool of semiotic analysis is the distinction between **denotation** and **connotation** – basic meaning and added meaning. A classic example is freedom fighters versus terrorists. The denotations are similar: people who oppose a powerful adversary through violent means. But the connotations differ: Where 'freedom fighters' are fighting a just cause, the ends of 'terrorists' are illegitimate. The distinction was formalized by the French philosopher and semiotician Roland Barthes (1973/1957), and laid out in a model (Figure 2.3). One of his most famous illustrative examples was the photograph in Image 2.3.

Figure 2.3 builds on Saussure's distinction between expression and content, or signifier and signified (*signifiant* and *signifié*). In the first or lower level of the figure, we find 1. Signifier and 2. Signified, which together make up 3. Sign. In Image 2.3, 1. Signifier is the actual photograph on the cover the magazine *Paris-Match*. The content can be characterized as 'a young Black man saluting the French flag' (2. Signified). At this first level, the full sign (3. Sign) of the cover might be considered a neutral description: an image of a particular person doing something familiar in a recognizable context.

To Barthes, however, the image was anything but neutral. This first layer of meaning, he found, called up a further layer that raised troublesome political and historical implications. The image appeared on a magazine cover

Image 2.3 Cover of *Paris-Match* (1955).

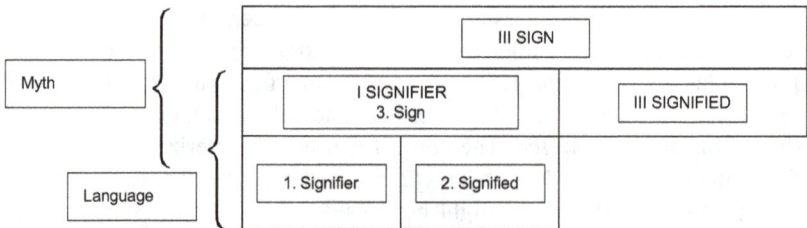

Figure 2.3 Denotation and connotation.

Source: Adapted from Barthes (1973/1957: 115).

in the mid-1950s, at a time when France still had colonies, and when it was not a given that colonialism must end, or that a Black person had the same human and civil rights as a White person. So, why did this image feature on the cover of a popular magazine? Barthes's answer was that the image signaled to readers that, actually, French imperialism was not a form of discrimination or repression: Black and White were united under the French flag as a symbol of freedom, equality, and fraternity for all citizens of the republic.

Barthes specified his critique with reference to the second or upper layer of Figure 2.3. His analytical strategy was to take the first sign (3. Sign) – consisting of 1. Signifier (the photograph) and 2. Signified ('young Black man saluting the flag') – and then treat this first-level sign as an expression with a quite different meaning. The first-level sign (3. Sign) now serves as an expression (I SIGNIFIER) at the next level of signification. At this second level, it takes on a further content: 'imperialism is a legitimate social order' (II SIGNIFIED). Together, I SIGNIFIER and II SIGNIFIED make up a more complex sign (III SIGN) speaking to and about the era in which people would be reading the magazine: France of the colonial period is (was) a legitimate social order.

Even though Barthes used a different terminology, it is helpful to retain **denotation** and **connotation** – they are standard terms in semiotic studies, and refer back to the Danish linguist Louis Hjelmslev (1963/1943), who was one of the central inspirations for Barthes's work. One of Barthes's original terms should be highlighted, however: **Mythologies** was the title of the seminal book in which the analysis of *Paris-Match* appeared (Barthes, 1973/1957). While traditionally associated with religious and other metaphysical worldviews, mythologies should be understood here in the broader sense of ideologies – political, economic, and cultural worldviews – and it was in this last sense that Barthes spoke of mythologies. As evidenced by the full set of analyses collected in the 1957 book, he had an exceptionally keen eye for how small, contestable ideas – myths – may grow into comprehensive, reprehensible worldviews: mythologies. A seemingly neutral level of denotation was blended with a normative level of connotations, which, in the end, reaffirmed an ideology of imperialism.

Barthes's conclusion, at once theoretical and political, was that mythologies 'naturalize' certain worldviews, as if they could not be otherwise. The task of semiotic and other critical analyses of signs and texts, accordingly, becomes one of denaturalizing worldviews by deconstructing them. The primary purpose of analysis is critique rather than criticism – calling out the premises and implications of the worldviews in question, identifying alternatives, and communicating the findings to the audiences who are, at once, subject to naturalization and the subjects of social change.

Barthes's point of departure, as noted, was Saussure's variant of semi-otics. But his redevelopment of the model of signs also provided a common denominator for Saussure and Peirce. Figure 2.2, summarizing Peirce's variant, emphasized that semiosis is an ongoing, even infinite process. With Figure 2.3, Barthes indicated that the process of semiosis may get stuck. As practical remedies, textual analyses contribute to restarting semiosis. Communicating its insights to wider publics, semiotics delivers reminders both that the world can and should be represented in more ways than one, and that critical interpretations of predominant representations are part of the brief of media and communication studies.

Box 2.2 Exercise

The denotations and connotations of images

Like languages, images and other categories of signs carry several different levels of meaning. Barthes's (1973/1957) model captured two such levels – denotations and connotations – and he went on to illustrate their modes of operation in representations and communications (p. 39).

First, choose one (and only one) profile picture from a personal profile on either Instagram or Facebook. Make an analysis of the picture with reference to Barthes's model:

• Which denotations can be identified in the picture?
• What connotations may the picture give rise to?
• Discuss whether and how the connotations of the picture constitute a mythology or ideology regarding the person being portrayed.

Next, choose an advertisement appearing in your feed from the same plat-form. Make another analysis based on Barthes's model:

• Which denotations can be identified in the image(s) and text(s) of the advertisement?
• What connotations may the advertisement give rise to?
• Discuss whether and how the connotations of the advertisement con-stitute a mythology or ideology regarding the product or service being advertised.

In conclusion, consider differences and similarities regarding the mythologies or ideologies at work in the profile picture and the advertisement, respectively.

Texts and contexts

The three traditions analyzing language and other signs – rhetoric, hermeneutics, and semiotics – have a shared point of reference, namely, **texts**. Increasingly over the past half century, and across different national systems of education, 'texts' have come to be understood as so much more than printed fact or fiction. And this extended concept of texts is key to contemporary research on media and society. Texts are now defined broadly as meaningful expressions and artifacts – words, sounds, and images, but also heirlooms and building styles – all of which invite interpretation as constituents of social and cultural contexts. In a broadly textual perspective, the response to the first question from Chapter 1 (p. 3), '*where* is meaning?', would be: in photographs on the cover of magazines and in profile pictures and advertisements on digital screens, but also in grandparents' silverware, in paintings at museums, and in the official buildings of the institutions of political power and economic capital.

To begin to address the second question from Chapter 1 (p. 3), '*when* is meaning?', we turn now to the question of how several different texts relate to each other in processes and networks. In scholarship as in common parlance, texts are said to enter into **contexts** – literally con-texts or conjoined texts – a term that carries two different, if interrelated implications. First, a context is a social setting that helps clarify the meaning of a particular text – for instance, 'how r u.' An already existing relation between sender and receiver suggests the point of the text in the given instance. Second, texts are each other's contexts: We interpret this text with reference to other texts received in the past, which provide a frame of reference suggesting, perhaps, 'I am not angry with you anymore.'

Contexts are then, at once, **textual** and **social**. Texts establish social contexts, which, in turn, lead us to produce some texts rather than others. Contexts, moreover, extend across time and space when texts are articulated, shared, and disseminated via media of the first, second, or third degrees. As technological and institutional carriers of texts, media serve to both maintain and modify contexts from the local to the global level of social organization.

Intertextuality

The concept of intertextuality covers a great variety of interrelations between and among texts and contexts. Intertextuality, first of all, suggests that no text is an island – any given text is a particular instance of 'textuality,' variable in form and content depending on context. Just as clay lends itself to being shaped as either small vases or large sculptures, textuality manifests itself in short factual messages as well as in long fictional series. Studies of intertextuality specify the somewhat abstract claim that texts enter into contextualized processes of meaning production, retracing the concrete relations between texts in historical and cultural contexts – the process unfolds between ('inter') the texts.

The very idea of intertextuality was articulated in the circle around the Russian literary theorist Mikhail Bakhtin (1981; Bell & Gardiner, 1998), who developed his accounts of literary communication at the beginning of the twentieth century. What Bakhtin referred to as 'dialogism,' echoing the insight of hermeneutics that inter-pretation amounts to a dialogue between and among texts and readers, was later translated as 'intertextuality' by Julia Kristeva (1984/1974). Their central claim was that no text is self-sufficient, complete in itself. In contemporary terminology, each text represents one node in a network of texts, both contemporary and his-torical. Other texts can be seen and heard to resonate within the text in question, evoking associations – connotations – in and among readers.

Originating as an analytical category from literary studies, Intertextuality as a phenomenon became especially manifest with modern mass media, which have systematically reformulated and recirculated works and themes from the much longer history of arts and cultures. On the web and in apps, hyperlinks are current prototypes of intertextuality, which operationalize and automate the interrelations between texts and contexts: Clicking links, whether to order a meal or buy a pair of shoes, we act at a distance, embedding the purchases in the context of our lives while ascribing meaning to the action as well as the commodity or service.

Figure 2.4 lays out intertextuality in a model with two axes (the figure builds on Fiske, 1987: 108–127). The **horizontal axis** has been the center of attention in most analyses of intertextuality since Bakhtin, particularly within literary studies and other aesthetic disciplines (e.g., Genette, 1997). Research has examined how particular categories of meaning have been accumulated and passed on throughout the history of arts and cultures – text to text, author to author, and -ism to -ism – in

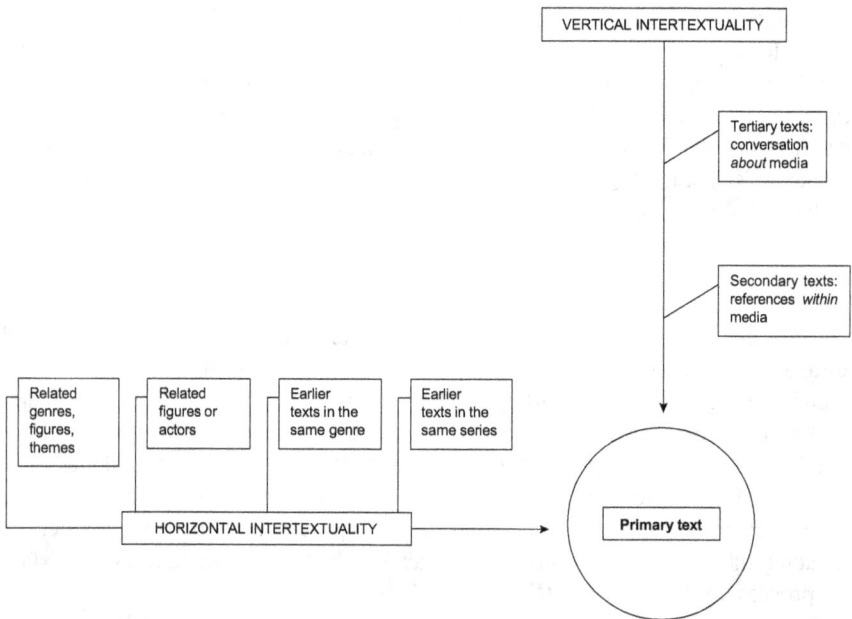

Figure 2.4 Horizontal and vertical intertextuality.

the shape of genres, characters, themes, symbols, and metaphors. Contemporary journalism and feature films, for instance, will draw on a rich legacy of conventions in describing, interpreting, and placing in historical and existential perspectives the wars and climate-related conflicts variously affecting different world regions (Chapter 1, p. 2).

Horizontal intertextuality feeds into **the primary text**, whether understood as a work of art or as a media product. **Vertical intertextuality**, in turn, addresses the circulation of meaning through texts, which is ongoing not only through historical time, but across social and cultural space too – the physical spaces in which people interact face-to-face as well as the virtual spaces of media. On the one hand, media institutions will refer to a comparatively small set of select or **primary texts**, for example, in advertisements for or reviews of feature films and in debate about the journalistic coverage of major national and international news events, from the images of the burning towers of the World Trade Center in 2001 to the empty streets and stores of early coronavirus lockdowns in 2020. These 'texts about texts' are the **secondary texts**. On the other hand, a great variety of interactions among ordinary users take place before, during, and after their media use. These additional, distributed, and multistep communications represent the **tertiary texts**. Along the vertical axis, both media organizations and media users participate in the production and circulation of meaning in society.

The present model of intertextuality (Figure 2.4) lends itself to criticism because of the emphasis placed on the 'primary' text, work, or media product. In certain respects, advertising and other 'secondary' texts can be considered at least as important, for the further circulation of news and entertainments, and for public expectations regarding their role and relevance in users' lives. 'Tertiary' texts, equally, ultimately draw on the same reservoir of cultural conventions that is the source of primary texts. Nevertheless, the model offers a useful device for designing concrete analyses of the interrelations between different media and texts as they enter into social and discursive **networks** (Chapter 6, p. 180). The model, in addition, helpfully recognizes ordinary media users among the origins of meaning – **humans as media** – as examined throughout this book.

Single texts, to be sure, remain relevant objects of analysis as instances of particular **genres** with specific social uses. To exemplify, the internationally successful Danish television series *Borgen* (2010–2022) about political infighting in parliament and within parties had broad similarities with daily newscasts about comparable events in Denmark and elsewhere. Newscasts rely on narratives; fiction films borrow techniques of representation from documentaries. The public service broadcaster behind *Borgen*, in other programming and online, took advantage of such family resemblances, for example, by having the main character of the fiction series, Birgitte Nyborg, tweet to the population of Denmark. Real-life Danish politicians, however, did not engage 'Birgitte Nyborg' in debate, nor could she speak or vote in parliament. Different genres of texts are circumscribed by different contexts even as the texts inscribe the contexts. As the following section explains, different genres invite distinctive forms of reflection and action – engagement with the world of politics through fiction, or deliberation regarding specific political agendas affecting the lives of viewers as citizens.

Box 2.3 Theories at issue

Texts and/or artworks?

Intertextuality and the extended concept of 'texts' might be taken to suggest that all texts are created equal – at least equally worthy of study. In practice, however, some texts are still considered more equal than others – more important and valuable. This is the case both if you ask ordinary users of media, and if you turn to scholars of intertextuality and other text-centered research.

Image 2.4a Mona Lisa. By Leonardo da Vinci.

Image 2.4b Mona Lisa. DALL-E.

Historically, a distinction between fine arts and popular entertainments has persisted, between unique works of art and commercially produced texts for mass consumption.

Image 2.4 bears out this distinction. Here, one of the most famous and familiar paintings in much of the world, *La Gioconda* by Leonardo da Vinci, better known as the *Mona Lisa*, appears side by side with a much later cartoon version: While the Lisa figure has also appeared, for instance, in installments of *The Simpsons* comic series, the present variant was produced through text-to-image modeling by the DALL-E artificial intelligence system (on such systems, see further Chapter 7, p. 212). Evidently, the painting is somehow primary – there could be no cartoon version without that original. But could or should the painting be considered more valuable or worthwhile in the perspective of contemporary users? Is it more important for scholarship to study the artwork than the commercial text? In any event, how is one supposed to undertake research about a painting situated deep in the Louvre museum in Paris, France, heavily guarded and surrounded daily by crowds of visitors? In fact, most people who are familiar with the *Mona Lisa*, only ever saw it as reproduced in books of art history and on the internet (on the technical reproduction of artworks, see further Chapter 1, p. 7).

This image helps distinguish the approach of media and communication research to texts and images from those of art history and other aesthetic disciplines – throughout this volume, we highlight three strategies of media and communication studies. First, the field proposes to explore the full **process** in which a painting or cartoon is produced, distributed, and consumed or used, asking, 'when is meaning?' Art history, traditionally, has given priority to the artwork as a **product** ('where is meaning?') with specific formal and thematic characteristics – even if art historians, to varying degrees, seek to place artworks in their historical and cultural contexts. These disciplinary emphases, among other considerations, have entailed fundamental differences in the choice of methods with which to examine the cultural artifacts – methods and differences which we elaborate in Chapter 6.

Second, the underlying distinction between artworks and mass-mediated texts is grounded in wider conceptions of **culture**. In public debate, it is not uncommon to encounter the view that, for instance, cartoons are hardly culture, and certainly not art. The divide – which we return to in Chapter 7 – is theoretical, but also normative, bearing witness to deeply held convictions about the beautiful and its interrelations with the true and the good, among the users of arts and media, and among the scholars studying these phenomena.

Third, we therefore elaborate, in Chapter 7, on media and communication studies as products of the historical societies from which they originate, and in which they remain embedded. In significant ways, media and communication research responds to questions being posed by contemporary technological and social developments – when Leonardo painted the *Mona Lisa*, there were no cartoons to compare it with. And, when researchers feed their answers back to society, they participate in shaping these same technological and social developments – through the texts they communicate to audiences willing to read and listen.

Genres and actions

A genre can be defined as a set of textual conventions for representing, expressing, and experiencing a particular segment of reality. As such, genres serve as informal contracts orienting and governing communication between and among people. Such contracts are comparable to the hermeneutic concept of pre-understanding (p. 34): To even begin to communicate, we need a framing within which a great many things are presumed and prefigured. Genres frame communications.

The concept of genres has a very long history, beginning with rhetoric in classical Greece. It has been applied to spoken, written, printed, electronic, and digital forms of communication, especially in humanistic scholarship on literature and other art forms. The original focus was on epic, dramatic, and lyrical forms of expression and interaction. Contemporary interdisciplinary research has taken a steadily growing interest in how a broad range of genres 'interpellate,' invoke, or address their participants in communication, establishing and maintaining social relations between texts and their recipients as well as among media users and other communicators (Bawarshi, 2000; Miller, 1984, 1994; Yates & Orlikowski, 1992). The approach includes social media, which can be understood as genres that 'enunciate' or anticipate users and their interactions in the context of everyday life (Lomborg, 2011). In a sense, genres provide 'manuscripts' for social actions that are ongoing in and of communication, or which may follow the immediate communicative contact. Examples range from dating apps to websites delivering consumer bargains and stock prices. Genres are textual forms with social functions.

For media and communication studies, it is useful to examine three aspects of any given genre (Williams, 1977):

- Formal composition
- Characteristic subject matter
- Mode of address

Whereas genre studies have traditionally focused on the formal composition of texts (for example, prose compared to poetry) and their characteristic topics or themes (romantic love and religious faith), recent research has come to emphasize the modes of address and potential actions associated with particular genres (Image 2.5). One current example is *Wikipedia* (McDowell & Vetter, 2022), which offers (more or less) factual knowledge about numerous topics in a standardized format, and which large numbers of internet users depend on as a first stop for resolving either disagreements with others or their own doubts. Distinctive features of *Wikipedia* include both the possibility of creating new entries and contributing corrections to existing entries, and the documentation and continued accessibility of successive versions of entries, enabling continued reflection and deliberation about the truthfulness and relevance of entries. Another example is the health information provided by public authorities during the **Covid-19** pandemic from 2020 onward. The same disease was countered with diverse communicative strategies in different national settings, including public information campaigns with distinctive modes of address designed to orient citizens' actions (Maarek, 2022).

Genres and modes of address constitute a key juncture of texts, media, and society. We began this chapter by locating texts 'inside' the media. But, in a sense, the texts *are* the media: Texts are the concrete carriers of the meaningful relations between and among individuals and groups that make societies possible. Chapter 1 underscored (p. 3) that meaning is *both* a product *and* a process. Chapter 1 further elaborated how the two perspectives on texts and media have given rise to separate and, in part, conflicting conceptions of communication as, respectively, transmission and ritual. But the two distinctive conceptions are often neglected or conflated in the **communication models** informing so much education and research about media. Communication models present themselves as close to common sense for many, even most readers of this book. To specify the role of texts in communication, however, it is necessary to revisit a few variations on the basic communication model. And to do so, we need the concept of **discourse**. Texts become discourses when they are communicated in and through media.

Image 2.5 World banking. Photo by Rosenfeld Media on Flickr.

The interactive potential of the internet has transformed the way in which people 'do' banking. Much of what used to happen face-to-face, when individual customers would enter the local branch of a national banking institution to withdraw cash, pay their bills, and perhaps make an investment, increasingly is performed online and across borders. Small businesses, similarly, rely on a wide variety of digital services, to secure microfinancing and to conduct import and export transactions on globalized markets. One example is the M-PESA service (M for mobile, 'pesa' for money in Swahili). Originating in Kenya in 2007, it expanded to become, by 2010, the most successful mobile financial service in the developing world with branches across a range of African nations.

Media and discourses

The concept of discourse permeates contemporary research on societies and cultures (Tannen et al., 2015). The present book defines discourse as the concrete uses of language, images, and other signs and symbols in social contexts. Compared to 'text,' which typically refers to a delimited entity communicating in and of itself, 'discourse' directs attention to the interdependencies between what is being communicated and the wider context of communication: senders, receivers, social settings, and historical and cultural backgrounds. A summary way of expressing the distinction is to say that a particular text – a song, a fairy tale, or a joke – may be articulated in many different variants or as different discourses (Bordwell et al., 2024; Chatman, 1989). **Discourse analysis** explores such variations and their interrelations with the rest of the communicative context. Across contexts, the same text translates into multiple discourses.

One prominent approach to discourses and discourse analysis underscores that, regardless of the many and superficially different discourses of a culture or historical period, they nevertheless tend to reproduce the same underlying **Discourse** – which defines and delimits what can and will be thought and said in communication. This variety of discourse analysis has a family resemblance with Barthes's examination of the connotations and mythologies of signs as communicated; both approaches seek to identify and deconstruct the worldviews at work. The central inspiration for this second approach to discourse has been the work of the French philosopher, Michel Foucault (1972/1969), who spoke of such worldviews as **orders of discourse** that, for a given period, remain dominant, but that, over the long historical haul, are replaced by new orders of discourse. A combination of Foucault's approach with a close reading of language and texts has been developed under the heading **critical discourse analysis** (Fairclough, 1995).

In this book, we approach discourses as the concrete manifestations of texts in communicative practices, as part of social contexts of interaction. The next, analytical question is whether and how standard communication models may help clarify the relationship between texts and discourses – between a delimited message and an entire communicative interaction. Communication models are, indeed, well suited for that analytical and conceptual task, but only if we begin by comparing, contrasting, and integrating two classic models. Figure 2.5 performs such an integration.

At first glance, Figure 2.5 is quite simple and familiar. It indicates a Sender and a Receiver exchanging a Message through a Channel. These four elements cover most of the first of two basic communication models, namely, the social scientific perspective of **transmission**, which was summarized in Harold D. Lasswell's (1948) formula: Who says what, in which channel, to whom, with what effect? The last element – an effect – is not explicated in Figure 2.5, but the premise is that if

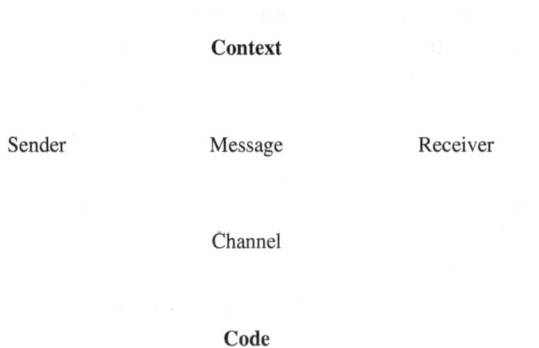

Context

Sender   Message   Receiver

Channel

Code

Figure 2.5 An interdisciplinary model of communication.

you receive a message, it will have some kind of effect, perhaps simply becoming aware of and experiencing an object or event, whether manifest or imagined.

Beyond Lasswell, Figure 2.5 incorporates a second model. Its origin is the humanistic perspective on communication as **ritual** – the position that communication is a way of sharing meaning through texts and other categories of messages, rather than transmitting information from A to B. In most respects, the two basic models coincide or overlap. One of the most influential communication models originating from the humanities, advanced by the linguist and literary scholar Roman Jakobson (1960), included the elements of Sender, Message, Receiver, and Channel (albeit in a different terminology). Jakobson's model, however, stood out on two important points, marked in **bold** in Figure 2.5.

The first distinctive element is the **code**, that is, a set of principles for selecting and combining signs, so that the entire configuration of the message acquires a particular meaning. Language, images, music – all of these forms of expression rely on specific codes, which, further, can be seen to vary widely across cultures and historical periods. Jakobson was particularly interested in the codes characteristic of poetry, and one of his points was that there is, in fact, no such thing as a separate poetic language. When poems come across as poetic, it is because ordinary language is used in extraordinary ways, so that readers or receivers feel uncertain as to what, in fact, the message is – multiple or ambiguous meanings are housed in one message. A related and equally important point, for Jakobson, was that poetic language is not restricted to poetry or literature generally. Most people regularly grow poetic in everyday communication, more or less intentionally – joking, flirting, and advertising all feed on poetic language.

The last section of this chapter returns to a special kind of code – the **binary code**, 0's and 1's – which has enabled new varieties of communication between and among humans and machines. It is the articulation and translation of signs in and through computers – from so-called machine code via several levels of programming to user interfaces – which deliver messages in codes that are comprehensible to humans.

The second distinctive element of Jakobson's (1960) model is the **context**. Texts deal with something – contexts. Also Lasswell (1948) assumed that communication addresses various aspects of reality. But a decisive difference between the two models is that 'context' carries different implications in the two perspectives. Jakobson's explicit reference to context was meant to underline that, thanks to texts, contexts are represented in a communicable, socially exchangeable form. Texts select and combine particular elements of reality in representations. Jakobson was positioning himself 'inside' texts, looking 'out' on reality. That perspective is comparable to the most common approach in studies of intertextuality (p. 43), which takes as its premise that humans come to understand reality through the weaving of texts in meaningful patterns. At the center of Jakobson's humanistic communication model is the text in itself, containing only traces of real-world contexts.

In comparison, the premise of Lasswell's (1948) transmission model is close to common parlance. Here, 'contexts' are the concrete realities being represented in texts: the material and institutional structures surrounding communication, the

Referential

Emotive   Poetic   Conative

Phatic

Metalinguistic

Figure 2.6 Communicative functions.

private and public spaces of people's lives. In this social-scientific perspective, the contexts of communication include physical infrastructures, international tech corporations, and national legislation regulating the operation of media in society (which are the main topics of the following Chapter 3). In sum, the transmission model observes texts from the 'outside,' standing in society and looking 'into' texts, so as to better understand how and why they are structured in particular ways to carry communication in society.

It should be added that Jakobson identified additional communicative functions, seven in all, one for each element of his communication model. These functions lend shape, to varying degrees, both to individual texts and to communicative processes. Figure 2.6 lays out the seven functions. The Emotive function marks the Sender's presence in the text, just as the Conative function registers its orientation toward the Receiver. The Phatic function makes sure that the Channel is open and working; Senders may clear their throats or repeat themselves. And if a portion of the Code may be difficult to understand, Senders can rely on the Metalingual function to explain a word or statement. The Referential function registers the link of the communication to the Context being represented. Finally, the Poetic function, as already mentioned, raises questions regarding the meaning of the Message: Ambiguous statements and transferred senses introduce a degree of openness into communication, for better or worse.

We are now in a position to summarize the relationship between the two communication models – their distinctive understandings of texts and discourses. Texts become discourses when they are communicated through media, acquiring social functions. Such functions are signaled 'inside' the texts and can be read off – this is the strength of humanistic models of texts and communications. It is equally important, however, to consider in which forms and to what extent various communicative functions manifest themselves 'outside' texts, in society – that is the strength of social-scientific models and studies of communication. *Their* central questions have been what humans do *with* media, and what media do *to* people (Katz, 1959). The two models, in combination, provide analytical resources for research to account for the discourses of media, at once, as vehicles of textual contents and communicative forms with social functions.

Metatexts, metadata, and metacommunication

The preceding section noted how, according to Jakobson (1960), the metalingual function serves to explain what particular linguistic signs mean, for example, foreign words or loan words. Media and communication research goes on to examine entire texts from a metaperspective – this book contains many metatexts in the form of summaries and interpretive accounts of classic texts about influential theories. Metadata, similarly, are data about data, for instance, indications of when a particular message was sent, and who sent it. Most generally, metacommunication is communication about an ongoing communication: Through choices of words, tones of voice, and body language, we constantly suggest to others what is the meaning or intention behind what we are saying.

'Meta' means 'after' or 'beyond': As reviewed in earlier sections of this chapter, textual analyses can bring to the surface meanings and intentions that lie beyond, below, or behind the literal meanings of words (and images) in media, relying on models and concepts from rhetoric, hermeneutics, and semiotics. This final section presents a complementary model for the analysis of texts and signs, specifically as they enter into digital media and communication.

Digital communication systems lend themselves to a continuous documentation of their operations, both as technological structures and as interactions between humans and computers, through 'cookies' or little computer files placed on users' devices: How often do particular users visit particular social media, who do they interact with there, for how long, which sites and services had they previously accessed, where did they go next, and so on? Answers to such questions can be gathered from **metadata**. And the reasons for meticulously documenting all of these data are, at once, technological and commercial: As we elaborate in the next chapter, the minimal metadata registering clicks and likes are worth very large sums of money, if and when they are collected, processed, and communicated to the right recipients in the right formats.

Communicatively speaking, metadata lie 'beyond' or 'on top of' the content or information being communicated. The underlying activity is **metacommunication** (Bateson, 1972; Jensen, 2022), or 'communication about communication,' which facilitates the conduct of communication as commonly understood. Importantly, metacommunication is carried on alongside and aligned with communication as such: In face-to-face interactions, people will have regular eye contact, and they will explain, in one way or another, why, at a certain point, they end the interaction. But, in the case of everyday conversations, the 'metadata' literally disappear into thin air.

Digital communication systems, in contrast, host and document several varieties of metacommunication. Here, the technology registers and stores the metadata, in and of the use of the technology for communication and many other purposes. On the one hand, the system automatically notes what users are up to, as far as

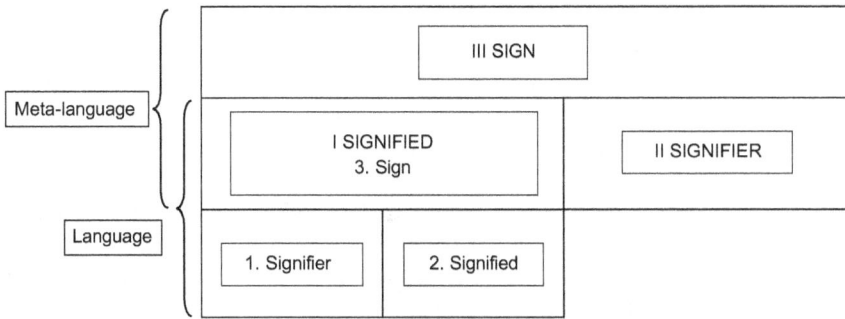

Figure 2.7 Metalanguage and metacommunication.

searching for information or sharing messages is concerned – what users are doing, in itself constitutes a form of communication, which later will be analyzed and recycled by others: system administrators, advertisers, researchers. On the other hand, users themselves add metadata to the system – they metacommunicate when they like, share, and comment on what others are saying and doing.

Earlier in this chapter, we illustrated the insight of textual traditions of scholarship that the meanings and implications of signs come in layers – in relation to the model and analysis of denotation and connotation (p. 39). In fact, the originators of this first layering of meaning – Hjelmslev and Barthes – outlined a comparable model of metacommunication. In Figure 2.3, the full sign at the first, denotative level (the image of a young Black man in uniform saluting the flag) was treated, at the next, connotative level, as the signifier or expressive component of yet another sign with a contested signified or content added ('imperialism is a legitimate social order'). Figure 2.7 is nearly identical to Figure 2.3, but not quite: For the analysis of this and other signs, the devil is in the details.

A closer look at Figure 2.7 reveals that it differs from Figure 2.3 in one, crucial respect: In Figure 2.3, SIGNIFIER 2 was placed to the left, but in Figure 2.7, it is situated to the right – and SIGNIFIED 2 now stands to the left. In this second round of analysis, the sign at the first level (still the image of the young Black man saluting the flag) at the next level up becomes the signified or content of yet another sign, to which an additional signifier or expressive content is added and attached. In this way, we are able, in practical terms, to find the image via a search engine such as images.google.com: A query (August 1, 2024) for the terms 'Barthes, Black, man' returned precisely this image at the top of the listed results. Associated with texts as well as images are metadata, which function as codes – and when selected search terms are entered as data, the codes provide additional metadata for processing the query through algorithms, delivering this particular image to our screens for further examination. Having communicated and metacommunicated through Google, we as authors were in a position to access the image to do something with it – include it in a book, characterize its denotations and criticize its connotations, and communicate with others, including you, the readers of this book, about its theoretical and social implications.

Metacommunication, in conclusion, can now be compared and related to the three basic forms of communication – one-to-one, one-to-many, and many-to-many – that we introduced in Chapter 1. In digital media, metacommunication represents a fourth type – **many-to-one** communication. When millions and billions of people enter particular search terms in particular combinations, over and over again, the Google search engine registers both the terms and the combinations. Over time, search results are adjusted and adapted as the system 'learns' what people are looking for. In other digital systems, too, users communicate many-to-one or 'into the system' (Jensen & Helles, 2017). As far as the systems are concerned, the goal is to enhance searches and improve the user experience, but also to collect ever more data about what users are doing with media, in order to do something to them.

This chapter has centered on the texts, discourses, and data – including metatexts, metadiscourses, and metadata – that are the concrete carriers of communication in society. The following chapters elaborate on the wider social circumstances that condition how signs are articulated and communicated in practice. Texts are, in a sense, there to be found 'inside' the media; society, similarly, manifests itself 'inside' the media. Chapter 3 reviews the technological, economic, and organizational factors shaping the infrastructures of communication for different categories of media.

Box 2.4 Exercise

Your communication into the system

Metacommunication in digital media generates a distinctive kind of product – metadata or data about data (p. 54). Metadata are essential to the mode of operation of digital systems – in technological and communicative as well as economic respects. They are sometimes referred to as 'big data,' in view of the colossal amounts of information that are processed through algorithms and other digital techniques in order to target advertising for products and services to particular groups of users as well as individual users – you.

This exercise illustrates how metadata enter into far-flung circuits of communication involving several categories of stakeholders. In these circuits, so-called third-party services – 'trackers' – are key: Those services have built a business on harvesting, analyzing, and reselling metadata to advertisers and other communicators seeking an audience. In technical terms, this happens through signs that are registered via http cookies at web pages and software packages in apps.

1. First, choose two apps that you would like to examine and compare – and which you yourself regularly use. Then go to the web page Exodus

Privacy (https://reports.exodus-privacy.eu.org/en/) and conduct a search for the two apps. For each app, you will be able to navigate a dedicated page telling you which, and how many, third-party services ('trackers') the app in question incorporates (e.g., Facebook Ads and Google Analytics); what purposes they serve for the app (e.g., advertising); and the sorts of data and metadata about users (e.g., their location and their photo archive) that the app and, hence, the third parties have access to.

2. Describe and compare the two apps with particular reference to their use of third-party services and the resulting data access: Which third-party services have access to user data through the app? What ends are these third-party services pursuing? Which kinds of data and metadata about users are available for harvesting?

The exercise can be turned into an assignment or paper, for instance, by including all apps found on one student's smartphone, or the five most common apps in a study group or class. This approach enables a characterization of the exposure to tracking through smartphones that affects individual users as well as groups – which, in turn, may be understood and studied as target groups in terms of their sociodemographic features (see further Chapter 6, p. 164).

3   Society in the media

Media are technologies

'The computer didn't do it.' That was the message of an advertising campaign that the tech company IBM ran in 1981 (Image 3.1). The image presents a police lineup of the kind that American movies and crime series have made familiar also outside the United States – but with the distinctive addition of a computer among the potential suspects.

At the time, computers were already essential tools of business and public administration, but they only became common consumer items from the 1980s onward. Massive mainframe computer systems were stoking fear of potential abuses with public consequences. While IBM, in the nature of the matter, would like to sell more computers, the purpose of such corporate advertising was to nourish an understanding of computers as neutral instruments and natural partners in collaborations involving ever more people in ever more contexts. The year 1981 was also when IBM introduced its line of PCs, which helped promote the widespread adoption of computers by households through the terminology behind the abbreviation: **personal computer**. And when Apple, in turn, launched the first Macintosh computer in 1984, the advertising campaign appealed to a notion of 'one person, one computer' in parallel to the core principle of political democracy: 'one person, one vote' (Jensen, 1993).

IBM was addressing the common worry that new technologies would have unforeseen and unfortunate consequences for humans and their societies. A classic literary statement of this concern was the English author Mary Shelley's 1818 story of Dr. Frankenstein, who dared create another human being for his own uses. Technologies of communication, in particular, have provoked **media panics**, in which a medium serves as the point of reference (or scapegoat) for a critique of contemporary social developments, for example, the (excessive) use of computer games or smartphones by young people (Drotner, 1992). Intervening in public debate, IBM and other tech companies may profit by making the point that, in a sense, it is the people using computers, not the computers as such, that are responsible for any abuses.

DOI: 10.4324/9781032655109-3

Computers can't commit crimes.
But they can be misused.
    That concerns us at IBM, and it should concern anyone involved with computers today. Because keeping computers secure is the responsibility of everyone who uses and manages them.
    At IBM, we continue to develop security measures that can help keep information safe.
    For instance, IBM computers can demand identification in any number of ways, including passwords, keys and magnetic ID cards. They can flag errors. Catch omissions. They're able to inform you of attempted intrusions and help an auditor do his job. Encryption devices can turn information into secret codes that are virtually impossible to crack.
    We're also researching new safeguards, such as electronic signature verification.
    True, there's probably no such thing as total security. But with proper precautions, computers can be more than just safe places to keep information. They may well be the safest. **IBM**

Image 3.1 The computer didn't do it. IBM ad, 1981.

This advertisement – reproduced from Time *magazine in 1981 – bears witness to changing technologies of representation and communication. The basis of the illustration was a photocopy of a microfilm, which during the twentieth century served as a way for libraries to archive print media, so that they could be used as source materials in historical research, sometimes in fragments and mostly in low resolution. For reproduction in this book, several copies of the advertisement, which extended across two pages, have been scanned digitally and then pieced together, with old and new media working in concert. The physical copy of the book (if that is what you are reading) is an **analog** medium, but most of the preparation (writing and editing) and production (layout and printing) was supported by digital technologies.*

More controversially, a similar point has been made about weapons. Like media, weapons are used and abused, sometimes with fatal consequences. The political lobby around the U.S. National Rifle Association (NRA) sums up its response in the argument 'Guns don't kill people – people kill people.' The counterargument – that it is evidently easier to kill other people with a gun in your hand – is met with additional questions: 'How are ordinary, law-abiding citizens supposed to defend themselves against people attacking them with a gun?' Following one more school shooting, in Newtown, Connecticut, on December 14, 2012, the head of the NRA,

Wayne LaPierre, at a press conference offered what he took to be a conclusive argument: 'The only thing that stops a bad guy with a gun is a good guy with a gun.' Since then, mass shootings in the United States have continued (totaling 604, with 754 people killed in 2023), and the causes of, and potential solutions to, gun violence have remained issues of public debate.

The impact of technologies on societies is never a matter of simple causes and effects – that is the conclusion of decades of social-scientific and human-istic research. But the challenge remains one of understanding – interpreting and explaining – how, exactly, the two sides of the technology–society equation inter-sect and interact, as technologies are developed to serve social ends, and as they are put into social practice at scale.

Box 3.1 Theory

Medium theory

'The medium is the message.' This famous slogan pinpoints an important research tradition addressing the interplay of media and society, so-called medium theory. The slogan was coined by the Canadian literary scholar and cultural theorist Marshall McLuhan, who during the 1960s gained both con-siderable influence on media theory and fame through the media. Beyond a number of widely read books (McLuhan, 1962, 1964), he succeeded in communicating his message to much larger publics through the central mass media of the period: television and radio.

The point of the slogan was to suggest that the specific content of the messages of any given medium is less important than its general form. *Form* carries *content* – each medium comes with a particular view of the world. Listening to the news on the radio at home in the morning is a rather different experience than checking an app on one's smartphone on the way to work, or consulting websites on the PC during the workday, or getting a summary from television news in the evening. It is not only that the events reported as news will have developed throughout the day – different media afford distinctive experiences because of their forms and expressive features.

Departing from this basic insight, McLuhan drew far-reaching conclusions about the historical development of media and their place in society. From the 1950s, television gradually became the central medium of contemporary communication environments – a standard against which other media would be measured – at least in North American culture. To McLuhan, that shift introduced a welcome challenge to print culture, which had been dominant for centuries, and which, in his analysis, carried a limited *and* limiting linear logic: The receivers of print media were being forced, in effect, to follow the sender's text, letter by letter, line after line, page up and page down. Instead,

McLuhan associated alternative forms of culture, even a new historical era, with the new (at the time) electronic media, which could be seen and heard to offer innovative visual and auditory forms of expression. Recalling IBM's advertising slogan of 1981 (p. 59), we could restate McLuhan's claim – or at least his wish and his hope – as 'Television did it!'

McLuhan's arguments were rather heavy-handed, inferring more or less directly from the media's changing forms of expressions to changing worldviews among their audiences. Part of the background was his training in literary studies, which traditionally have concentrated on the interpretation of texts rather than the examination of actual readers and readings. In contrast to his mentor, Harold A. Innis, whose works covered history and economics, McLuhan did not rely on historical source criticism (see further Chapter 6, p. 174), nor did he undertake empirical research on the social contexts of media and communication. In hindsight, his predictions about the dawning of a new historical era of communication and culture stand as inspired and inspiring essays rather than traditional scholarship. McLuhan took inspiration from the fundamental social and cultural changes taking place around him (the 'youth rebellion' associated with the year 1968), and from their representation in the media, above all television, which disseminated and debated these shifts far and wide. Like McLuhan, also later theorists of media and communication have articulated the hopes and dreams of their times. During the 1990s, many scholars and authors looked to the internet as a **cyberspace**, a different realm of reality empowering individuals and enabling their personal and cultural expression (Bell & Kennedy, 2000; Benedikt, 1991; Jones, 1998) – the concept derived from a novel (Gibson, 1984). During the 2000s, the notion of a **Web 2.0** (O'Reilly, 2005) proposed to recover and reinvigorate the internet for more and better user participation. And during the early 2020s, the potential merger of physical and virtual realities was summarized in the idea of a **metaverse** (Ball, 2022), once again informed by science fiction (Stephenson, 1992).

Despite the questionable generalizations and essayistic exaggerations advanced by McLuhan, subsequent theory and empirical studies have redeveloped the implication that was first identified by Innis and McLuhan: Depending on the material technologies available during particular historical periods, some forms of communication, culture, and society have been conceivable – others inconceivable. The alphabet and other systems of writing had enabled the accumulation and critical assessment of human knowledge, which previously had been passed on from generation to generation through oral tradition in the form of 'good stories' (Goody & Watt, 1963; Havelock, 1963). The printing press, crucially, came to circulate both religious scriptures and publications analyzing and criticizing religion to vastly increased numbers of people, feeding into wider cultural and social shifts, including the Protestant Reformation in Europe (Eisenstein, 1979).

The internet and digitalization writ large currently invite comparison with writing and printing as necessary, if far from sufficient conditions for social change of a comparable scope and scale.

As investigated by Innis (1951; 1972/1950), particular technologies and communicative practices have been associated with particular types of societies, which, in his rendering, have tended either to remain stable over **time** or to extend across **space**. Inscriptions in stone last a long time, but do not travel well; papyrus and paper are easy to carry and transport, thus facilitating the dominance of distant provinces by centralized political powers, but they are vulnerable to floods, fires, and decay over time, and they lend themselves to appropriation by local oppositions in provinces speaking out against the center. In the second half of the twentieth century, television served to redefine the experience of space and time, specifically the distinction between private and public spheres, by introducing moving images of far-off, foreign locations to young and old within families and households (Meyrowitz, 1985). The internet, in its turn, constitutes a worldwide archive of information and a suite of services for interacting at all levels of local and global society, involving individuals, organizations, and institutions across space and time.

'Medium theory' is the summary term for the approach to media and communication studies outlined here (Meyrowitz, 1994). (A related, somewhat broader research tradition considering media as psychological and cultural environments is 'media ecology' (Strate, 2016)). Digitalization in general and the internet in particular have brought renewed attention, in recent years, to the theoretical and analytical perspective of medium theory. This perspective considers different phases of world history in terms of the changing modes of expression or 'languages' of predominant media and communicative practices (Manovich, 2001). Such languages, importantly, are **remediated** (Bolter & Grusin, 1999): The forms and contents of one medium are recycled by subsequent media. And the recycling works both ways: YouTube videos reflect more than a century of film history; current television programming has adopted the use of several overlapping 'windows' within a single screen image from computers and the internet. Whereas medium theory has sometimes been criticized for an excessive focus on one medium at a time ('from writing to printing to television to computing' (Strate, 2016)), the ongoing society-wide and worldwide digitalization of media and society represents an opportunity for research to examine the continued coexistence of different media in contemporary communication environments.

Determination in the first instance

Research on the relationship between technologies and societies, sooner or later, faces the question of **determination**: Which elements (for instance, the diffusion of the internet) were responsible for changes in which other elements (for example, the 'Arab Spring' of political transformation in countries of the Middle East during the 2010s)? And which mediating mechanisms might explain the concrete interaction of these several elements (infrastructures, levels of education, national economies, longer cultural legacies, or other factors) (Howard, 2010)?

It is tempting to conclude that, when all is said and done – **in the final instance** – *either* 'technologies shape societies,' *or* 'societies shape technologies': New media of political communication empower citizens – or citizens empower themselves by developing new technological resources and engaging in new communicative practices. The question of determination remains one of the most intensely contested, in media and communication research, and across other disciplines and interdisciplinary fields examining the relationship between technology and society (for overview, see, e.g., Biagioli, 1999).

A reformulation of these questions helps prepare more nuanced answers. One of the founders of the research tradition of **cultural studies**, Stuart Hall (1983), introduced a distinction between determination in the final instance and determination in the first instance. In doing so, he was challenging a common tendency in Marxist and other critical social science to take as its premise that, in the final instance, it is the economic basis of society, not its political and cultural superstructures, that govern developments, changes, and, indeed, the course of world history. As a model for explaining social developments, that approach could be said to take its lead from detectives in crime fiction: *Follow the money!* Although Hall certainly agreed that economic conditions explain a great many social structures and processes, he preferred an analysis moving 'in the opposite direction': first a description of the economic (and other material) circumstances, then an explanation of what particular social groups and persons actually do and say, recognizing the various degrees of freedom, unpredictability, or **indetermination** associated with specific domains such as media and communication. As one illustration, telecommunications companies around the world have cashed in on the innumerable texts sent via mobile phones since roughly the year 2000 (and which are still being sent, day in and day out, even while messaging applications have been taking over much of the traffic). But, in fact, texting was never thought of in advance or planned as the first 'killer application' of mobile media and communication. The technological potential was discovered as if by accident, was embraced not least by young users, and soon came to be taken for granted in everyday communication within and across age groups (Gow & Smith, 2006; 55; Ling, 2004).

The principle of determination in the first instance can be specified with reference to three different mechanisms: affordance, emergence, and momentum. These mechanisms begin to specify how technological and other social factors intersect and interact to produce media as permanent institutions in the structure of societies.

Affordances

The term 'affordances' refers to the common experience that, when humans encounter objects in the world, whether in nature or in social settings, the objects seem to afford, offer, or invite some uses rather than others. Taking a walk in a wood, for instance, we may use a branch that has fallen from a tree as a bench to sit on and have a rest; the same branch can later serve as a bridge across a stream in the wood. The outside of a car, similarly, affords a bench for the two main characters of a feature film to have a conversation in between two action-packed scenes; next, the car becomes part of a bridge allowing the protagonists to jump from car to car in pursuit of the truck up ahead with a criminal at the wheel.

For a start, people will use objects as they find them (branches) or as the objects have been designed to be used (cars). Throughout human history, however, objects have been remade for seemingly endless purposes: Trees are turned into newspapers; cars become part of political demonstrations and art installations. It is, above all, this long trajectory of individual and collective interventions into and engagements with reality – from objects that were simply picked up and applied, through basic tools that have been designed and redesigned for a proliferating variety of jobs, to complex technological systems supporting local as well as global social interaction – that distinguishes the human species, enabling us to rule (other) animals and the Earth (so far).

Recognizing very long processes of natural evolution and historical change, the concept of affordances originally was developed within the discipline of biology to capture the great many ways in which humans interact with their natural environments (Gibson, 1979). More recently, it was transferred to media and communication research to challenge an understanding of technology advanced by **postmodernism**, which takes as its premise that technologies are open to limitless reinterpretation and remodeling. As elaborated and applied by Hutchby (2001) to media and communication, the concept of affordances offers a middle ground between the radical **constructivism** of postmodernism and a similarly absolute form of determinism. Hutchby noted how, on the one hand, both individuals and social groups gradually discover and learn the affordances of communication technologies, and how, on the other hand, communities and societies come to imagine and prepare further affordances to be designed and integrated into technologies. From its introduction in 1979, the Walkman afforded a way of making music not just transportable (the transistor radio had accomplished this three decades earlier), but also personal (a personal stereo) (Bull, 2000; Gay et al., 1997). With smartphones, music players became one of many apps, a medium within a metamedium (Chapter 1, p. 8).

As with trees and cars, the affordances of smartphones are malleable; friends will share a headset to listen to the same music, then and there. As a technology and a social institution, moreover, the Walkman lent itself to adaptation, from cassette tapes via CDs to archives of MP3 files streaming from digital clouds. Lastly, a further conception of **social affordances** (Hsieh, 2012) suggests the point that affordances arise not only in the encounter between an individual user and a specific technology, but as part of configurations of technologies and users as they come together to accomplish common purposes in and across social contexts. The first Walkman afforded users the option of creating their own soundscapes, free from the madding crowds and noisy surroundings of the big city. Subsequently, users have come to enjoy additional options, for instance, sharing their musical preferences with others, at a distance and through the playlists of online services such as Spotify (see Image 3.5, p. 90).

Emergence

Media emerge when general technological potentials are given a concrete social form. The social form, importantly, is not an incidental add-on or plug-in, but a constitutive part of the formation of the medium. The very first prototypes of new media had social forms and cultural meanings: At early film screenings around 1900, before there was even an institution of cinema, 'film' featured as one item on a program of diverse entertainments in the context of a theater or tivoli (Thompson & Bordwell, 2018). It was not until the following decades that film assumed what came to be considered, for close to a century, its 'natural' form, namely, long and rounded fictional narratives shown to the general public for a fee. From the outset, documentary genres had raised high hopes regarding the enlightening potential of this new visual, easily accessible medium, but documentaries were soon relegated to a minor substream of film history. Since World War II, as films increasingly have been embedded in other media (television, video, DVD, streaming) enabling private and personal viewing – old software on new hardware in ever more contexts – fiction has remained the primary attraction.

Media history is ripe with examples of how the actual uses of communication technologies have been, if not accidental, then certainly far from given from the outset (for overview, see Winston, 1998). In each case, a range of circumstances – physical, economic, political, and cultural – ended up producing particular media in particular historical settings. **Emergence** denotes this complex process. The concept originated from **systems theory**, which seeks to characterize general features and mechanisms shaping complex systems, natural as well as societal, not least the transitions or 'quantum leaps' between different levels of complexity (Seidl & Schoeneborn, 2016): How did physical and chemical processes emerge as life in a biological sense? How did the sounds uttered by early humans turn into full-blown languages? How did the basic technical potential of sending data packets via digital networks end up facilitating global streaming services such as Netflix?

Let us return for a moment to the local origins of film. In the early days of the medium, until 1927, film was silent, which meant that the many different languages of the world were not among the factors deciding the global success (or failure) of individual films. This presented a unique window of opportunity for small nations. Denmark (a country with, at the time, a population of only 3.5 million) had been home to many successful silent films, but the introduction of 'talkies' had economic and cultural as well as personal consequences (Dinesen & Kau, 2006). The silent stars had to develop their voices (if they were able to), so that the spoken

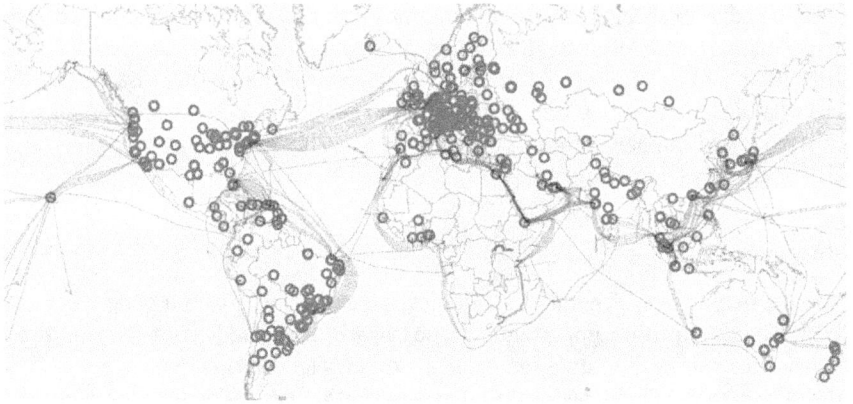

Image 3.2 Digital crossroads. Courtesy of ITU Library & Archives.

> *Internet communication has frequently been associated with an abstract and separate sphere of 'cyberspace,' and with an understanding of data as residing in 'the cloud.' Like other media of communication, however, the internet depends crucially on physical points of connection and repositories of information. One of the central components of the global internet is the so-called Internet Exchange Points (IXPs), connected by submarine and other cables, comparable to the lines through which communication by telegraph began close to 200 years ago. The internet is a network of networks, which rely variously on cabled and wireless technologies, and it is the IXPs that join local and regional networks into a global grid. As this map of the distribution of IXPs around the globe indicates (International Telecommunication Union, 2023), the whole world is connected – but some parts of the world are more connected than others. There is a distinctive concentration of IXPs in three centers of the world economy: East Asia, Europe, and North America. Such differences bear witness to further **digital divides** of a social nature, which persist both between and within countries, and which entail fundamental inequalities in the access to political, economic, and cultural information, and to other essential resources hinging on information and communication (see further Chapter 4, p. 111).*

word might match their visual appearance. Directors and companies also had to think again about the interplay of sound and image in old and new genres. Indeed, the international economy of moviemaking was transformed when language came to decide the size of potential markets and, hence, the budgets of films. Little Denmark had established itself as one of the great nations of the silent era. With the introduction of sound, it proved much harder for Danish companies to prosper on international markets. Sound film, in short, emerged as a different category of medium than silent film.

Momentum

The third and final mechanism behind the principle of technological determin-ation in the first instance (p. 63) takes effect in the long run. The understanding of consequences as 'effects' – one billiard ball hits and sets in motion another billiard ball – is deeply ingrained in human perception and cognition, so deeply that it may get in the way of more nuanced conceptions of how technologies may affect various institutions, practices, and discourses of human communication. However, alternatives to simple determinism sometimes rely on equally debatable premises and arguments. A famous example – 'butterfly effects' – derives from the natural sciences, and refers to the possibility that, in principle, a butterfly moving its wings in one geographical location could initiate an earthquake or other natural disaster on the opposite side of the Earth (Gleick, 1987: 9–31). This line of argu-ment presupposes, first, a very long chain of interrelated causes and effects and, second, a system in which one action or agent may reconfigure the system as a whole. The two elements come together within various traditions of **social con-structivism**, which have been influential in studies of the integration of technolo-gies into social systems (an early agenda-setting overview is Bijker et al., 1987) (on comparable notions of the construction of meaning at the level of texts and discourses, see Chapter 2, p. 50). The key premises of social constructivism have been that technologies remain entirely open to reinterpretation and redesign (as noted with reference to postmodernism in the section on affordances, p. 64); that such reinterpretation and redesign are essential for progress in human existence and social coexistence; and, not least, that the users of technologies are able, as social agents, to decisively reshape the available technologies as they are applied in practice. This line of argument runs the risk of reaching an opposite extreme of indeterminism, as if users were at liberty to reconstruct technologies as they please.

It is reasonable to seek a middle ground between the extremes of determinism and indeterminism, particularly regarding the long-term consequences of tech-nologies as social infrastructures. Toward this end, an important and influential contribution was presented by Thomas P. Hughes (1983), based on studies of the introduction of electricity into Western societies in the period between 1880 and 1930. In addition to recognizing the several stages of developing, implementing, and maintaining specific technologies, Hughes found that technologies are best understood not as single and separate devices, but as 'technological systems' interacting with other social systems. His further point was that, once invented and introduced into social practice, these technological systems acquire an immanent force or **momentum** that manifests itself over time and at different levels and sites of society. Accordingly, it is essential for research to examine the consequences of technologies as **processes** rather than **events**.

Hughes's (1994) conclusion, building on his own studies as well as those of other scholars, was that 'young' technological systems lend themselves, at least in certain respects, to social-constructivist perspectives, whereas 'mature' systems align better with a moderate version of technological determinism. In the latter case, infrastructures of electricity, water supply, and communication establish a set of ground rules for social interaction, constituting what the discipline of physics defines as **inertia**: It takes a great deal of concerted effort to alter the direction and force of a moving object and, similarly, of the consequences of a technology once it is firmly in place. For one thing, it takes time to develop, implement, and subsequently update or rebuild the physical networks carrying telephony, television, and internet services. For another thing, technological systems of an infrastructural scale depend on considerable economic investments, which, in turn, normally require preceding political decisions on state or public involvement, and perhaps new legislation. In the end, then, how individuals and households are able to turn on their lamps, tap water, and access images and sounds on various screens, raises fundamental ideological issues to be debated and political decisions to be made.

Because the social consequences of technologies manifest themselves over time, and are difficult to anticipate, there are many examples of failed predictions regarding the future trajectories of technologies. At the beginning of this chapter, we noted how, at the beginning of the 1980s, computers had become part of many people's working lives, but were not yet a household item (p. 58). The first, so-called mainframe computers, which were about the size of a family home, had been manufactured by IBM and other companies since the 1940s. But a future in which a large proportion of the world's population would be carrying a much smaller, much more powerful computer in their pockets, would have been inconceivable at the time, even for professionals within computing. One famous, failed prediction – 'I think there is a world market for maybe five computers' – has been attributed to the chief executive of IBM in 1943, Thomas Watson, but its precise source has not been established (http://en.wikipedia.org/wiki/Thomas_J._Watson, August 1, 2024).

Predictions such as this underscore the main message of the present section: The *affordances* of a technology must *emerge* and acquire *momentum* before either researchers or practitioners will be in a position to make qualified assessments of its short-term commercial potential and likely long-term social consequences. Rather than ridiculing past predictions with the benefit of hindsight, we are well advised to first examine their provenance (on source criticism, see further Chapter 6, p. 174), and next reflect on our own presumptions regarding technologies of the present day. Advertising and trade publications – for obvious commercial reasons – are filled to the brim with hype concerning the many blessings of a seemingly endless sequence of new products and services. Each prediction represents an opportunity to analyze its premises, and to assess its plausibility in the light of lessons from earlier historical periods.

Box 3.2 Analysis

The remediation of film

Film is a classic example of how different technologies have variously replaced and complemented each other. In historical perspective, the remediation of media (Bolter & Grusin, 1999) entails both a recycling and a reinvention of previous forms of representation and communication. And, for film as well as other media, the introduction of new technologies has presented additional opportunities for monetizing the same or similar contents and services (raising a number of economic issues that we consider in the following section).

Film constitutes, at once, a medium in its own right and a content carried by other media. A film, therefore, may end up living if not nine, then five lives:

- *Cinema.* If you ask directors and others with a special affinity for film, they are likely to insist that a film can and should be experienced at the cinema, particularly if you are viewing it for the first time. Common also in public debate, the position builds on the premise that, compared to other media, film represents a distinctive form of expression holding special artistic or aesthetic value. The premise also has served to justify the classic marketing strategy: first, a wide and deep experience before the big screen, and later, a more mundane and partially distracted experience through various smaller screens at home and on the move.
- *DVD/video.* For several decades, video recorders and, later, DVD players allowed average consumers to watch films, either bought or rented, in the privacy of their own homes. While many households around the world still have the necessary hardware and software – playback devices and collections of tapes and discs – and whereas these technologies still enable the distribution of and access to niche films with small and specialized audiences, hard copies of films for personal viewing are in decline as a mainstream medium and a central moment in the distribution chains and business models of the film industry.
- *Television.* Television traditionally has been the last stop in the tour of a film through various media. Films represented, and still represent, an important attraction for viewers and, hence, a selling point for television stations when planning programming schedules. The shared commercial interest of film and television companies has led to a great deal of collaboration between them in various national settings, delivering coproductions to be shown, in turn, at the cinema and on television.
- *Internet.* As in the case of other traditional or legacy media, the production and circulation of film have been redefined by digitalization and the internet. The increased transmission capacity of digital networks has enabled the distribution of moving images, not least feature films and television series, to the individual household – so-called **video on demand**. Where, previously, consumers would rent single films, the standard has become subscriptions to **streaming services** such as Netflix and Disney+, which draw on extensive back catalogs of films (and series) for viewers to access anytime and, increasingly, anywhere through mobile devices.
- *Multimedia.* Lastly, a comparatively small set of extraordinary films have furnished the manuscripts, so to speak, for other media products, as part of comprehensive marketing strategies. A famous historical example is the

Disney enterprise (Wasko, 2020), which turns 100 years as we write these lines. Beyond films and cartoons, the Disney corporation, among other formats, has developed television series and designed computer games building on familiar figures and themes across multiple media and genres. In this respect, films sometimes equal works of world literature that have lent themselves to recycling and reinterpretation through many iterations and media (on film, as well, with Harry Potter as one example). Filmic works as 'primary' texts, moreover, are disseminated through a range of 'secondary' texts (Chapter 2, p. 45). And, when circulated further through social and other media, films give rise to the production of 'tertiary' texts among their audiences.

In order to begin its lives, a film takes preparation of and investment in its production and distribution. First, all media production requires a wide range of professional competences covering technical designs, aesthetic choices, administrative functions, and more. In economic terms, such competences constitute commodities that each has a designated value built through **education** – human labor is a commodity that is produced and prepared through training, and which enables the production of other commodities for sale and profit. In culturally comparative and historical perspectives, the competences in question have been considered, variously, the responsibility of either the individual or the collective. In a number of European countries, education for the arts, including film, has traditionally been supported through publicly financed schools and academies, as part of a national commitment to cultivating and preserving cultural legacies. In the United States, in comparison, students of film as art and practice typically fund their own training, as an investment in their own future. Similar considerations and social choices apply to the training of journalists: Who should be responsible for producing and maintaining the competences that condition the continued operation of the press and journalism as social institutions and a 'fourth branch' of political governance (see further Chapter 4, p. 100)?

Second, the institutional and organizational processes of producing and distributing films have been organized according to two prototypical models. On the one hand, in European and some other countries, **public support** has traditionally been available to see films through the different phases of their lives – from the writing of manuscripts, via the production on sets in studios and in the field, to postproduction and marketing. On the other hand, the American model associated with Hollywood has operated on purely commercial terms, approaching films in economic and legal terms as a commodity like any other. Underlying the two models of the production of culture, and of the professional competences informing culture, are two philosophies of how best to fund and regulate marketplaces of ideas, images, and words – through the market or the state. Certainly, the two philosophies still come in several variations and combinations in different countries and regions of the world. From Bollywood and Nollywood (Image 3.3) to the United States, public funds are allocated to art films, recognizing film as more than entertainment and escape. Film inhabits the contested borderlands of fine arts and popular cultures (see further Chapter 2, p. 46). Throughout Europe, too, the production and distribution of film depend crucially on commercial markets. Nevertheless, the two philosophies remain central to national and international policy debate as it applies to and affects media and communication. Chapter 4 returns to the normative theories that guide both policy and public debate concerning the appropriate ways of regulating film, other media, and entire communication systems. The following section prepares that discussion by reviewing the basic economic mechanisms that shape the funding of (and the profits from) media and communication.

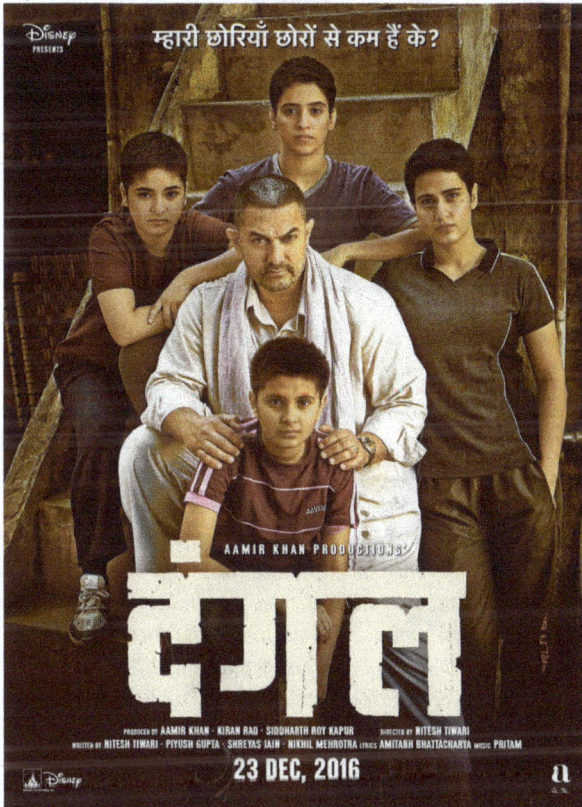

Image 3.3a Hollywood, Bollywood, Nollywood. A movie poster from the film *Dangal*. Walt Disney Co/Everett/Shutterstock.

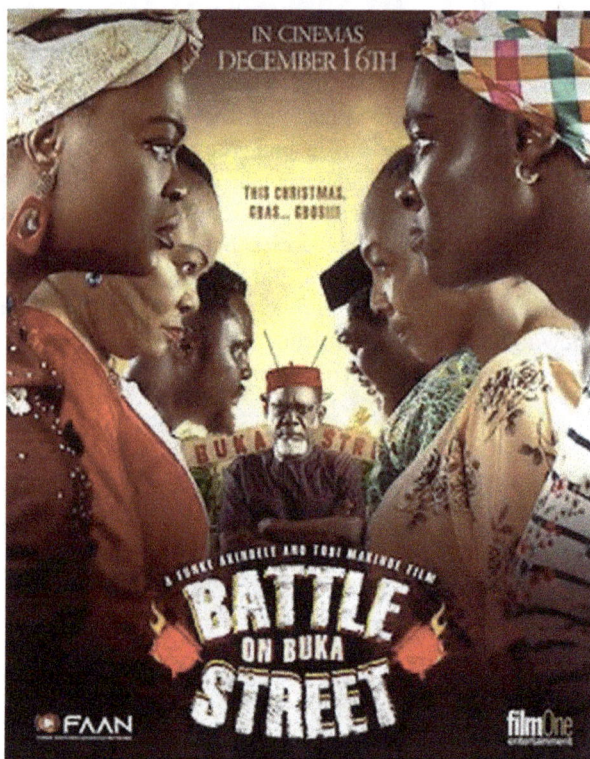

Image 3.3b Hollywood, Bollywood, Nollywood. A movie poster from the film *Battle on Buka Street*.

'Hollywood' is a familiar shorthand for the American film industry, his-torically located in and around Hollywood, California, USA. Nicknamed 'the dream factory,' Hollywood has been exporting hopeful narratives throughout the twentieth century and into the twenty-first. Around the globe, other centers of film production have prospered, as well, by addressing different cultural traditions and social circumstances. Bollywood, for one, was named after the Indian city formerly known as Bombay, now Mumbai, and produces the largest number of titles annually of any national film industry (close to 1,800 before the Covid-19 pandemic, up again to about 1,600 in 2022 (Statista, 2023)). The film Dangal, depicted here through its poster, was released in 2016 and became the highest-grossing Indian film of the year. Nollywood, for another, derives its name from Nigeria, but the term has been used more broadly to also refer to films catering to the Nigerian diaspora, and to films originating from Ghana, too. Nollywood is represented here by the 2022 box office success, Battle on Buka Street. The latter terminologies *have been contested, in part, because 'Bollywood' and 'Nollywood' might suggest that the two traditions were derivative and secondary to Hollywood. The -wood suffix, however, has remained widely popular as a way of branding local film industries in a globalizing world: Wikipedia (2023) features a long list of -woods, which, at the time of writing, included 25 in Asia, ten in Africa, and five in Latin America.*

Media are economies

'There's no business like show business' is both an evergreen (Irving Berlin, 1946) and the title of a film classic (Walter Lang, 1954), and it has become a set expression in English. The entertainment business and other media never cease to fascinate both practitioners and audiences. People *in* the media spend a great deal of time speaking *about* the media: rock stars sing about rough times on the road; film directors depict fake newsmaking and other bad habits behind the scenes; and fiction authors write books about authors writing books. And yet, audiences seem to want to hear the songs, watch the movies, and read the books.

Media, in one sense, are businesses like any other, pursuing standard business models and commercial strategies to make a profit. In another sense, however, media practitioners and media users normally agree that, compared to the manufacture of other goods and services, the production of meaning holds a privileged position in society at large. Media articulate and circulate meanings and identities that define who we are, as individuals and communities. As such, media attract more than their share of public and political attention and policy debate. A central agenda and recurring challenge is how different media, old and new, may be financed in a sustainable fashion. As the words of a song from another film classic, *Cabaret* (Bob Fosse, 1972), remind listeners: 'Money makes the world go round.'

Money and media are linked as a business practice and a form of communication, not least, through advertising. Advertising has been part and parcel of the modern media since early newspapers in the 1600s. Throughout the centuries, the potential impact of advertising on the contents of media and the quality of their communications has given rise to ideological debates, public quarrels, and a great many research projects. Particularly for television and radio, studies have established how genres and schedules are shaped in fundamental ways, both on and behind screens and speakers, by the presence of advertising in the system. The narratives of crime and comedy series follow the ebb and flow of advertising breaks; talk and music radio channels are punctuated, time and again, by a word from their sponsors.

The contents and forms of advertising do vary significantly between countries and world regions; traditional print and electronic media (and additional formats such as billboards in cities and along highways) still carry a substantial number of commercial messages. However, the shift in advertising content and spending to digital media and online communication, within a relatively short time frame, represents a decisive transformation of media economies. Table 3.1 sums up developments since 2017, and includes projections for the period until 2027. At the time of writing, digital media and communication already account for approximately three-fourths of the money spent globally on advertising, up from less than half in 2017.

Advertising, however, is only one of the moving parts of media economies. Situated within local as well as global markets, advertising addresses audiences in the context of experienced historical and cultural legacies. Money starts flowing if, and only if, the supply of communicative goods and entertaining services is matched by the right demand: interest, attention, and purchasing power.

Supply and demand

Supply and demand are familiar terms in everyday conversation as in economic theory. Even if media are a unique business, they deliver goods and services that are bought and sold in mundane and concrete transactions. Behind the seemingly simple notions of supply and demand, several economic mechanisms decide, first, which media, genres, and discourses will be supplied and, next, which of these are in sufficient demand for them to go round.

An initial step is to recognize not one, but two types of supply and demand – they are laid out in Figure 3.1. The first type is the most evident: A medium supplies a particular content or service, for instance, a feature film at the cinema or a sub-scription to a streaming service. In both instances, the audiences are consumers demanding, and willing to pay for, the experience of films, as retailed or as archived and available on demand.

The second type of supply and demand is equally important: Audiences 'supply' their attention – which is in high demand from advertisers, who will pay the media for enough attention from individuals, preferably categorized according to their sociodemographic characteristics as consumers. Although this 'supply' can be considered indirect and largely unintentional, it matters a great deal for the structures and operations of media economies. All media carrying advertising depend on the same basic model – payment for attention. As suggested by advertising jargon referring to 'eyeballs,' advertisers pay media for the documented attention of enough consumers oriented toward the right screens at the right time and to the right extent.

	Media as suppliers of commodity	Users as suppliers of commodity
Supply	*Content* (information, news, entertainments, communication services)	*Attention* (a documented number of individuals attending to a particular media content or communication service)
Demand	*Payment by audiences* (*de facto* interest in receiving a particular media content or using a particular communication service, translated into monetary form)	*Payment by advertisers* (and other economic agents, e.g., sponsors: *de facto* attention, documented and translated into monetary form)

Figure 3.1 Two types of supply and demand.

Because a majority of media in the world today are fully or partially financed by advertising, media and communication researchers have long insisted that, in economic terms, the primary product of media is not their contents but their audiences (we return to digital versions of the basic structure, p. 81). As originally argued by Dallas W. Smythe (1977), media produce attentive individuals, who can be sold to advertisers looking for consumers who will attend to and, ideally, purchase their products and services. In this analytical perspective, the contents of media are, if not irrelevant, then at least secondary to the advertising at the center of the communicative encounter: Content constitutes a means to an end, namely, the meeting of consumer and commodity.

Smythe (1977) belongs to the tradition of **critical media and communication theory**. Its combined theoretical argument and political critique suggests that, in a sense, audiences are 'working' for the companies behind the advertisements and commercials, and could even be said to end up paying twice for the same commodity: First they lend their attention to advertising (producing profit for the medium), and as a group, at least in some cases, they go on to pay for the commodity (producing profit for the company advertising it). The argument extends, perhaps even more clearly, to digital media such as Google (Lee, 2011). The search engine attracts continuous and massive attention, because users are looking for information about numerous objects and events that are associated, often quite specifically, with particular (categories of) commodities. Consequently, Google (always) makes a profit on the attention oriented to the advertising linked to search results; advertisers (sometimes) make a profit on the commodities that users take an interest in and search for. Table 3.1 indicates the extent to which this model of advertising has come to serve the interests of Google and other digital platforms.

Table 3.1 Global spending on digital and traditional advertising

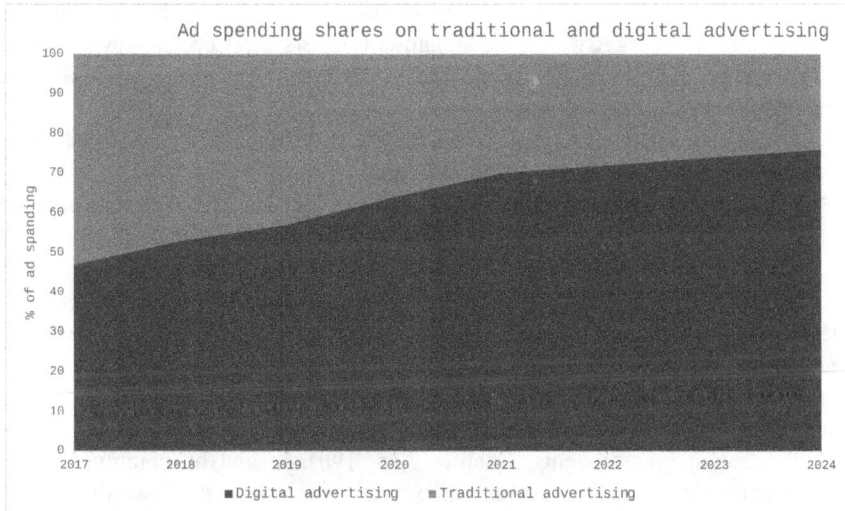

Source: Data interpreted from Statista which can be found at: www.statista.com/outlook/dmo/digital-advertising/worldwide

One response to such critical analyses has been that, while media do trade in attention, their users are at liberty to choose both media and commodities as they see fit. Platforms and advertisers will suggest that the economic model delivers free content along with focused access to consumer information within a generally pleasurable experience of contents as well as commodities. Chapter 4 returns to the resulting, ongoing debates – regarding the freedom of choice for consumers and the quality of contents and experiences – which unfold in national and international media, and whose premises and arguments are specified in so-called normative theories of media and communication.

In summary, two different and distinctive economic processes underlie the basic concepts of supply and demand for media and communication. These processes are conditioned, further, by three sets of economic as well as political and cultural factors. At the most general level, communication depends on material **infrastructures** – roads and digital networks – so that morning newspapers and magazines, films, and games, may reach their intended and interested users. As consumers taking advantage of these infrastructures, moreover, the population in question must have a certain **level of income**, so that they are in a position to afford media contents and communication services, above and beyond the basic necessities of life. The same population must represent a relevant **level of education** covering not just basic literacy, but also background knowledge regarding the sorts of topics and themes being reported and represented in the media, so that they may demand both media hardware and software in the form of contents and services.

Second, as businesses media are embedded in larger **politically** regulated systems of **legally** implemented principles and procedures. These systems cover, for example, tenders for radio channels and mobile services, the enforcement of contracts among the producers and distributors of film and television, and agencies of consumer protection reviewing advertising in different media. In addition, feeding into the **market** where media and consumers meet up, are several other markets, large and small. The wares and services being exchanged, wholesale and retail, range from **material** cables to the **immaterial** rights of copying works of art and other contents, once again subject to rules and regulations established by national legislatures and international treaties.

Third, economies run on more than cool cash. Not least for a domain such as media and communication, the establishment of supply and demand is a **cultural** process. Media production and media use are each informed by rich repertoires of narratives and symbols that constitute premises and preconceptions guiding the preparation and consumption of particular contents and services. More than a sequence of rational choices matching discursive means to social ends, the process of communication is interwoven with the exploration of personal identities and the affirmation of cultural allegiances (as further suggested by the public's involvement in media events, Chapter 7, p. 196). In and by communication, people cultivate themselves and the communities to which they (would like to) belong.

Box 3.3 Exercise

What's the price of media?

People pay for media contents and communication services in two distinctive ways – with money in the shape of coins, bills, and credit card transfers, and with their attention through the time they devote to advertising. This exercise reviews the resources you spent on media and communication over the past year in terms of money and time. The point of reference can be yourself as an individual or a larger group, for instance, your household, a group of friends, or a class attending the same course.

1. First, describe how much money the person or group spent on different media throughout the year. It may be difficult to either recall or look up the precise figures, but please make an estimate – and remember to include the full range of media, from subscriptions of television streaming and music services to visits to the cinema and online purchases of specific items. (In some countries, people must pay a license fee for access to television and radio, or programming may be supported through tax payments allocated to broadcasters on an annual basis. Please include such fees and taxes, and try to calculate the average amount per tax-paying citizen that is paid to broadcasters annually in your country.)
2. Next, describe how many hours the person or group spent on all forms of advertising (including, e.g., sponsored messages) during the past year. This may be even harder to determine – please consider such elements as sponsored links in apps and search engines, commercial breaks on YouTube as well as on television and radio, banner advertisements on websites and in newspapers and magazines, and billboards in city streets and along highways.
3. Lastly, calculate the relationship between a) the amounts spent on media and communication and the person's yearly income (or the average income of the group); b) the relationship between the time spent attending to advertising and the total time spent on media supported by advertising.

The exercise can be turned into an assignment, paper, or project in one of two ways: by comparing several individuals or groups, or by comparing the money or time spent by the person or group in question to the national average. In some countries, this last figure is available from national statistical bureaus or other public or private agencies.

Image 3.4 Facebook goes public. Photo by ProducerMatthew on Wikimedia Commons.

Media are often very valuable companies, in part, because investors expect promising new media to earn even more money in the future. Facebook (now owned by the Meta Corporation), which was launched in 2004 and made available to the general public in 2006, soon became a success with rapidly growing numbers of users around the globe. On May 18, 2012, the company had its so-called initial public offering (IPO), or stock launch; was valued at a record amount of $104 billion; and was welcomed by the NASDAQ Stock Exchange via this screen outside the Thomson Reuters building in New York City. But in the period following its launch, Facebook's stock dropped dramatically, and the incident provoked both lawsuits addressing irregularities relating to the IPO and public debate about the hype surrounding big tech companies – all of which investors, consumers, and citizens could follow on their smaller screens.

Three models of media economy

Though media economies are complex and diverse, three main models of financing and regulating media institutions have consolidated themselves over the course of several centuries (McQuail & Deuze, 2020: 258–262). Being outcomes of an interchange between emerging technologies and existing social structures, they represent a series of political compromises and practical solutions to the shared question of how to organize communication across time and space, and across private and public spheres of human existence and social coexistence. Predictably, each model has been subject to variations across cultural space and adjustments over historical time, in response to other social developments and the introduction of still more technologies and institutions enabling and extending human communication.

Press

The printing of books and newspapers, from the outset, was a commercial endeavor undertaken by privately owned and operated enterprises. The availability and accelerating accessibility of newspapers and other **periodical** publications (appearing daily, weekly, or monthly – long before current online media performing continuous updating of news and making information accessible 24/7) stimulated both personal reflection and public deliberation, including debates about the appropriate social uses of the media carrying these processes. In political as well as philosophical discourse, a position took hold that freedom of expression for print media would be served by a second kind of freedom, namely, freedom from any deciding influence wielded by state, church, or nobility. Instead, the free market, arguably, could promote, even ensure, the free articulation and exchange of ideas and arguments among presses and their readers. The bulk of contemporary print, broadcast, and digital news media remain premised on the assumption that free, commercial markets are necessary conditions of free, communicative expression and exchange. The position is summed up in the common understanding of the press as a **fourth estate** of governance, which serves as a critical watchdog acting on behalf of private citizens to keep a tab on the public powers exercised by legislatures, executives, and the courts (see further Chapter 4, p. 100).

Three sources of income are associated with this first model, with the press as the prototype, but with relevance for several other media, as well:

- **Sales** – buying the daily newspaper, visiting the cinema, and purchasing films, music, and books online, which may then be watched, listened to, and read either online or offline
- **Subscription** – typically monthly or yearly payments made for access to news media and magazines, increasingly through the internet, as well as subscriptions to streaming services
- **Advertising** – advertising for goods and services addressed to readers (and listeners and viewers), in addition to classified ads listing vacant jobs.

Broadcasting

When radio (during the 1920s) and later television (during the 1950s) were first introduced as mass media for the general public, the need to regulate these media had a primary, technical basis. Within the territory of any given country, stations can only broadcast programs (and advertising) within a delimited spectrum of frequencies, which translate into a small number of channels per area or community (and market). Where printing presses produce newspapers, magazines, and books as entities that are distributed separately, radio and television channels may disturb the signals being transmitted by other channels, thus interfering with *their* freedom of expression (and income). Consequently, states undertook to regulate broadcasting both within and between their territories, granting concessions or

specified rights for particular channels to broadcast to the population of a community or country. One additional motivation for such public oversight of broadcasting
was the perception, still widely held, that the images and sounds of television and
radio are more direct and powerful means of representation and communication
than the printed word, hence requiring regulation according to publicly accepted
norms and guidelines.

The twentieth century witnessed the implementation of two main variants of
the regulation of broadcasting, each resting on a distinctive economic model.
The **North American variant** entailed the right for private entrepreneurs (ABC,
CBS, NBC, etc.) to establish radio and television channels, and to integrate
advertising with programming, subject only to broad guidelines regarding the
contents of either programming or advertising. In the **European variant**, in
comparison, semi-public companies such as the BBC in Great Britain – so-
called **public service** media – were entrusted with broadcasting a diversity of
enlightening, educational, and entertaining contents, financed through license
fees (or taxes).

Beginning in the 1980s, the introduction of satellite and cable systems in many
countries served to reconfigure the two historical variants. In the perspective of
viewers and listeners, the North American variant could be seen and heard to take
over, leaving public service broadcasting as a residual format in the European
setting, along with state-governed broadcasting in a considerable number of auto-
cratic regimes (see further Chapter 4, p. 108). Television subscriptions came to
include a combination of national and international channels, including from
neighboring countries, mostly supported by commercials, in addition to specialized
channels dedicated to sports and films in particular. With the local and global
breakthrough of the internet from the 1990s, distinctions between different types
of television and other media, and between different sources of income, have been
increasingly blurred.

With traditional flow or broadcast channels as the prototype, television and
radio have four primary sources of income:

- **Commercials** – here again, the buying and selling of viewer and listener
  attention is key, comparable to the case of advertising in print (and digital)
  media. Commercials typically appear in blocks, within or between programs,
  and remain the main source of income for radio and television stations
- **License fees / taxes** – as mentioned, particularly in Europe, broadcasting has
  been, and still is, funded, in part, by taxes or fees for the use of communication
  devices such as radio and television sets and personal computers. The income is
  then allocated by states to national public service media
- **Subscription** – payment for access to one or more channels, typically emphasizing films, sports, and special interests – so-called video on demand (VoD).
  In rare instances, payment may be for a single program or event, so-called pay-
  per-view. Today, subscription to television (more rarely, radio) **channels** can be
  seen to overlap with subscriptions in the press model above: Subscribers go on

to select a single film, series, or program, that is, delimited **works**, parallel to articles in the press model

- **Sponsoring** – a brief reference to a company or a display of its products or services, securing the television or radio channel a smaller payment than for commercials. And, in contrast to advertising proper, sponsoring cannot include endorsements of specific products or the companies behind them.

Common carriers

The third and final model of media economy has become increasingly central to local and global communication environments following the breakthrough of digital and mobile media. The term 'common carrier' captures the foundational principle of telephone systems, in which all conversations are simply transmitted without interference by the telephone company in either their contents or their forms. Traditionally, the cost of transmission was paid for by the person initiating the call. But, as the technological distinctions between, on the one hand, voice telephony and, on the other hand, networks for the distribution of 'data,' 'films,' and other 'contents' have been dissolving, the economic model has been shifting, too. Telephone conversations are conducted via the internet; networks that had been established to bring cable television to the households of a local community carry radio and television channels as well as internet connections.

The end result has been a merging and rerouting of money streams as part of a sprawling **network economy** (Benkler, 2006; Castells, 2009). **Subscriptions** remain the ticket to various networks, which may be operated, however, simultaneously by multiple providers of basic services, mobile telephony, and access to a proliferating range of specialized services – music, news, gaming, and more. **Advertising** in apps and on websites, similarly, has become a staple of the internet, too, with fuzzy boundaries to **sponsoring**: Brief presentations and logos invite users to click their way to company sites for more information and purchases. The internet, moreover, has brought specifically digital business models to media and communication. One example is **recommender** systems, familiar from the Amazon enterprise, which relies on data about users' earlier searches and purchases to recommend ever more searches and purchases, originally of books, later of a broad range of commodities: 'If you liked A, you may also like (and buy) B.' Another example of digital business models is **personalized commercials** – advertising that, based on cumulative records and analyses of data about users, is fine-tuned and targeted at small segments of consumers and, in principle, the individual – you.

The economy of the internet, in sum, revolves around users' communications and actions online. Chapter 1 presented three prototypes of communication – one-to-one, one-to-many, and many-to-many. Chapter 2 added many-to-one communication as a distinctive feature of the operations of digital media: Users leave behind traces that lend themselves to detailed documentation, analysis, recycling, and reuse by many different interests with economic stakes in the internet. Seizing this business opportunity over the past two decades, an industry has grown up to service the resulting **marketplace of attention** (Webster, 2014), which trades in massive amounts of data registering who attends to what, where, when, for how long, and in which combinations and sequences. This business, in turn, has generated research and public debate, nationally and internationally, on **surveillance** as a pervasive social practice. Central to these debates have been critiques of a system of 'surveillance capitalism' (Zuboff, 2019) in which users themselves deliver – *are* – the commodity, reemphasizing the points made by Smythe (1977) and earlier in this chapter about audience attention as a commodity. Chapter 4 returns to this and other debates relating to normative media theories (p. 107). Digitalization has restated and reactualized classic questions of who can and ought to do what to whom through media and communication (Katz, 1959), and, by implication, who can and ought to surveil whom.

Box 3.4 Exercise

What Google knows about you

When people use digital services, they leave behind traces – of conversations, searches, posts, likes, and so forth. Since 2018, citizens of the European Union can, General Data Protection Regulation (GDPR) in hand, request to download the data that particular platforms hold about them. (In some other countries and regions, comparable protections have been introduced or are emerging.) This exercise illustrates the nature and potential uses of the data stored by digital platforms.

1. Go to https://takeout.google.com/ and download your personal data (it may take minutes, hours, even days to retrieve the data files, depending on the amount of information accumulated about you).
2. Review your data: What does Google know about you? How precise are the data? Are you surprised by some of the data?

Personal data sets are relevant for other stakeholders than tech giants such as Google, including academic research on use patterns and their social implications. So-called data donations (Ohme & Araujo, 2022) grant independent researchers access to data that otherwise would be reserved for the platforms collecting them (see further Chapter 7, p. 210). Data donations, thus, enable studies that assess the nature and extent of digital data collection, and which perform further critical analyses and interpretations of the way in which personal data are being monetized.

The exercise can be extended by performing the same steps – requesting, reviewing, and comparing your own data – from other platforms such as Facebook or Amazon.

Media are organizations

Because they depend on considerable technological and economic resources to operate, media typically make up large, specialized, complex organizations of individuals collaborating to get out messages and services. As such, they represent a contrast to 'authors' as traditionally understood. Since the Romantic period of the early 1800s, people creating and communicating culture – 'artists' – have often been cast as solitary geniuses (in fact, artists have always depended on the finances and goodwill of royalty, churches, or state authorities). With the emergence of modern media institutions, it became increasingly evident that the production and circulation of meaning in society relies crucially on a division of labor. Even the most brilliant inspiration – for a film manuscript or the design of an app – is the beginning of a long, laborious process involving professionals and specialists with diverse knowledges and competences. Their collaboration, in turn, is circumscribed by social structures – organizations – in which some have a greater say than others as departments, sections, and the organization as a whole seek to accomplish predefined tasks by specified deadlines.

To clarify the relationship between individual organizations and wider social structures, this section takes a few steps down the ladder of abstraction – *from* technologies and economies as comprehensive social systems *to* the many small, meaningful actions that get the job of communication done, internally within media organizations, and externally as they address and relate to audiences, advertisers, and other stakeholders. Technologies and economies delineate a territory for media and communication; within the boundaries of that territory, organizations accomplish the concrete production of contents and services at five different levels (Lotz & Newcomb, 2021).

Five levels of media production

Individual agents

Even though authors are nowhere near as important in 'media' as they are in 'literature,' it is, nevertheless, important to recognize the general agency and specific contributions of individuals to media organizations. Through their crafts and competences, employees deliver essential raw materials for what amounts to an industrial mode of production in modern media. A case in point are the writers drafting and reworking, over and over again, the manuscripts on which, for example, the episodes of television series are based. In a study of the production of a television series depicting the friendship of a Black and a White woman in the United States from the 1960s until the present day, Lotz and Newcomb (2021) noted how the manuscript for each new episode was first vetted at a 'tone meeting,' in which the writer, director, and producer all joined the conversation to establish a common tone. The end result was a collective interpretation of the manuscript, anticipating the subsequent and similarly collective production of the series by a larger team. In later stages, other contributing writers could refer to lists of 'tone suggestions,' displayed in the producer's office, where they were taking turns rewriting the text at all hours. Industrial modes of organization and creative processes, then, are not contradictions in and of themselves.

With digital and interactive media, the dualisms of producers and users, senders and receivers, have been blurred. For one thing, anybody with access to the internet can express themselves in ways comparable, in principle, to artists and intellectuals of the past – through social media, online discussion groups, fan communities, and so on. For another thing, proposals and drafts by ordinary users – **user-generated content** – feed into both professional media production and collective projects such as *Wikipedia* (McDowell & Vetter, 2022). Media and communication research has summarized these shifts in the concepts of **prosumption** (combining production and consumption) (Toffler, 1980) and **produsage** (production and usage) (Bruns, 2008).

Individual productions

Like individual authors, individual 'works,' while relevant, are less central to the analysis of media and communicative practices than for the study of literature and other arts. Media studies, instead, focus on the types of content and forms of expression – genres, series, flows, networks, and so on – that a given work or product represents. Media studies, in addition, devote special attention to the interrelations between the texts and contexts of media, including, importantly, the organizations circumscribing and the professional competences generating the texts.

Still, some works do attain a special status, whether as sources of intertextual inspiration (Chapter 2, p. 43) or as points of reference for public debate. One robust example of the first kind is the James Bond figure, which has regularly inspired new films and associated news coverage and public debate for more than half a century since the premiere of the first title (*Dr. No*, 1962). As part of a comprehensive study of the Bond phenomenon, Bennett and Woollacott (1987: 177–184) showed how the team behind the production of the individual movies understood their daily work routines as being guided by a 'Bondian' ideology: Their constant awareness and ongoing interpretation of a long legacy manifested itself in seemingly mundane choices and routines. Regarding the other role of individual works – as points of reference in public debate – prominent instances of video games (e.g., *Grand Theft Auto*) and television series (e.g., *Paradise Hotel*) have been repeatedly criticized as expressions – even causes – of a cultural decline among its users or of society as such (see further Chapter 2, p. 46). Such debates, in turn, may inform, question, and reshape practices of production and marketing: To what extent should video games be designed to glorify violence as an avenue toward luxurious lifestyles; to what extent should reality television shows expose participants in personally embarrassing situations to the general public?

Particular organizations

Media organizations of a certain size, over time, develop distinctive ways of organizing their activities and producing their services – which audiences subsequently recognize in the forms and contents of their output. The programming offered by a particular television channel, for instance, projects a specific 'house style' (Ellis, 1982): There are small, yet significant variations among the several national channels typically available in a given country, both as they are presented and broadcast in flow mode, and as they are configured on websites and through apps. Similarly in the case of social media, although many elements and functionalities of Facebook and LinkedIn are identical, the focus of their coverage and their styles of engagement address users as private individuals and professionals, respectively (even while Facebook affords job searches and LinkedIn may lead to romantic relations).

Many media organizations, moreover, enter into larger wholes framing and affecting the organization and the products of their individual parts. **Media conglomerates** – corporations covering several different media such as film, television, and games, typically in multiple countries – have long been a central part of the global media and communication environment. Digitalization has entailed even wider and deeper integration of a diversity of companies variously emphasizing the production and distribution of information products and communication services, and of the necessary hardware and software: Apple, as a case in point, is the producer of computers, smartphones, smartwatches, and more, as well as an ecosystem of contents supported through iTunes and the App Store.

Specific media industries

Like industries producing either groceries and other day-to-day necessities or household appliances lasting years and decades, different media industries fill particular functions and perform specific tasks for individuals and society at large – from entertainment and journalism to marketing and market watching – which, again, shapes the organizations in question, their practices, and their discourses. The classic example of the media domain is the press, which for centuries has been considered a critical infrastructure of information and argument in the context of political democracy. Recognized across practically the entire left–right political spectrum, the unique institutional status of the press, in addition to legislation affirming freedom of expression in much of the world, has motivated more or less generous schemes of public support in some countries, covering, for example, news media devoted to local current affairs and minority communities.

The entities producing film and television, traditionally, have been distinct and distinctive industries, in part, because of the comparatively smaller budgets available per hour and minute of television screen time. On television, crudely, form precedes content: Production is circumscribed by tradable and translatable formats, genres, and programming schedules, which define what is need-to-have and nice-to-have, respectively, at what length and in which qualities. Film, in comparison, enjoys greater degrees of freedom, even if the average feature film can be seen to abide by genre conventions that lay down rules of the road for writing, shooting, and editing the narrative, delivering an implied 'contract' with cinemagoers and viewers about the nature of the experience on offer. Against the general background of digitalization and the specific development of streaming services, the practices of film and television production are currently converging. Beyond media such as film and television, convergence is affecting other industries and sectors, too, as they integrate digital technologies into internal workflows as well as external communications, becoming quasi-media in the perspective of their collaborators and consumers.

Private and public sectors

In a final analytical step, media and communication studies are obliged to consider organizations as parts of a wider **political economy** – the complex and contested interchange between private, commercial entities and the public, political agencies regulating markets through legislation and executive and administrative measures. This interchange unfolds at local and, increasingly, global levels; it conditions single media industries as well as entire national and regional media systems; and the mechanisms of political economy are making themselves felt throughout the chains of command and professional routines that guide the decisions and actions of individual media practitioners each and every day. For many years, film, television, and radio have been subject to rules and regulations regarding copyright, sponsorship, and state support, for example, within federations such as the European Union. Over the last two decades, the internet has brought additional challenges of how to navigate markets and cultures that are, at once, local and global, in political as in economic terms (challenges that we take up in Chapter 4).

A central fault line remains between state-supported and entirely commercial organizations – the line applies to the domain of media and communication as well as to other sectors depending on technological systems as instruments of social planning and, at best, progress for citizens. Since 1945, one site of political-economic contestation has been whether film qualifies as a commodity, an art form, or both, and if so, how exactly. Insisting on an understanding of film as art, the European Union and its member states have allocated substantial resources to national and regional film industries so that they might compete with 'Hollywood,' that is, the pivotal position of the United States in the international production and distribution of feature films, certainly across the Atlantic. In other parts of the world, as well, Hollywood remains a major economic force, offering films and television series with high production values at comparatively low cost, although other centers such as Bollywood and Nollywood have made their mark as alternative sources of narratives grounded in local and regional cultures (Image 3.3). In a future perspective, an overriding, open question is how different nations and regions of the world – with Europe, China, and the United States as three powerhouses of geopolitics and the world economy at the beginning of the twenty-first century (Jensen & Helles, 2023) – may seek to promote not only continued prosperity, but communicative and cultural flourishing for their citizens, through which measures of political, economic, and technological cooperation or confrontation.

The internet represents, at once, a symbol of and a site of struggle for addressing and resolving these issues. A point of departure for research and debate is given by the understanding of the internet as a common carrier (p. 81), operating according to a principle of **network neutrality** (Tewksbury & Rittenberg, 2012:157): treating all users, all types of content, and all services as equal, neither censoring nor favoring some of the many media, communicative practices, and other social interactions carried by the internet. One challenge to net neutrality occurs at the level of nations and regions of the world. As more of the physical infrastructure of the internet (e.g., fiber cables and data centers) has come to be owned and operated by private interests such as Alphabet (Google), Meta (Facebook), Microsoft, and Amazon, the resulting markets allow for some companies and service providers to basically pay their way toward more favorable conditions, for instance, in terms of transmission speeds and the cloud storage of contents. Such arrangements, in several further steps, are likely to further deepen existing **digital divides** between different nations and socioeconomic groups within nations that are able to finance premium services (or not) (Scheerder et al., 2017). A second, even more funda-mental challenge relates to the received understanding of the internet as a global infrastructure (or not): At the intersection of ongoing political, economic, and technological confrontations between world powers, there is a real possibility that, at some point in the future, citizens of the world will be accessing separate or only partially connected internets (Hall & O'Hara, 2021).

Box 3.5 Analysis

Producing music

Music – and sound generally – perhaps surprisingly, are among the least studied aspects of media and communication, including in a production perspective (Jensen, 2006; Sterne, 2012). After all, music is an essential ingredient of most media – film, television, radio, and internet – of the **soundscapes** (Schafer, 1977) of supermarkets and department stores, as well as of the personal commu-nication environments that many people create for themselves every day with their smartphones and earbuds. And yet, media and communication research has developed few methods and models to account for the production, uses, and experiences of music (for a recent overview, see Hesmondhalgh, 2022).

One explanation for this state of affairs is the fact that musicology – which would be a natural source of analytical approaches in the area – traditionally has been even more centered on 'works' than comparable aesthetic discip-lines such as literary studies and art history (Goehr, 1992; Kramer, 2002; McClary, 1991). In recent decades, however, more theories and empirical studies have come to address how music communicates to and with its users, particularly for popular music (Shuker, 2016). Indeed, the addition of digital media to contemporary communication environments has made it imperative to study music as so much more than works or texts. Music, increasingly, is produced, disseminated, and engaged with on digital platforms, and it is actively and creatively employed by audiences in diverse social and cultural contexts.

The concept of **composition** suggests an analytical approach to music as a communicative process unfolding in social contexts. The anthropologist Ruth Finnegan (1989: 160), distinguished three varieties of composition:

- *Individual composition* is the most common understanding of 'composition': A single individual creates a sequence of sounds (with or without words), typically structured with a specific set of instruments in mind, to be performed for an audience at a later point in time. In this understanding, an essential part of the process is the detailed, formalized notation of the composition. A key example is the 'classical' music of the Western world – symphonies, sonatas, operas, etc. – as handed down with reference to written and printed scores, and performed as part of recurring repertoires continuously for centuries.
- *Collective composition.* The composition of musical works also is accomplished through collective efforts. The process consists, to an extent, in trial and error – which applies to individual composition, too, and to the preparation of many other communicative discourses. Building on their common experience, groups of composers develop distinctive forms of musical expression as they perform parts, alone and together, gradually building wholes. While the final outcome can be documented in notes and scores, it need not be. The contemporary prototype of collective composition is rock and pop music, broadly speaking.
- *Composition-in-performance.* A third variety is composition that only occurs in and of the performance, then and there. Though the participating musicians already know both the essential elements and the potential range of variations, in a sense they produce a new work every time they combine and enact the details, adding nuance in the moment. In this case, too, notation of the full composition is a potential rather than a necessary step. Whereas, in the contemporary West, the prototype is the standards and variations of jazz, throughout history different communities and cultures have practiced a great variety of compositions-in-performance.

Overlaps between and hybrids of the three prototypes are common, to be sure. Classical music is improvised by virtuosos; rock music is rendered in scores and plans including minute details for the next tour of a star.

This is in addition to technologies of recording, editing, and distribution that afford at least two additional approaches of producing and communicating music.

First, in recent history, a fourth variety has been common – **remediated composition-in-performance**. Here, as in the case of jazz, music is composed in and of the performance, which further incorporates forms of expression from other media (on remediation, see Chapter 1, p. 8). Music that was originally composed by others, as well as additional sources of both natural and engineered sounds, enter into recordings and live performances across a number of genres. Examples count techno music and the work of disc jockey producers; other instances are avant-garde musical practices, which for decades have employed communication technologies to challenge the tradition of Western classical music 'from within.'

Second, some uses and reuses of music in and by digital technologies constitute **composition-in-use**. The interactive and programmable affordances of digital media allow users to shape their own consumption and craft the experience of music in context, for instance, through playlists and recommendations coming from others on social media and through online music services. Digital technologies, to an extent, allow ordinary audiences to 'coproduce' music – as it is sounded and experienced.

Studies of the 'production' and 'reproduction' of music hold further social implications. Chapter 1 introduced the characterization by the philosopher Walter Benjamin (1977/1936), of the altered status of artworks in 'the age of technical reproduction,' whenever more copies of the same literature, painting, music, and so on have been disseminated through printing presses, photographs, film, radio, and later media following Benjamin's lifetime. On the one hand, the works of art thereby lose what Benjamin referred to as their **aura** – their special qualities of originality and authenticity. On the other hand, their greatly increased availability held the promise of a democratization of art and culture – via print and electronic media, many more people were now able to *receive* and experience cultural artifacts that previously had been reserved for the few. In the present 'age of digital reproduction,' the nature and status of artworks is in question once again: In principle, the users of digital media are in a position also to *send* works to many others; in practice, most users have much wider and more convenient access to the long legacy of musical and other works, along with the capability of controlling their contexts of use – what to listen to, where, when, in which sequence, with whom, by whose recommendation, for what personal and social ends (Image 3.5).

Top artists   Top songs

1 Arcade Fire   1 Sara Jo
2 Alex Cameron   2 Ronja Røverda...
3 The Beatles   3 Best Life
4 Sebastian   4 STOR MAND (...
5 The National   5 Prescription R...

Minutes listened   Top genre

12.264   **Rock**

Spotify   SPOTIFY.COM/WRAPPED

Image 3.5 Musical mirrors. Courtesy of the authors.

> *Early file-sharing sites such as Napster, which enabled people to freely share songs, but did not observe standard rules of copyright, represented a transitional phase in the public's use and experience of music – from physical records, cassette tapes, and CDs, to online distribution. With Apple's iTunes service and other providers, the communication of music via the internet was given a sustainable, legal, commercial form. Services such as Spotify, Apple Music, QQ Play (in China), and Boomplay (on the African continent) allow users both to shape their own consumption of music and to follow that of others. Music is a form of communication that many would like to communicate with many others about. On social media and websites, Spotify users, for instance, will share their personal 'Spotify Wrapped' playlists – a collection of their most frequently played musical numbers from the past year, in this case covering evergreens familiar around the world (The Beatles), local classics (Sebastian), as well as children's favorites making themselves heard on parents' lists (Ronja Røverdatter).*

Emergent media organizations

Chapter 1 characterized society as a communication system. In the first section of the present chapter, we described how media emerge from particular historical uses of the affordances of specific information and communication technologies – and how media, over time, acquire a social momentum. We are now ready to combine these two perspectives in a summary of how media operate as organizations: Media organizations are small, delimited communication systems that contribute to the larger, expansive communication system that is society. Like societies, organizations are produced, maintained, repaired, and transformed in and by communication (Carey, 1989b/1975).

The interrelations between media organizations and the rest of society are themselves established through communication: The organizations host innumerable **internal** communications so that they may operate day in and day out, as well as a much smaller set of **external** communications addressing consumers, clients, partners, other media, and the public at large. Without the conversations in editorial meetings, there could be no news in the next hour or on the following day. Without ongoing dialogues with advertising agencies, media would have no advertising to place in their apps and on their home pages.

All organizations, in fact, can be understood and studied as communication systems. The field of **organizational communication** (Scott & Lewis, 2017) examines the communicative processes and structures that make the highly diverse organizations which constitute modern societies cohere, internally and externally. Modern organizations – supermarkets, banks, hospitals, political parties, and more – rely on a range of technologies to accomplish their internal and external communications. And, because organizations across the board depend on the same or similar digital technologies, these technologies are promoting an integration of otherwise quite distinct sectors of society into a new category of communication systems (see the analysis in Box 3.6).

And yet, media remain special – a particular kind of organization and a specific social institution. Chapter 4 focuses on media as single institutions – from the cinema as an art form to the press as a political forum – as well as their combination in a comprehensive and distinctive institution facilitating communication throughout society.

Box 3.6 Theories at issue

Media systems and communication systems

Considering the totality of media in a given country, media and communication researchers have traditionally referred to its **media system**. Individual media are parts of a larger whole – a 'system' – that enables, constrains, and defines the terms of communication in society. The media – the parts and the whole – moreover, interact with several other, similarly complex systems, specifically the economic system ('the market'), as examined in this chapter, and the system of political governance (including 'the state'), which Chapter 4 turns to next. And, as would be expected, countries with different historical legacies and cultural traditions are home to different media systems as well.

One of the most influential accounts of media systems (Hallin & Mancini, 2004) identified three types: a liberal model (in the United Kingdom and the United States), a social democratic welfare model (in Northern Europe), and a pluralist, polarized model (in Southern Europe). A central criticism of this typology, since its introduction two decades ago, has been that the framework takes key societies of the Global North not only as the point of departure, but as a standard by which to compare and contrast the interplay of media, markets, and states generally. The authors subsequently addressed these concerns through an edited collection of analyses of media systems 'beyond the Western world' (Hallin & Mancini, 2012). Another point of contention, regarding this and other studies of media systems, has been a persistent tendency to focus narrowly on news media and factual genres, blindsiding other contents and communicative practices relevant to the structures and power relations of local and global society. Last but not least, studies have revolved around the classic mass media – press, radio, and television – although the authors of the foundational publication have proposed ways of addressing the internet as transformative for systems of political communication, too (Hallin, 2020; Hallin & Mancini, 2017; Mancini, 2020).

An alternative approach shifts the emphasis from specific media to general forms of communication – one-to-one, one-to-many, many-to-many, and many-to-one – referring instead to **communication systems** (Jensen & Helles, 2023). Such systems cover the full range of media and genres, including entertainment and gaming, in addition to face-to-face interactions and the highly differentiated and widely distributed actions that users engage in at work, in family matters, and throughout everyday life. The premise of this second approach is that all of these actions and interactions are part and parcel of the place of media and communication in society: Issues of social power and personal and cultural identity are crucially at stake in communicative practices unfolding in many genres other than 'news' and 'current affairs.' And, in line with medium theory (p. 60), the emergence of communication systems suggests the importance of long historical as well as culturally comparative studies of the technological, institutional, and discursive conditions of human communication, beyond the genres mostly associated with political democracy.

Medium theory took part of its inspiration from the breakthrough of television as a new 'central medium' of North American and other Western cultures; the internet has played a comparable role in emerging studies of communication systems. So far, research on communication systems has challenged the tradition of media systems studies by submitting that, in the twenty-first century, media systems as defined by Hallin and Mancini (2004) should be understood as parts of larger wholes: Communication systems are reconfiguring and redefining media as systems and social institutions. Chapter 7 returns to the dynamic in which developments on the ground within the domain being studied, thus, frame not only the agendas of empirical studies, but also the theoretical frameworks in which findings are interpreted (under the heading of 'double hermeneutics,' p. 214).

4 Media as institutions

Media and other institutions

What is an institution?

When people speak of 'institutions,' they commonly refer to the basic building blocks of society – parliaments and stock exchanges, healthcare systems and universities, churches and families. But the definition of an institution is often less than clear, in common parlance and in research. For the study of media as institutions, it is particularly important to recognize a distinction between general **institutions** like 'the press' and concrete **organizations** such as the Reuters news agency, the Al Jazeera news channel, and the *People's Daily* newspaper (on organizational communication, see further Chapter 3, p. 91).

This chapter on media institutions and the following chapter on media users, both rely on complementary perspectives, one historical, the other systematic. To clarify the nature and operation of institutions, the present chapter first provides a brief **historical** account of the origin and development of the concept, and next presents a **systematic** framework for comparing several competing definitions of institutions, and assessing their relevance for media and communication research.

Institutions are human-made and socially constructed. To begin an answer to the heading of this section – what *is* an institution? – it is helpful to restate the question in terms of the origins or causes of institutions. *Why* do societies have institutions in the first place? Aristotle, the philosopher of Greek antiquity who coined many of the ideas and approaches still informing modern science and scholarship, distinguished four kinds of causes:

1. *Efficient causes* bring about particular events.
2. *Material causes* are the matter or materials that make events possible.
3. *Formal causes* are the forms that matter assumes when it effects events.
4. *Final causes* are forces that initiate other causal chains, and which, to Aristotle, represented general principles governing the world in the widest sense, its structure and development over time.

DOI: 10.4324/9781032655109-4

Image 4.1 The World Wide Web as an institution. Courtesy of the Computer Science & Artificial Intelligence Laboratory.

Chapter 3 included a map of the internet Exchange Points (IXPs) that connect many smaller networks into the global internet (Image 3.2, p. 66). While the internet consists of such material connections and cables, like the press it is also an immaterial institution: Institutions exist everywhere and nowhere in particular. That also applies to the institutions administering and ensuring the continued operation of the internet and the transmission of innumerable, uninterrupted streams of bit, for example, the international entity known as the World Wide Web Consortium (W3C). This is both an **organization** *with local chapters and an* **institution***: Similar to law courts and parliaments, the W3C oversees technical and other standards facilitating the many local uses of the global web. The photograph shows part of the 'team' behind W3C when they received an Emmy Award on its behalf in the United States. Without them, there would no organization and no institution – but the W3C exists on a different scale and in a different sense than these concrete individuals.*

One familiar institution – that of a law court – is typically depicted, on television news, as an official building, the camera perhaps panning to an inscription indicating its jurisdiction. Here, the efficient cause is the contractor developing and the workers constructing the building. Concrete, wood, and other materials make up its material cause, plans of the building its formal cause. And the final cause is the end or purpose of having a space in which various legal procedures can be conducted to address the disagreements and disputes among individuals and groups that all societies encounter, and must consider and resolve. The institution of the law court is there to be found, 'inside' the physical building, but no judge, lawyer, plaintiff, or visiting citizen can actually touch or point to it.

Aristotle thought of final causes as overdetermining, unifying, indeed, as divine principles. Contemporary philosophy and scholarship, in comparison, distinguish concrete causes from guiding principles with anticipated end results. Causes, to one side, are typically associated with universal regularities and unavoidable mechanisms, for instance, laws of nature such as the force of gravity. The natural world bears witness to a wide variety of causal principles, but it does not have any identifiable, final ends. Ends, to the other side, are experienced by human beings – whether persons, groups of people, nation-states, or international congregations – and articulate the intentions behind the actions undertaken by either individuals or collectives. The borderlands of ends and causes is a wide 'gray area,' which is the subject of much social-scientific and humanistic research, examining phenomena such as collective decisions, public opinion, and cultural tendencies, all of which are expressed and negotiated in and through media and communication.

In the example of the law court, its ends grow out of earlier, complicated political processes that involve citizens and elected officials defining its brief; the law court can be seen to perform its role according to certain historical (but not universal) laws; and most people, in most cases, will feel bound by the outcomes of legal proceedings. And, even if some may resist the verdicts pronounced by law courts, they still entail obligations that are enacted through prison sentences, fines, and compensations: Being enforced, the verdict becomes a cause. The law court, then, is an objective or manifest fact, not in the same sense as the courthouse building, but because people ascribe meaning and consequence to law courts, their procedures, and their decisions. Media, equally, carry meanings and consequences, as they participate in informally adjudicating the appropriate ends and means of human existence and social coexistence.

Institutions generally can be understood as a distinctive category of facts – social facts – an idea deriving from one of the founding figures of the discipline of sociology, the Frenchman Émile Durkheim (1982/1901). Institutions are the most fundamental and stable structures of society. Institutions are produced, maintained, repaired, and (mostly very slowly) transformed (Carey, 1989a), through the ongoing interactions of the members of society, and through the meanings that they ascribe both to the interactions and to the accumulated institutional structures. The point is not that people are constantly thinking of and talking about various social institutions to guide whatever they end up doing. Most people will obey the law most of the time, but do not give this much thought. However, if challenged and questioned, they are quite capable of explaining why they should not be brought to trial for most of the things they do and say, day in and day out. Institutions such as law courts and current legislation are part of the extensive silent or practical consciousness that people constantly rely on (see further p. 98).

From time to time, this silent or practical awareness will rise to the surface and become top of mind, specifically when people have individual doubts or experience disagreements with others. In such instances, media and communication acquire an essential social function. To begin, we check the encyclopedia and other trusted sources, or we ask others for advice, or reason with them. But if either doubts or disagreements turn out to be somehow fundamental, or if the issue affects many people or significant interests, it is essential to communicate – at greater length and in sufficient detail – so that communities may arrive at a consensus or, at least, a shared understanding of the matter at hand and an agreement on how to proceed toward a decision. Different from, but comparable to the role of law courts in society, this is precisely one of the central social uses of media. Media make up a unique social institution, facilitating individual reflection and collective deliberation on other social institutions and practices, their ends and their consequences.

Institutions, agents, and structures

This opening discussion of institutions recalls the brief presentation in Chapter 1 of the theory of social structuration (Giddens, 1984) (p. 19) – we are now in a position to specify the place of institutions in the wider process of social structuration, with reference to media as institutions that, literally, mediate between persons as social agents and the social structure and process of structuration they all share and participate in. An important insight of the theory of social structuration is that neither the particular institutions nor the social structure as a whole are complete systems unto themselves that people simply enter at birth. On the contrary, the countless 'micro' actions of individuals, groups, and organizations are crucial contributions to the production and maintenance of 'macro' society. Giddens summed up this insight in the concept of 'the duality of structure.' The two aspects of the duality are **agency**, namely, humans' diverse capabilities of acting in social contexts, and **structure**, that is, the accumulated and collective product of human and social actions over time. And, as highlighted in Chapter 1, media and communication relate structure and agency. Through the different degrees of media, people anticipate, articulate, and orient themselves toward particular actions, with (potential) implications and (practical) consequences for the future structure of society, however minimally in the case of each action.

Giddens, further, distinguished three levels of consciousness. **Discursive consciousness**, first, carries an explicit recognition that something is the case, and that, accordingly, the person in question has particular options of going on to act (or not to act). Discursive consciousness is typically articulated in speech or verbal language, that defining medium of the first degree (Chapter 1, p. 6). The concept of **the unconscious**, next, derives from Sigmund Freud's account of the many unspoken, unrecognized, yet powerful forces underlying and driving human psych-ology. **Practical consciousness**, finally, is the important, if understudied, grey area between the discursive and unconscious levels of human consciousness. A very large proportion of what we each think, say, and do over the course of an ordinary day, and during a lifetime – alone and together – is guided by implicit premises, received customs, and rules of thumb. But, if prompted by others, we are able, in most cases, to express our practical consciousness in discourse, making it explicit and exchangeable. (In this regard, practical consciousness differs from the uncon-scious, which is only accessible, if at all, through psychoanalysis or sustained self-reflection.) To exemplify, in many families and households, its members will listen to the news on the radio in the morning (or each person may receive updates through the media of their choice), not least to keep an eye (or ear) on the time until they need to leave. If updates report on delays in public transportation or backed-up roads, people will quickly and effortlessly transition from practical to discursive consciousness, thinking of and likely talking about best solutions and next steps. In those circumstances, the radio (and other media) contribute to the maintenance of such essential social institutions as the family, the labor market, and the educa-tional system.

Like many other social actions, communication, in sum, is ingrained *in everyday life*, producing an orientation both toward the general, familiar structure of society and toward the specific options which that structure affords individual social agents in the contexts where they find themselves – for gainful employment, political influence, self-development, and many other worthwhile endeavors, *in society*. The interrelations of media, structure, and agency are laid out in Figure 4.1 – which elaborates on Figure 1.3 (Chapter 1, p. 19). The box at top right identifies the three forms of consciousness, which, in various respects, inform how people act, and which are articulated and inscribed in communication through the three degrees of media at bottom right. Media, thus, afford resources for individuals and collectives to describe, plan, and organize their agency, constantly enabled and constrained by the social structure embedding them.

Social structure has two aspects – resources and rules – as indicated at bottom left in Figure 4.1. **Resources** come in two varieties. **Allocative** resources, also known as scarce or limited resources, are concrete. There is a limited gross national product (GNP) available in any given country to sustain the life and welfare of its citizens. A similarly delimited public budget is available for various social services as well as the diverse infrastructures and investments that enable the generation of GNP year after year. All these resources are scarce in the sense that they can only be allocated and consumed once. In a broader sense, all of the resources available within the territory of a country and, indeed, all of Earth's resources are allocative. As contemporary environmental movements have it, 'There is no Planet B.' The question is how a country or people, or humanity as such, will decide to maintain and distribute its allocative resources. And, because the answers entail outcomes of wealth and poverty, life or death, they give rise to continuous communication and contestation, and international conflicts and wars.

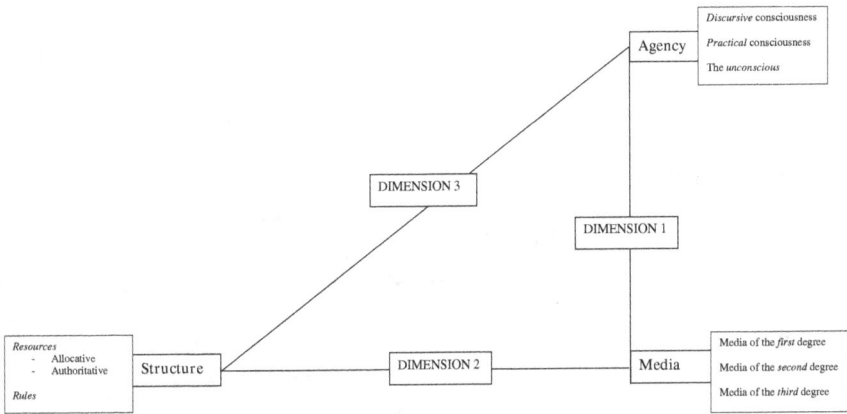

Figure 4.1 Media and the structuration of society.

Physical and symbolic struggles over scarce resources involve a further category of **authoritative** resources: They carry authority, but not in the sense that a judge, a doctor, or an expert panel has the authority to decide an outcome. Authoritative resources, instead, are mobilized to decide *who*, in fact, is an authority, and *what* will count as the last word in a particular domain and instance. A primary example of authoritative resources is the knowledge, skills, and competences that are generated and disseminated throughout the educational system, from kindergarten to PhD programs. These resources shape individuals as social agents, who, in turn, participate in and structure society in their various roles as voters, workers, taxpayers, and so on. While media, certainly, are a source of allocative resources (generating more income for some social agents than others), structurally speaking the media, first and foremost, constitute authoritative resources: Media articulate the meaning of power and negotiate the relative power of different meanings.

Rules, finally, are generally accepted principles and procedures that govern how individuals as well as organizations and institutions could and should act in different social contexts – from the classroom to the courtroom to the newsroom. Some rules apply specifically to allocative resources, for instance, legislation regulating economic markets. In the media business, a classic issue is how to ensure and promote not just formal, but real freedom of expression. If one or a few companies control many different media, or all or most of the steps in the chain producing and distributing information or entertainment, say, in the case of news or film, the final outcome may be a (formal) problem of (lack of) economic competition, a (real) problem of (lack of) political and cultural diversity, or both. A recent example was the rise of a good deal of research and public debate during the 2010s and 2020s addressing 'platformization' (van Dijck et al., 2018): the domination of central junctures in the global flows of communication by a small set of operators such as Alphabet (Google) and Meta (Facebook).

A different set of rules applies to authoritative resources: How ought media to select and combine the various contents and services on offer? Here again, both **formal** and **informal** rules make a difference. Various formal, legislative frameworks are enforced, in different countries and world regions, to limit libel, racism, and hate speech, and to regulate complicated issues of copyright or **intellectual rights**. But many rules guiding media and communication remain informal. Journalists, in particular, are expected to practice the art and business of journalism according to guidelines of best practice; such guidelines, however, vary considerably among nation-states and across cultural contexts pursuing different philosophies of news as an essential ingredient of political, public communication.

More than a special kind of business (Chapter 3, p. 73), media are constitutive elements of another special social institution – the **public sphere**. As such, media are themselves subject to ongoing debate and evaluation of the rules they (ought to) follow in supporting public debate and serving the public interest. At best, media are self-reflective and open to interventions from ordinary users and professional practitioners alike. The following sections examine the interrelations between the media and the public sphere, and between media institution(s) in the singular and the plural. The press, whether print, broadcast, or digital, is one institution with a historical affiliation to the institution of political democracy. Taken together, the modern media make up a comprehensive institution-to-think-with – about society, the world, and life in general (see further Chapter 7, p. 193). And the public sphere is an institution that includes, but extends beyond the media, entering into a distinctive configuration with the other institutions of modern societies.

The public sphere as an institution

The **public sphere model** (Figure 4.2) (Jensen, 2021a: 18) provides a mapping of the place of media in contemporary society. Highly influential in international media and communication studies, the model can be said to identify social structures so self-evident that research may end up taking them for granted, when designing empirical studies or debating their implications for either theory or policy development. The original work behind the model, by the German sociologist and philosopher Jürgen Habermas, traced the growth and transformation of a **bourgeois public sphere** in Europe from the 1700s until the present day (Habermas, 1989/1962). As a general account of social and cultural processes stretching across centuries, the model has retained much of its explanatory value, lending itself to studies of print, electronic, and digital media, genres, and communicative practices. Habermas himself (2006, 2022) has remained an active participant in intellectual and public debate about the potentials and limitations of media as vehicles of political communication and participation. (An assessment of Habermas's works on media and communication, published across three-quarters of a century, can be found in Jensen, 2021e: Chapter 3.)

	Society		State
	Private sphere	*Public sphere*	
	Intimate sphere	*Cultural public sphere*	The (agencies of the) state ensure(s) the material infrastructures; overall economic stability; law enforcement; and regulation of conflicts by economic, coercive, legal, and ideological means
Object	Religion, sexuality, emotion, friendship, etc.	Preaching, art, literature, music, etc.	
Institution	Family	Organizations, clubs	
	Social sphere	*Political public sphere*	
Object	Private economic activity, production and sale/purchase of commodities, including labor	'Politics' and 'the economy,' including social issues	
Institution	Private enterprises and stores	Parliamentary organs, representing political parties, and the press	

Figure 4.2 The public sphere model.

The model, first of all, highlights a special 'sphere,' space, or social domain in between, on the one hand, the authorities and agencies of the state and, on the other hand, the enterprises and endeavors of individual citizens. In this public sphere, everybody and anybody – individuals and groups, political parties and grassroots movements – have the right and the opportunity to present and promote their viewpoints, and to engage with others in debating the ends and means of human coexistence in the widest sense. Like other institutions, the public sphere is not tied to any specific location, but is enacted across space and time, in and by media and communication.

Public spheres began to take shape, as mentioned, from the 1700s onward as part of the development of modern political democracies and market societies in the Western world, symbolized by events on both sides of the Atlantic: the American and French revolutions. Early on, the public sphere established a buffer zone of sorts between citizens and the state; in later stages, the public sphere came to serve as a shared space in which the boundaries between the private domains of citizens and the powers of the state could be negotiated. The understanding of what qualified as 'private,' however, was contested from the outset, and has remained ambiguous, as suggested by Figure 4.2: 'Private' enterprise or business is covered by a **social sphere**, whereas the 'private' lives of citizens, unfolding at home with family and friends, is said to occur in an **intimate sphere**.

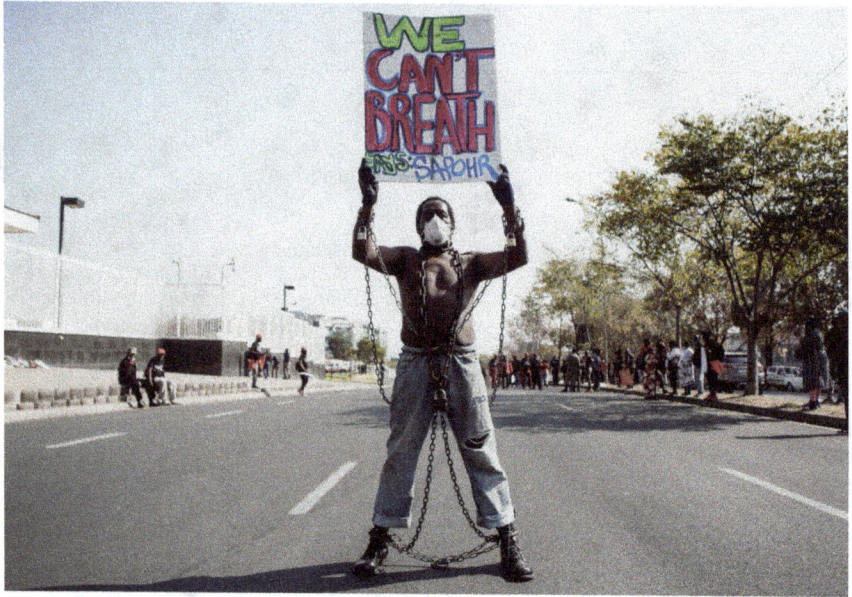

Image 4.2 Political places and times. Gallo Images/Getty Images.

'The public sphere' spans diverse forms of information and communication about political and cultural issues, through media of all three degrees (Chapter 1, p. 5), locally and globally. This photo from the website of National Public Radio in the United States captured a moment of a demonstration by members of the Economic Freedom Fighters, a political party in South Africa, protesting the murder of George Floyd by American police a few days earlier, on May 25, 2020, and expressing solidarity with the #BlackLivesMatter movement (see the analysis of the U.S. incident in Chapter 6, p. 175). While occurring on a different continent, news of the murder was rapidly disseminated, on the African continent and elsewhere around the world, through media of the second and third degrees, giving rise to embodied manifestations such as this in media of the first degree: a human being carrying chains and a handwritten placard repeating some of the last words spoken by George Floyd. Recalling the excruciating history of slavery, in North America, Africa, and elsewhere, demonstrations and other communications reached out across space and time to speak out against a legacy counting the policy of apartheid in South Africa, which lasted until the 1990s, and racism persisting in the United States and other countries of the Global North.

Second, literally *everything* is open to discussion in the public sphere. Citizens are invited to raise questions regarding *what* – which opinions – they themselves and others could reasonably hold, *about* which political, economic, and cultural agendas, as well as *how* opinions about the various agendas ought to be articulated and communicated. The very practice of communication, then, its forms and its contents, are included among the topics of legitimate debate. Accordingly, the public sphere and the media carrying communicative practices acquire a self-reflective and, at best, self-corrective potential.

Because of the great variety of issues to be addressed, with diverse implications for the lives of individuals and social groups, Habermas and later theorists have commonly subdivided the public sphere into two segments, one **political**, the other **cultural**. The premise is that some communicative practices revolve around human beings as persons with a cultural presence in the world, in an existential sense associated with family life and with religious and other 'eternal' perspectives on the very meaning of human life. Other communicative practices focus on the more immediate material and practical circumstances of individual well-being and social welfare, targeting the political decisions and market conditions that, in combination, shape the distribution of scarce (allocative) resources in society and govern the configuration of (authoritative) resources in patterns of power and influence.

The different profiles and purposes of the two sub-spheres are reflected in different **genres** of communication (Chapter 2, p. 48). Prototypical 'cultural' genres include fictional narratives such as feature films, novels, and reality tele-vision, but also video games and additional entertainments in different formats across platforms and cultural settings. 'Political' genres, in comparison, empha-size factual accounts, from classic news reports to television documentaries, along with debates between politicians in podcasts, and among citizens on social media. (Misinformation and disinformation are further examples of political genres, even if they deliver the opposite of facts about society and the world – Chapter 5 returns to current research and public debate about mis/disinformation and its potential effects, p. 149.) It should be added, though, that the distinction between political and cultural genres is far from clear-cut: Cultural genres such as television fiction series frequently carry political messages; political genres of news and current affairs draw on audiences' cultural backgrounds to make a point; and both cultural and political genres feed into the democratic processes that the public sphere as a whole, ideally, nurtures.

Third, and importantly, the public sphere model is no neutral description of society as it was, or is, structured. On the one hand, the model helpfully lays out the basic **elements** of modern society – the elements are all there to be found and examined further in research on contemporary media and societies. On the other hand, the **relations** between the elements that the model suggests were, and are, debatable. Growing out of a specific historical and cultural context, the model represented an idealized understanding of how society *could* and *ought* to be structured. It was this understanding that ignited and informed political revolutions across Europe and North America in the 1700–1800s. These revolutions sought to consolidate basic rights of freedom of expression, additional freedoms of trade and occupation, the election of political representatives through democratic procedures, and the rule of law, limiting and regulating interventions by the state into the lives of private citizens. Still, women and entire social classes and ethnicities were excluded from public spheres and political democracies in most of the world well into the twentieth century. Even today, also in formally democratic societies, not all citizens enjoy real or equal access to the public sphere or to the political institutions and practices deciding the terms of their private lives.

And yet, the public sphere model represents a common denominator of sorts, even common sense, for most people most of the time. It is a worldview, circumscribing and inscribing citizens' interactions with each other, with the media, and with other social institutions. Like media, worldviews are subject to change. But, because the public sphere model is thoroughly ingrained in everyday life, in cognition and action, any change takes time, and will remain subject to challenge and calls for a return to the status quo. Media and politics are sites of strongly held beliefs and deep conflicts of interest. And their intersection, unsurprisingly, is the source of some of the most contested issues both in the theory and in the practice of human communication.

Media and politics

The media of politics

Media offer daily coverage of political developments, debates, and decisions, telling stories, not least, about the victories and defeats of political parties and their leaders. Politicians, in their turn, take a continuing interest in the media as means of contact to and communication with voters, other political figures, interest groups, and stakeholders from society in the round. And the three-way encounter of media, politicians, and citizens is itself bounded by legislation regulating different media and shaping the general infrastructures of communication in society, for instance, through state support or tax exemption for certain media and genres (see further Chapter 3, p. 86). In all these respects, media (of the second degree) have historically operated as media of and for politics: Communication is an essential component of the production, distribution, and regulation of most of the (allocative and authoritative) resources that all humans and societies need and want. As participants in modern public spheres, however, the media have become ever more central both to the political process itself and to the legitimation or critique of its outcomes.

Politics, briefly, is a distinctive set of human actions and social practices that define and allocate the values that apply to society as a whole (Easton, 1953). In and through politics, society identifies the (more or less) common *ends* of social coexistence and the *means* of attaining them. (In a wider sense, also decisions made by company boards regarding coming investments and artworks addressing human alienation in cities have political implications, and the following section returns to these wider notions of politics. The present section focuses on politics as traditionally understood and practiced.)

Image 4.3 Partygate. Courtesy of *The Daily Mirror*.

Media have traditionally provided the public with insight into the institutions and practices of politics, increasingly including the private lives of politicians (Thompson, 2000). And, in some cases, private events have public consequences. On December 1, 2021, a tabloid newspaper, the Daily Mirror, *broke the story that the U.K. prime minister at the time, Boris Johnson, along with members of his staff, had violated the restrictions imposed on everybody to combat the Covid-19 pandemic that had started in 2020, meeting for drinks and having a general good time. Public criticism, declining support for the prime minister's Conservative Party, and formal inquiries into the events ensued, ultimately leading to Johnson's resignation both as prime minister in 2022 and as a Member of Parliament in 2023.*

Box 4.1 Exercise

The media and parliamentary politics

Make an analysis of the role of the media in an event involving the parliament or legislative assembly in your country – a recent election, a contested piece of legislation, or a political scandal of some sort:

- First, describe the event and the values that different participants and stakeholders take to be at stake in the event
- Next, select at least two parties located differently on the political spectrum in your country
- Collect data concerning these parties' positions in and perspectives on the event:
  - From the parties' own websites
  - From two or more news media: the internet, newspapers, magazines, radio, television
  - From social media or discussion fora on news sites

For the basic exercise, data from a single day of news coverage and social media posts will do. For a project or paper, you may analyze communication across the media selected for an entire week. Begin by describing differences and similarities among the various media. Next, identify and discuss the 'agendas' (Chapter 5, p. 135) that are taken, by each medium, to be central to the event, including any agendas inherited or repeated by one medium after another.

Like media, political institutions call for analysis both in the singular and in the plural. Systems of political governance in their entirety serve to characterize the country or society in question, for example, in comparative studies of democracies and autocracies. But for studies of the place of media in political processes, it is normally helpful to single out a particular institution – the parliament, the cabinet or government, the courts, or the administrative agencies of the state. Media will typically cultivate distinctive relationships with each of these institutions, through networks of named contacts as well as anonymous sources. In Chapter 2, we examined the case of Cambridge Analytica abusing personal data about internet users to serve political clients, which was exposed by a whistleblower and covered by media around the globe. State agencies, too, are called out by whistleblowers from time to time. One of the most widely publicized and debated examples was Edward Snowden's 2013 revelation of the massive surveillance of individuals routinely performed by the U.S. National Security Agency (NSA), nationally and internationally. This last case raised the fundamental issue of whether and how persons working in and for state agencies such as the NSA ought to deliver **input** to the media about problematic and potentially illegal, even unconstitutional practices, which may then be disseminated as **output** to the general public, to stimulate political and public debate and, perhaps, to reform established practices. The Snowden case presented a genuine communicative dilemma: Identifying and documenting a (potential) transgression by a state against citizens (of one or more countries) may, in itself, compromise the security of both the state and its citizens.

In Chapter 3, we reviewed different ways of organizing and funding media. When it comes to the conduct of politics, advertising-supported or commercial media, and state-supported or public service media all operate in the same marketplace of attention (Webster, 2014) (if not in the same marketplace for advertising (p. 73)). In the marketplace of political attention specifically, it is often less important to advance a specific viewpoint or position, and more important to set a particular agenda (on the agenda-setting function of media, see Chapter 5, p. 135). Whoever raises an issue or question to public attention – be it a politician, a spin doctor, or a journalist – and does so at the right time and from the right angle, holds an advantage and gains added influence on subsequent debate by defining what will count as relevant answers in the first place. To exemplify, agricultural policy, in many countries, quickly translates into a balancing of 'the economy' against 'the environment' – as farmers, environmental organizations, and political parties with different leanings are well aware. As a result, the various interest groups in the agricultural domain will promote their own agendas through reports, press releases, and other communications that selectively highlight some legal principles, some scientific findings, or some version of common sense. Over time, struggles over agendas may decide not only the tenet of public debate, but also subsequent legislation and its enactment in policy and practice, ultimately affecting both the economy of agricultural enterprises and the environments in which farmers and other citizens and species live. In light of the climate crisis enveloping the planet (see further Chapter 1, p. 2, and Chapter 2, p. 28), the economy–environment balance has become a source of particularly acute and contested agendas for communication and politics in the twenty-first century.

Political communication, thus, points well beyond concrete solutions to practical problems, and beyond specific disagreements about the nature of the problem at hand and the scope of the proposed solutions. The juncture of media and politics brings up existential questions regarding the basic survival and welfare of individuals and collectives, further motivating research to consider the potential contribution of media and communication to good lives and just societies. The resulting research questions are inherently normative: Where, for example, *should* societies draw the lines between 'public' and 'private' affairs, and to what extent *ought* 'economic,' 'political,' and 'cultural' considerations inform and guide the innovation and regulation of digital infrastructures? In response, media and communication research has outlined a politics of media.

The politics of media

Normative theories differ from other theories by addressing not only what media *are*, how they actually work, but how they *ought* to operate to serve the interests of individual citizens and, simultaneously, the public at large (Christians et al., 2009; Jensen, 2021e). Normative theories have a long history, stretching back to ancient notions of sustained dialogue as a source of human insight into what is true, beautiful, and good, an ideal that was first articulated in Plato's rendition of Socrates' dialogues. The European Renaissance and Enlightenment each reaffirmed the capability of humanity to individually and collectively exercise reason, to understand both the past and the present, and to shape a common future. In subsequent centuries, the ideal of progress through reason was linked, through twists and turns, to a further ideal of democratization. Not just well-educated thinkers and well-heeled social classes, but literally everybody and anybody could be seen to command reason, and should be enabled, as a human right, to participate equally in the governance of society and the definition of ends and means for the future: Anybody is somebody (Scannell, 2000).

It was not until the 1950s, however, that normative media theories were synthesized and systematized in a typology of different positions regarding the organization of communication in society. The background was the Cold War, which entailed confrontations between contrasting models of the good life and the good society, with implications for the media and other social institutions alike. The foundational work was published in the United States, premised on an anti-Communist agenda (Siebert et al., 1956). The authors, nevertheless, delivered a robust account of four basic models, which have proven their continuing relevance and have been widely applied in empirical studies of media institutions in different countries and regions of the world. While focused on the printed press – which, at the time, served as the central vehicle, not least, of political communication – since then the typology has been updated to inform studies of electronic and digital media, as well:

- *Authoritarian media theory.* The first normative theory provided a background and contrast to the other theories developed over the course of history and synthesized from the 1950s onward. Authoritarian media theory has rarely been articulated and advocated in detailed or explicit terms, instead representing the social hierarchies that first printed books (from the 1400s) and later newspapers (from the 1600s) came to challenge and, in part, transform. Medieval society and its communicative practices had been grounded in a cosmology, at once political and religious, in which, presumably with God's blessing, the monarch or king resided at the top of the hierarchy, presiding over all of his subjects, who were supposed to remain in their 'natural' place within this 'eternal' order. Like power, information would flow from the top to the bottom of society. The contents of 'media,' to the extent that they existed and were distributed in public spaces, were subject to prior restraint – censorship – which was administered by a small set of trusted individuals on behalf of the sovereign. Today, authoritarian principles are still being widely practiced in different kinds and degrees of dictatorship and autocracy around the world.
- *Liberal media theory.* The first sustained challenge to authoritarian models of media and communication was informed by liberal ideals. Liberalism, briefly,

is the tradition in the history of ideas that takes persons, their expressions and their enterprises, as primary values of human existence and social coexistence, and which marked the transition from traditional to modern forms of social life. Increasingly, individuals were conceived as ends in themselves, holding certain inalienable rights; individuals, further, were considered rational agents with capabilities of collectively articulating and achieving such human rights. A common metaphor for the communicative processes at work has been the **marketplace of ideas** (Peters, 2005). The premise of the metaphor was (and still is) that generic economic markets for the exchange of goods and services will ensure the optimal conditions for people to also exchange ideas and opinions, so that they may serve their own political and cultural ideals and interests. Anyone finding that they cannot gain a hearing for *their* ideas in existing media might start their own 'presses' as businesses, at least in principle, recently in practice through websites and on social media. A second, related premise was (and is) that all of this economic and intellectual competition will aid publics in arriving at consensual solutions to shared social problems. (These same premises informed the long-term development and consolidation of the public sphere model, too, p. 100.)

- *Totalitarian media theory*. The occasion for comparing and typologizing normative media theories, as noted, was the Cold War, specifically the emergence of communist media systems in some parts of the world. It is debatable whether authoritarian and totalitarian societies could, in fact, be considered different ideologies regarding the appropriate functions of media, in light of the record of various fascist regimes from the 1930s onward. Referred to by Siebert et al. (1956) as 'totalitarian,' the proclaimed mission of communist media systems, however, has been one of transforming society and culture in fundamental ways, rather than of reaffirming existing social and cultural hierarchies. And, while contemporary authoritarian media systems may operate according to commercial principles, in whole or in part, communist media systems traditionally have been funded and controlled by the state. Following the popular uprisings in Eastern Europe beginning in 1989, and the dissolution of the Soviet Union from 1991, the People's Republic of China has maintained a hybrid media system combining a regime of firm state control with commercial business models (Zhao, 2012).

- *Social responsibility theory of media*. After 1945, the premise of liberal media theory – that market competition would stimulate intellectual competition – was becoming increasingly implausible. First, economic concentration, in many countries, had resulted in fewer and more interlinked media outlets, undermining the credibility of ideals of an open 'marketplace of ideas.' In response, both news media and journalistic associations came to emphasize their professionalism, as articulated in policies and codes of ethics, and supported through considerable economic and organizational resources, which, arguably, put established media in a position to nevertheless deliver a diverse and balanced coverage of current affairs to their readers, listeners, and viewers. Second, radio

Image 4.4 The Great Firewall. Photo by William Olivieri on Unsplash.

The Great Wall of China was originally built as a defense against military aggression from the outside. Today, the Chinese state is preoccupied, not least, with limiting outside influences on Chinese citizens through the internet, especially in the case of international news and political debate, but also for additional categories of content such as pornography. The technological and administrative response has been dubbed the Great Firewall, referencing the digital security systems that businesses, public institutions, and other organizations will maintain between their internal communications and the global internet. Western tech companies, meanwhile, have been accused of complicity in designing and implementing various elements of this 'solution' to China's domestic 'challenge,' despite their origins in the United States and its liberal media model (in pursuit of the market opportunities also associated with the liberal model). Chapter 3 elaborates (p. 87) on the internet as a geopolitical battle ground between China and the West at the beginning of the twenty-first century, even while the two sides share a common interest in continued economic cooperation and development.

and television, particularly in Europe, had long been subject to detailed regulation by states. As mentioned in Chapter 3 (p. 79), such regulation had originally been enforced for technical reasons, because of the limited bandwidth available within the borders of each country; in later stages, continued regulation came to be motivated, not least, with reference to the public value of assuring diversity and balance in the available content across a range of factual and fictional genres, for majority and minority cultures alike. **Public service** media – radio, television, and additional online formats – today represent the clearest case of media institutions organized and operated according to the normative theory of social responsibility.

Beyond the four 'classic' positions that had been identified in the 1950s, two further normative theories have been added in view of the introduction of new communication technologies and changing social structures from the local to the global level (McQuail, 1983). One theory recognized the special economic and cultural circumstances of nations in the Global South; the other theory embraced the potentials of new media for greater public participation in society-wide communication:

- *Development theory of media.* At the end of World War II, a number of Western countries still held colonies in the Global South (see further the analysis of colonialist and imperialist ideologies in Chapter 2, p. 39). As the process of decolonization accelerated from the 1960s, an important agenda for research and public debate became the future role of media, as resources of nation-building within these newly independent countries, but also as carriers of viewpoints from, and representations of, these nations to other national and international publics. Two positions were pitted against each other, respectively advocating a free flow of information globally and self-determination for the peoples of the Global South. Western media, specifically international news agencies, but also 'Hollywood' (Chapter 3, p. 71) and other transnational media interests, sought to largely maintain their dominance to ensure (what they took to be) the 'free' exchange of information on 'free' market terms. In contrast, much of the Global South – seconded by the Eastern bloc centered in the Soviet Union – insisted that alternative arrangements were imperative to begin to address the historical inequalities between the Global South and North, in communication infrastructures as in other social domains. International regulation of the flows of information and entertainment in the world, arguably, must counteract entrenched imbalances in the global supply of narratives and perspectives from and about the many cultures of the world. Following lengthy and conflicted discussions in the context of the United Nations (MacBride, 1980), research and debate are still ongoing, the contested issues largely unresolved. Since the worldwide diffusion of the internet, discussions have come to include a new category of divides between rich and poor nations and world regions – **digital divides** (Scheerder et al., 2017) – which, in turn, may deepen familiar divides of income and education.
- *Democratic-participant theory of media.* Overlapping with the age of decolonization and subsequent debates about North-South communications, media establishments in many Western countries were in for another round of reckoning, as a growing number of voices in contemporary public debate began to question their relevance as meaningful, substantial resources for citizens' political and cultural participation. Diverse 'anti-authoritarian' protest movements – feminist, youth, student, and **1968** rebellions – engaged with the media, simultaneously as representatives of social establishments and as channels potentially

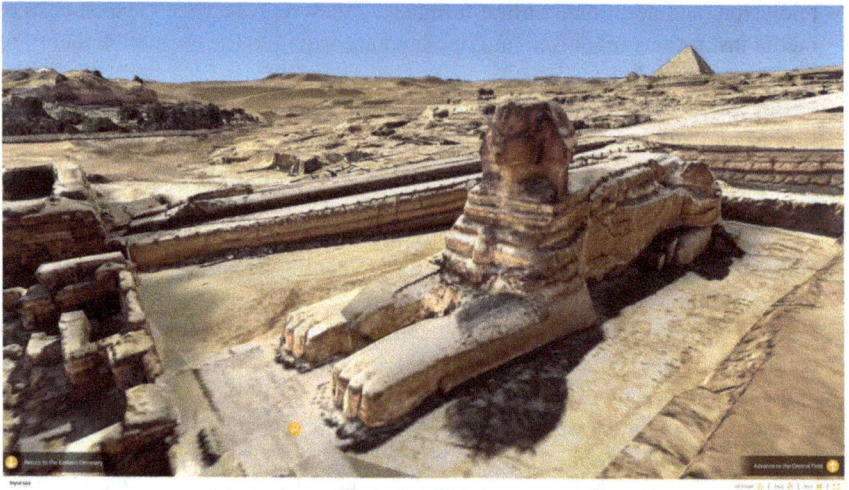

Image 4.5 A cultural public sphere. Preliminary model of the Sphinx. Courtesy of the Giza
Project, Harvard University.

> *Although public debate is most commonly associated with the institutions and*
> *practices of politics, media are also sites and sources of a cultural public*
> *sphere, which engages with ethical, aesthetic, and existential questions*
> *concerning the nature and implications of classic ideas of truth, goodness,*
> *and beauty. Such questions are addressed in several modalities and multiple*
> *genres of fine art – literature, theater, classical music, visual arts (Chapter 2,*
> *p. 46) – as well as in popular culture carried by mass and social media.*
> *Modern media have facilitated encounters with fine art and popular culture*
> *side by side, and virtual travels across other traditional divides – 'our' culture*
> *and 'their' culture, cultures of the past and the present. And digital media have*
> *recently enabled new ways of 'going to the museum,' for instance, through vir-*
> *tual tours of the pyramids of ancient Egypt.*

carrying and amplifying critiques. Redoubling the challenge of social responsibility theory to liberal media theory, democratic-participant theory went on to
fundamentally question the social responsibility of established media. A widely
shared vision was to give **public access** to ordinary citizens, who would thus
become producers for and editors of mass media, chiefly radio and television,
but also 'grassroots' print media (Downing, 2000; Glessing, 1970), extending
the historical ideal of democratic participation to the social means of communication (Enzensberger, 1972/1970). The interactive functionalities of digital
media, predictably, have lent renewed attention to and support for democratic-
participant theories of media and communication (Jenkins, 2006; Lievrouw,
2023; Rheingold, 1994).

Box 4.2 Theories at issue

Freedom from, freedom to

Many day-to-day debates about media and society are informed by the same two basic perspectives on social structure and human agency. To one side, a **consensus** model takes society to be a largely well-oiled whole in which media will serve their specific functions well without too much oversight by or intervention from state or public agencies. To the other side, a **conflict** model highlights the need for continuous and sustained critique of the social status quo, including through media and communicative practices, whose transformative potential, therefore, must be protected and promoted so that they may help identify and guide the necessary reforms. Most simply put, the question is whether the **state** or the **market** should fill the role as the primary guardian of the freedom of the media.

'Freedom,' however, is an ambiguous term, covering two concepts with quite different practical implications. First, in a 'negative' sense, **freedom from** something, focuses on the extent of the interference by states and other authorities, quantitatively and qualitatively, into the endeavors of private citizens, for instance, the way in which media enterprises are organized and run. In common parlance (and in a good deal of research), this is the typical understanding of freedom. Chapter 3 noted the related normative position that a 'free' economic market advances 'free' political discussion – freedom of expression and intellectual and cultural freedom generally. In a second, 'positive' sense, **freedom to** something, depends on the availability of adequate material and immaterial resources and circumstances for doing and being certain things in life, from personal security to systems delivering health services and education for all citizens.

The negative definition of freedom-from summed up the strategy of the European middle classes as they fought for political and economic rights from the 1700s onward, and it was promoted by the early press in opposition to the establishments of feudal states. A positive redefinition of freedom-to – in the form of increased public intervention into national economies, the establishment of state-funded social services, and financial support for some cultural institutions and practices – was the end result of massive national and global economic crises, most notably during the 1930s, which led to the most disastrous world war to date. A common interpretation of this historical trajectory, extending across two centuries, is that the modern prototype of society, combining industrial capitalism and representative forms of democracy, survived repeated crises and wars thanks to a redefinition of freedom – from freedom-from to freedom-to – and its implementation in major social institutions.

The distinction between freedom-from and freedom-to pervades social scientific and humanistic disciplines and areas of research, including philosophy, political science, and media and communication studies. One particularly influential formulation was presented by the philosopher Isaiah Berlin (1969/ 1958), who introduced the terminology of 'negative' and 'positive' freedom (but who only recognized negative freedom-from as 'real' freedom). Since classical Greece and Rome, thinkers have debated how societies could and should govern themselves, not least with reference to the kinds and degrees of positive and negative freedom that should be granted to individuals as part of their membership of and coexistence within local, national, and global communities (de Dijn, 2020).

Societies around the world, today, bear witness to distinctive balances between freedom-from and freedom-to, which have remained subject to contestation and negotiation, including in the domain of media and communication. In recent decades, public and policy debates have referred to strategies of **privatization** and **deregulation** that would limit, once again, the role of state agencies in regulating and structuring media and other social institutions. In practice, however, the relevant question is rarely the quantitative variant of 'more or less' regulation, and certainly not 'regulation or not,' but rather several qualitative distinctions and decisions as to *what* exactly is to be regulated *how*, for instance, through national film legislation or international agreements regarding network neutrality (Chapter 3, p. 87). For deliberation on the appropriate answers in particular national and cultural contexts, the normative theories of media and communication have remained important references and yardsticks: Media regulation in any given country typically represents a combination of several normative principles and associated procedures. Next time you hear a politician or some other stakeholder claim, in public debate or as part of an electoral campaign, that their positions and policies will serve freedom, you will know what the follow-up question is: freedom-from or freedom-to, and in whose interest?

Box 4.3 Analysis

BBC – from the Beeb to the iPlayer

Established in 1922, the BBC, or British Broadcasting Corporation (originally Company), soon became a fixture of everyday life for British citizens, colloquially known as the Beeb. Over time, it developed into a model of public service broadcasting (Chapter 3, p. 80) for other countries in Europe and elsewhere, and it has remained a global provider of news and information through the BBC World Service. As such, it might be considered an 'institution,' having maintained its local and global position for more than a century. But, theoretically and analytically speaking, the BBC is a media organization, which has been shaped and reshaped through shifting technologies, variable economic markets, and changing political forms of governance. (A large body of research on and resources about the BBC is available, including its own telling of that history, www.bbc.com/historyofthebbc/. For overview, see Hendy (2022).)

The BBC represents a microcosm of the expansion and diversification of media organizations since the early twentieth century. Like other broadcasters, the BBC has multiplied its number and variety of radio and television channels, while simultaneously capitalizing on the synergy between media and channels, internally in its production and distribution chains, externally through the BBC brand promising, not least, quality news and television series to national as well as international audiences. The BBC microcosm, however, stands out in today's media macrocosm in two important respects. First, its position of strength was built on a mandatory **license fee** paid by U.K. households for the reception of radio and (later only) television. While commercial sales of its programming and services now make up a substantial part of BBC revenue, the license fee remains the primary source of income. The BBC, thus, is the prototype of the social responsibility mode of organizing mass communication (p. 111), still thriving in a predominantly commercial media and communication environment. Second, the BBC stands as a **global medium**, above and beyond its exports of news and series. In addition to a sustained presence on the internet, the BBC has upheld its commitment to serving news and information in multiple languages via radio to publics around the world.

- *Radio.* Founded in 1922 as a radio broadcaster, the BBC retained its national monopoly (for radio) until 1973, when advertising-supported radio was first introduced in the U.K. Both before and after that transition, the number and profiles of BBC channels have changed repeatedly, today including 10+ national channels, formatted in terms of their contents, styles of presentation, and listener demographics, in addition to a plethora of regional and local channels. The BBC's most distinctive contribution to radio as a medium of communication, however, remains the BBC World Service. Begun in 1932 as the BBC Empire Service, in the era of colonialism (see further Chapter 2, p. 41), and broadcasting in English only, in 1938 it began offering programming first in Arabic and subsequently in a growing set of world languages. At the time of writing, the service covers 40+ languages and claims 200+ million weekly listeners. Whereas the imperial origins of the BBC World Service might be thought to call its contemporary vision and mission into question, the professionalism of its journalism and the size of its audiences suggest its continued stature as a trusted source of international news and current affairs.
- *Television.* BBC television first encountered competition, in 1955, with the introduction of the commercial Independent Television (ITV) national network. The 1980–1990s witnessed further deregulation of the medium

and competition from additional channels distributed by satellite and cable technologies. And yet, BBC channels have remained at the top of the charts in terms of the total size of audiences, compared to ITV, the channels of the Sky company, as well as other content providers. One explanation of such resilience has been the formatting of different channels for different audience segments, as also pursued by the BBC's radio channels, and as a scheduling strategy adapted to a communication environment in which public service and commercial media compete side by side for the same scarce attention (Webster, 2014). A distinctive feature of the formatting of BBC Television, adopted by other public service broadcasters, too, is a set of channels dedicated to the young: BBC Three catering to youth, CBBC to the 6–12 age range, and CBeebies to children below 6 years of age.

• *Internet*. Like other public service and commercial broadcasters around the world, the BBC has made its services available on the internet, accessed through smart television sets, smartphones, and other digital devices. What started out, in 1994, as a web presence centered in and supporting its television and radio programming, has grown into the comprehensive BBC Online network, which incorporates elements such as BBC News and BBC Sports as well as the video-on-demand unit, the BBC iPlayer, and BBC Sounds including live radio, audio on demand, and podcasts. Digitalization has enabled the BBC to extend and enhance its classic three-part service to the public – to inform, educate, and entertain, in the words (and in that order) of its first director-general, John Reith. These same digital initiatives, however, have brought complaints, which have been voiced regularly by commercial competitors over the past century, namely, that the BBC holds an unfair, state-sponsored advantage, particularly in the digital, multichannel market that broadcasters and other communicators have come to share – which leads, finally, to the governance of the BBC.

The BBC is a semi-public, so-called statutory corporation, that is, an organization established by the state, but operating without direct intervention from the government, which does, however, set the license fee. Within the resulting financial resources, the **BBC Board** outlines a framework for the activities of the organization, to be implemented by the **Executive Committee**. Its operations, moreover, are overseen by a regulatory and competition authority, the Office of Communications (**Ofcom**). The special status of the BBC (and comparable public service organizations in other countries) is a historical instance, as mentioned, of the normative theory of social responsibility (p. 111): The BBC is charged with performing an essential communication service to the public at large, subject to regulation by authorities that ultimately have political origins, and which must legitimate the nature and extent of regulation to that same public in democratic elections. While subject, over the years, to criticism from both the left and the right of the political spectrum, the BBC has managed to maintain both its political backing and the popular interest, and remains a versatile **organization** participating in the structuration of multiple **institutions**, locally and globally: British media generally, the British press specifically, national institutions of arts and culture, and an international public sphere.

Single media in composite communication environments

Converging media

A distinctive feature of the decades around the year 2000 was, first, a growing integration of previously separate media – what research and public debate described as **convergence**. Second, digitalization was enabling communication by an expanding roster of social agents and interests – individuals as well as businesses, public institutions, and civil society organizations – in ways that challenged the classic understanding of media, the press in particular, as institutions monitoring *other* institutions. Recognizing both of these shifts, this last section of the present chapter returns to the two aspects of media as institutions that we introduced briefly in Chapter 3 (p. 91): the convergence of single media within one media institution ('the media system'), and the interweaving of media and other social institutions in a wider 'communication system.'

One of the insights of medium theory (Chapter 3, p. 60) is that the set of media that are available at a given historical time and in a particular cultural context, together constitute an 'environment.' Similar to the natural environment, a media environment presents particular terms – potentials and constraints – for humans to communicate with each other, individually and collectively. If nature is the site of a physical or material metabolism, the media could be said to perform a cultural metabolism. What we communicate, and how we communicate, feed into who we are, as persons, communities, and societies. And, when media converge, people are enveloped by new communication environments.

Convergence, to begin, is a polysemous or ambiguous concept – with five primary meanings (see further Jens F. Jensen, in Jensen, 2016: 18–21):

- *Technological convergence* refers to basic digital principles that are applied to and reshape all media (if not necessarily to the same degree or in the same ways). It used to be a relatively simple matter to identify and separate the various technological elements that made different media possible:
  - *Services*, for instance, broadcasting, voice telephony, and databases;
  - *Networks* such as those dedicated to television (terrestrial, satellite, or cable), telephony, and the internet; and
  - *Terminals*, including television sets, telephones, and computers.

Each of these components has been subject to convergence:

- *Convergence of services*, first, refers to the contents of media, specifically their forms of expression and representation. With digitalization, text, sound, still, and moving images are all articulated in the same semiotic repertoire of codes (on semiotics, see Chapter 2, p. 35). The transition has been described as a transformation of 'atoms into bits' (Negroponte, 1995). Through the digital 'alphabet,' 0 and 1, contents previously wedded to either printed pages, celluloid, radio, or television signals are translated and recombined in some new (and many old) communicative practices.
- *Convergence of networks*, next, refers to the distribution of the entire spectrum of media and communication services through a single network; all varieties of content, equally, lend themselves to distribution via any digital network. Several different systems of distribution, however, are still in operation: land-based digital networks and cable systems; landline telephony and mobile telephony; in addition to DVDs, CDs, and downloads.
- *Convergence of terminals*, further, is in evidence when users rely on the same terminal for multiple communicative practices, either simultaneously or at different points in time. On the one hand, television sets work double shifts as terminals for broadcast television, streaming films and series, video gaming, and so on. On the other hand, different kinds of terminals accomplish the same communicative function: listening to the radio via a radio set, a laptop, or a smartphone.
- *Convergence of businesses*, finally, focuses on the organizational and institutional changes that follow from the other varieties of convergence. Publishing houses, film companies, music producers, telecommunications providers, software firms, and so forth, have all entered into larger media corporations and wider conglomerates. While conditioned by technological developments, this last variety of convergence primarily constitutes a commercial strategy, as media and other businesses look toward an uncertain future. Different sectors of national and international economies have sought to profit by investing in a range of products and services, while at the same time entering markets outside their traditional focus of interest. One example of business convergence was the fusion of the TimeWarner conglomerate and the America OnLine (AOL) network in 2000: TimeWarner had a large, attractive archive of entertainment; America OnLine had the networks for distributing it. But the fusion did not deliver the outcomes that had been hoped for, and by 2009, AOL was reestablished as an independent company.

It is essential, then, to approach convergence as a dynamic interplay of technological and social factors – as highlighted in Chapter 3 through the concepts of affordances, emergence, and momentum (p. 64). The first four varieties of convergence – the implementation of basic digital technologies along with the digitalization of services, networks, and terminals – *afford* new configurations of communication and other social interaction, which facilitate the further convergence of businesses.

Although actual opportunities for investment and income are far from given, technological convergence and business convergence, in combination, afford *additional* degrees of freedom and further development for single media companies and conglomerates alike. A case in point is the development of new products and services, which frequently originates from small start-up companies. While such companies are, again quite often, later bought by larger tech corporations seeking to scale their products and services, in several later steps an outsourcing of activities may follow, subcontracting to several smaller companies the design, production, and distribution of contents, applications, and advertising. Rather than converging into one super medium to end them all, the media that *emerge* represent a range of complementary and partially overlapping organizations.

Convergence, in sum, is best understood as several open-ended processes. Different media have been converg*ing* in different respects and to different degrees, but they have rarely converg*ed* into a final, stable state. As these processes continue to unfold as components of long-term digitalization, some media and communicative practices will be consolidated and reinforced – they gain *momentum* – while others will decline and, perhaps, disappear.

The last two decades have witnessed a historical round of technological and business convergence, specifically a convergence of media with other sectors of production, distribution, and administration that traditionally have not been dedicated to supplying and supporting communication services. Image 4.6 even claims that 'every business is a media business,' communicating high and low with customers and collaborators in their daily operations. The following section elaborates on business convergence as one indicator of an infrastructural development in which 'media' no longer are, and probably never will be, what they once were.

Digital communication systems

Chapter 1 identified three aspects of any medium (p. 9):

- *Materials.* All communication depends on material resources – the human body and its technological extensions (McLuhan, 1964). When referring to their smartphone as a 'medium,' people highlight the fact that its distinctive combination of materials – metal, glass, and other components – provides a point of access to searching information and communicating with others.
- *Modalities.* Communication between and among humans is enabled by particular modes of expression and experience, of particular contents and in particular forms. The smartphone is an 'audiovisual medium': We hear the person at the other end of the line, and we see the results of our Google search, perhaps a YouTube video.
- *Institutions.* The smartphone, last but certainly not least, participates in multiple social institutions: economic markets subject to regulation by political authorities, and an everyday crisscrossed by the multiple cultures of work life, family life, and everything in between. Digital media are interrelated, with each other and with other social institutions, in distinctive ways. One example is Alphabet

Image 4.6 Every business – and everybody – is, potentially, a media business.

The claim advanced by this statement, which is a common saying in business circles and some communication studies, rings true to the extent that companies continuously interact with diverse stakeholders – clients, competitors, policymakers, and the general public – in and by communication. Depending on the stakeholder in question, communication may unfold one-to-one, one-to-many, many-to-many, or many-to-one (Chapter 2, p. 56). Private persons, too, can make a business out of presenting themselves to small or large audiences, locally and globally, as exemplified by lifestyle influencers. Communications, however, also represent liabilities, rendering influencers and other businesses vulnerable to criticisms that may grow into so-called shitstorms. Like politicians who are exposed to crises through media coverage (Image 4.3, p. 105), therefore, businesses regularly need to come up with responses to keep their customers satisfied.

(Google), which, in addition to YouTube and the dominant search engine of the Western world, also owns Android (the most common operating system in the world of mobiles) and Google Play (the largest app store globally). Another example is Apple, which, in addition to upmarket hardware and software, delivers content to consumers via iTunes.

Interrelated media, admittedly, are far from a new thing. First, economic **concentration** has been characteristic of media and other businesses for decades. Rupert Murdoch, commonly referred to as a media mogul, started out as a publisher of newspapers in Australia, and went on to acquire several major newspapers in the

United States and the United Kingdom. Second, Murdoch gradually integrated multiple media and genres, from print and broadcasting to film and publishing, into a **conglomerate**, which was even split into two separate conglomerates in 2013: his (reconfigured) News Corporation counting ventures in publishing and Australian broadcasting, and 21st Century Fox comprising a further range of media. Other conglomerates have integrated media with additional and associated business domains: The Walt Disney Company is an entertainment conglomerate incorporating toys and theme parks, too. (And, in 2019, 21st Century Fox was acquired by Disney.) Third, like other businesses, media operate in steps or stages, for instance, from the production to the distribution and exhibition of films in cinemas. A company controlling several or all of these stages is termed **vertical integration** – from the top to the bottom of the process, and from the beginning to the end of the value chain.

So, then, do these entities constitute media – or not? One way of addressing this question is to define one's way out of the ambiguities resulting from open-ended historical developments: '*This* is a medium, *that* is not a medium.' Such an approach produces **definitive** definitions – this book takes an alternative approach delivering **sensitizing** definitions (Blumer, 1954). By exploring shifting configurations of the technological, modal, and institutional characteristics of different media, we submit, research is in a better position to account for 'new' media, and to compare these with 'old' media. Chapter 1 referred to the computer and the internet as metamedia (p. 8), which integrate all previous media of communication in and through a specific technology. But metamedia also add new media to the mix, suggesting a terminology of **adopted** and **born** media: The internet has 'adopted' a long historical line of old media, and has 'given birth' to new variants such as social media.

To conclude this chapter on media as social institutions, we return to the ongoing emergence of digital communication systems: How are contemporary technological, economic, and political conditions structuring – enabling and constraining – particular communicative practices? This last question shifts the emphasis from *media* systems to *communication* systems (Chapter 3, p. 91), in which the internet delivers society-wide and worldwide infrastructures for communication – one-to-one, one-to-many, many-to-many, and many-to-one. Digital communication systems incorporate both 'media' as traditionally understood and additional, converging, and emerging organizations and institutions of social interaction, for professional and personal ends, in private and public sectors, locally and globally.

Table 4.1 presents a matrix for studies of digital communication systems. It relates three general, structural dimensions of social organization – infrastructures, markets, and states – to four specific levels of analysis: access networks, backbone networks, applications, and data.

First, digital communication systems are determined (in the first instance, Chapter 2, p. 63) by available material **infrastructures** at a particular historical time. Next, these infrastructures, hardware and software, are shaped over time by the different economic interests competing for, owning, and controlling their various components through **markets**. Lastly, political measures introduced by **states** serve to regulate the economic and other social uses of infrastructures. The

Table 4.1 A framework for digital communication system analysis

	Infrastructures	*Markets*	*States*
Access networks	What are the existing access networks for digital communication?	Who owns and controls digital access networks?	How does the state regulate digital access networks?
Backbone networks	What are the existing backbone networks for digital communication?	Who owns and controls digital backbone networks?	How does the state regulate digital backbone networks?
Applications	What are the existing applications for digital communication?	Who owns and controls digital communication applications?	How does the state regulate digital communication applications?
Data	What are the existing types of digital communication data?	Who owns and controls digital communication data?	How does the state regulate digital communication data?

Source: Originally published in Lai, S. S., & Flensburg, S. (2023). *Gateways: Comparing digital communication systems in Nordic welfare states.* Nordicom, University of Gothenburg. https://doi.org/10.48335/9789188855848. Reprinted with permission from Nordicom.

three structural dimensions, together, condition all of the meanings, and all the powers, that are articulated and negotiated through countless communications.

The common denominator of the four specific levels of analysis is a practical question: How is it that digital systems come to enable human communication one-to-one, one-to-many, many-to-many, as well as many-to-one? The answers follow from an examination of four constituents: An **access network** relates individual users and their devices to the internet; a **backbone network** joins the many local users and access networks to the global internet so that they may connect and exchange information and ideas; **applications** such as web pages and apps enact a great variety of communicative purposes; and the outcomes depend on the transmission via the internet of digital **data** carrying contents to be interpreted and acted upon (data including, importantly, the 'contents' being displayed on user interfaces as well as the additional 'information' about users that they themselves communicate into the system).

The four levels constitute a hierarchy: To begin communicating digitally, you need, first of all, an internet connection (for instance, a cellphone with subscription to a mobile service) that allows data to travel far and wide through local and global networks. Next, this initial connectivity establishes an onward connection to the servers of a particular communication service (such as an app). And, lastly, the service processes each user's request for access to a specific kind and quantity of data (for example, a football score or directions to a particular location).

At the 12 intersections of the structural dimensions and the analytical levels in Table 4.1, questions for further research are articulated – for instance, 'what are the access networks in operation in my area?', 'who owns and operates the backbone networks?', and 'what are the policies by which state agencies in my corner of the world regulate the applications enabling digital communication?' The answers begin to map digital communication systems across time and space – history and geography. Depending on country and world region, the access networks may include mobile telephony as well as fiber-optic and DSL broadband connections; backbone networks are commonly owned and operated by regional telecommunications companies, but tech giants such as Meta and Alphabet are also investing in data centers and submarine internet cables; and applications are (sometimes) regulated by national and regional authorities through legislation covering political and cultural rights and protections.

Box 4.4 Exercise

Your digital communication system

Although the matrix in Table 4.1 was originally developed to map national and regional digital communication systems, it also helps to identify the infrastructures, markets, and political frameworks that circumscribe the communicative practices that individual citizens engage in and experience.

1. First, choose 3 or 4 of the 12 questions in Table 4.1 that you find most interesting.
2. Next, try to answer each question, starting from your own habits of communication. Public agencies in many countries make available online records of the types of access networks that cover particular neighborhoods (copper, cable, fiber), and about the companies operating these networks – identify your type of access network and your operator; do the same for your mobile connection. Or go the Settings of your phone to assess which applications you spend the most time on, and then check who owns and operates these applications. Or look into the legislation that applies to your preferred ways of communicating.
3. Finally, select two of the three structural dimensions, and discuss with your reading group or class how these dimensions interact to shape your daily communications (for instance, how does a particular piece of legislation apply to the operators in your local area?).

The exercise can be turned into a paper or a project by including a larger group of students or an entire class.

Digital communication systems are still emerging and gaining momentum. Two sets of communicative practices begin to suggest some of the social transformations underway. First, digitalization is reconfiguring the **internal** and **external** communications of private companies, public institutions, and other organizations. Whereas political parties, for example, still maintain firewalls between their intranets and the internet (see further p. 110), digital infrastructures facilitate the involvement of members, allies, and other stakeholders in formal and informal consultations. Grassroots organizations and popular movements, equally, engage their members and the public in online debate and deliberation. And businesses will promote their customers' brand loyalty through online communities and other continuous communications that may nurture a sense of belonging and being heard, perhaps stimulated by discounts and lotteries, too. Media businesses, such as tabloid news, invite the involvement and, sometimes, the active contributions of audiences to public communication, positively conceived as citizen journalism, more cynically called out as unpaid labor.

Second, as suggested by Image 4.6 (p. 120), digital communication systems are blurring the lines between media and **non-media**. Organizations that traditionally have not been considered 'media' – corporations, unions, and professional associ-ations, state and municipal agencies – increasingly participate in the political and cultural public spheres at large to promote their own long-term interests with ref-erence to the public interest. In doing so, they enter the ongoing production, main-tenance, repair, and transformation – the institutionalization – of society (Carey, 1989a).

Communication as institutionalization

Media represent institutions in society; the communications they enable and enhance, constitute a **process of institutionalization**. On the one hand, commu-nication maintains the media as such in institutionally variable forms – means of interpersonal contact, agencies of administration, vehicles of the arts, a fourth branch of governance, and an integrated infrastructure serving all of these social ends, spanning market, state, and public sphere. On the other hand, communica-tion, as carried by media of all three degrees (Chapter 1, p. 5), serves to repro-duce and reconfigure all other social institutions. Chapter 7 returns to the point that media exist *within* society – in specific historical times and cultural places. Society, in one sense, is an accumulated outcome or 'effect' of communication.

Chapter 5, next, elaborates on the effects of media and communication, in different contexts and at different levels of the social structure. Media institutions are part and parcel of the ongoing institutionalization of the rest of society; media use by people – as citizens, consumers, family members, and more – is an essen-tial aspect of their socialization as individuals. The question of effects – strong and weak, good or bad – is one of the most thoroughly researched and, simultaneously, one of the most contested aspects of media and communication in both research and public debate.

5   Media users

Users and effects

One question trumps all others as the social and scholarly motivation for doing media and communication studies – it is the question of **effects** (Katz, 2001): What difference do media make, in our personal lives and in social life? Where Chapter 4 addressed **structural** effects – the interchange of media with other social institutions – this chapter focuses on the effects of media on people.

Media can have effects on **attitudes** and **actions**; on **individuals** and **groups**; in the **short term** and **the long term**. Media effects can be either **wanted** or **unwanted**, depending on context and purpose – audience and user studies have examined the (more or less) wanted effects of advertising as well as the (largely) unwanted effects of violence and misinformation represented in the media. Importantly, a media effect may amount to a transformation, but also the maintenance of personal attitudes and social structures: **No change** must be counted among the effects of media and communication. Indeed, the very idea of 'effects' calls for further examination, both in theoretical terms (media are rarely self-evident or direct 'causes' of human actions), and in a historical perspective: The effects of one-to-many communication such as television viewing and of many-to-many communication through social media should be approached differently.

By way of introduction, it is useful distinguish four different conceptions of the people attending to and applying media and communication for various personal and social ends:

- **Recipients**. People always receive something from the media that they attend to, even as they can be seen to respond, more or less actively and deeply, to the communication on offer. Media provide access to diverse worlds of experience and insight far beyond the immediate input that people receive through their senses and from their surroundings.

DOI: 10.4324/9781032655109-5

- **Users**. People, further, use – engage with and apply – media for a wide range of purposes. We use specific media and genres to take care of various needs and address different interests. The personal and social uses of media consist both in literal 'interactivity' – selection from and navigation of media interfaces – and in the more or less committed and empathic interpretation of their contents and forms.

Image 5.1 Parades and propaganda. Everett Collection/Shutterstock.

Different periods in human history have been preoccupied with, and concerned about, different kinds of media effects – on people's attitudes, emotions, and actions – while at the same time assessing the effects differently, as either strong or weak. An important backdrop to contemporary media and communication research was the two world wars of the twentieth century, which seemed to suggest a considerable effect of war propaganda on the masses variably fighting and suffering. Propaganda made use of multiple platforms in the years leading up to the Second World War – parades such as the one depicted here, further represented in the German director, Leni Riefenstahl's documentary Triumph des Willens [Triumph of the Will] *(1935) about the Nazi Party's 1934 congress, and as covered in other 'new' and 'old' media of the time: radio and newspapers.*

- **Publics**. In and by communication, recipients and users become a collective – a public – that come together, via media, to exchange experiences and viewpoints about their common affairs in a shared social space – a public sphere (Chapter 4, p. 100). Beyond their moments of communicative interaction, publics constitute social agents, in economic, political, and cultural matters, with reference to both consensual and conflicting interests.
- **Market**. Alternatively, particularly in the perspective of senders, the recipients of media can be approached as a market. More than users of media, they are consumers – economic agents who may be willing to spend either their time and attention or their money (or both), initially on selected contents and communications, later on other goods and services on display.

These distinctive conceptions of the audiences or users of media and communication are reflected – theoretically, methodologically, and normatively – in the research traditions that we review in this chapter. The many potential applications of findings from research, for commercial and political ends, have produced diverse ways of posing the general question of 'effects.' And, with historically changing technologies and institutions of media and communication, assumptions concerning the nature and scale of any 'effect' have been changing, too.

Box 5.1 Analysis

The history of media effects

Public interest in how communication might be used to persuade people to think and act in particular ways, goes back to classical **rhetoric**, which has remained a source of inspiration for modern theories of communication (Chapter 2, p. 26). It was not until the 1800s, however, that **communication** was commonly referred to as a generic social and cultural phenomenon that could be examined and evaluated as such. Previously, it had been customary to consider the preacher's sermon, the minstrel singer's tales, and the books containing scientific knowledge and practical guidance as different categories of human action and social interaction. In an influential volume on the history of the very idea of communication, John Durham Peters (1999) showed how the concept of communication emerged in response to, and along with, new technologies – first the telegraph and the telephone, later film, radio, television, and the internet. In Peters's summary formulation, 'mass communication came first' (p. 6): It was only once technologically mediated communication had highlighted the common process and its technological and social variability, that it seemed natural to also include conversation and other everyday interactions under a heading of communication.

The understanding of 'effects,' similarly, has reflected the historical trajectory of modern media over the past 100 years. The earliest effects studies date from the beginning of the 1900s. While subject to alternative assessments (Neuman & Guggenheim, 2011), it is helpful to divide the different conceptions and studies of the effects of media and communication into four phases (McQuail & Deuze, 2020: 507–517):

1. *Powerful media*. Before the Second World War, media were often considered highly influential on individuals' perceptions of and behaviors in the world. Not least propaganda in times of crisis or war, as disseminated through broadcasting and print media, was a source of concern among scholars and commentators (e.g., Lasswell, 1938). The concerns, however, were largely substantiated through informal observations, rather than by systematic research.

2. *Media without power*. Following the formation of a field dedicated to media and communication studies, from the 1930s onward, media effects became a topic of sustained empirical research. Surprising to many, and contested by some, studies did not find any clear, strong, or direct links between the media as stimulus and the audience response (summarized in Klapper, 1960). The literature, instead, identified a variety of intervening social and psychological circumstances and contingencies, as illustrated by the coupling of mass communication and interpersonal communication in two-step flows (Chapter 1, p. 14).

3. *Effects in the plural*. From the 1960s onward, the concept of effects became increasingly differentiated to account for a range of cognitive, affective, and behavioral consequences of media use and communicative practices. The null findings of the previous period, moreover, were in for a reassessment. For one thing, the breakthrough of television in much of the Global North suggested to intellectuals as well as ordinary viewers that 'new' categories of media could have different kinds and different degrees of effect. For another thing, researchers looked beyond the potential effects of media on the attitudes and actions of individuals regarding specific issues, to also consider structural effects, for example, a reconfiguration of electoral and other political processes through the influence of media, in part with inspiration from critical social theory.

4. *Effects as processes*. Around 1980, research could be seen to gradually reemphasize the embedding of media use in wider social and cultural contexts. One inspiration for this reorientation came from qualitative studies of the reception and social uses of media (see further p. 138) and – more generally – of 'meaning production' as a process pervading and maintaining society and culture (Chapter 1, p. 3). Reception studies, briefly, explore how ordinary media users participate in the social production and circulation of meaning by interpreting and applying the textual

contents and discursive forms of media in everyday settings. Rather than asking *whether* media have effects, the premise of reception studies had become that media and communication necessarily have effects – the question is *which kinds* of effects, and *how* these effects manifest themselves, from the level of individual consciousness to the institutions and infrastructures of entire societies.

Since circa 2010, digitalization – of media and communicative practices, as well as of media and communication research – has marked the beginning of one more phase of effects studies: *5. Effects in and through systems.* The registration of user actions has become a standard operating procedure in digital communication systems. And the processing and analysis of the resulting data, through algorithmic procedures and artificial intelligence (AI), generate findings that, next, shape the further circulation of information in those systems according to a logic of supply and demand. At work is a systemic effect by which minimal user actions (demand) influence the provisions of the system (supply) – and vice versa. Critical studies of contemporary society have described this logic as the pivot of an overarching system of surveillance capitalism (Zuboff, 2019). (See further the Box 5.5 with an analysis of 'Users in systems,' p. 153.)

Effects and contexts

After this brief **historical** overview of the development of effects research, the following pages turn to different types of audience and user studies in a more detailed, **systematic** perspective: A systematics – a comprehensive characterization and categorization – of the main research traditions begins to compare their relevance, strengths, and limitations when it comes to addressing specific research questions.

The full systematics is laid out in Figure 5.1 – which calls for a bit of explanation. Each box within the figure carries the name of a research tradition, which provides an analytical perspective on a specific moment of the longer process of communication. But the moments, crucially, do not make up a chain effect in which one type of use or effect simply follows after or from another type. The figure, in other words, does not represent the process of communication *itself*, but depicts multiple research *perspectives on* that process. In fact, the various traditions of audience and user studies have been, and often remain, at odds regarding the definition and delimitation of the various moments of impact and their interrelations.

Nevertheless, the process of communication provides a common denominator for the many varieties of audience and user studies. First, there is an obvious difference between short-term and long-term effects – from a person's attention to and contact with a particular medium and message, to the cumulative impact of several

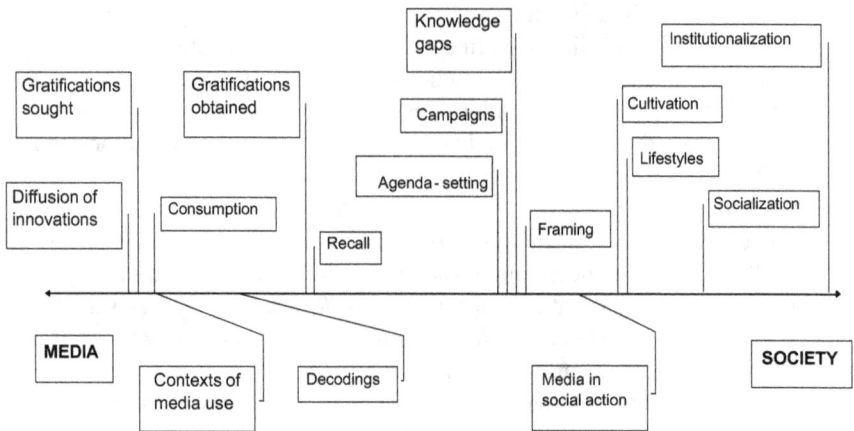

Figure 5.1 The process of communication, as defined by audience research traditions.

media on social institutions such as economic markets or state agencies. Second, whether explicitly or implicitly, all the traditions laid out in Figure 5.1 bear witness to an orientation toward a specific moment of the longer process of communication. Third, the visualization helps clarify which kinds of research questions, early or late in the process, each tradition is suited to address and analyze – and what it *cannot* capture. Chapter 6 returns to different empirical methodologies, which equally represent complementary perspectives on communication as an extended process of producing and circulating information and meaning in ways that make a difference, for individual media users as social agents and for the structure of society.

Toward the left in Figure 5.1, the focus tends to be on 'media' as such, their more immediate uses and the interpretations they invite and enable. Toward the right, the focus shifts to 'society,' that is, the entire social and cultural field that the media grow out of and feed into. And situated between the two poles of Figure 5.1 is a range of research traditions that have emerged to examine diverse aspects of the three-way give-and-take among the media, their users as social agents, and the social structure circumscribing both the media and the agents.

Above the line in Figure 5.1, we list the primarily quantitative traditions that have been collected under the heading of **the dominant paradigm** (Gitlin, 1978; Webster & Phalen, 1997). As the expression suggests, these traditions have attained, and retain, a dominant position in media and communication research, as reflected in international journals and conferences, and we review them first. Below the line, we include a further set of primarily qualitative approaches, which gradually have acquired a more prominent position in the field.

We begin by highlighting one premise for the following reviews of different research traditions: Media-user encounters can rarely be accounted for in terms of direct 'causes' and simple 'effects.' Media present a **potential** of meanings and potential actions, which users go on to **actualize** to varying degrees, typically in several steps of interpretation and stages of action. We, further, approach each of the moments identified in Figure 5.1 as a 'context,' in which the media-user encounter can be said and seen to unfold, from the very short to the very long term.

An example of an 'early' context is the moment when a user turns to the internet to learn more about, for instance, interesting and suitable educational programs or attractive investment opportunities. An example of a 'late' context are so-called knowledge gaps – between people who know a great deal, and others who know little, about social domains such as the educational system or economic trends. It might appear commonsensical that these gaps would close over time – after all, a mass of media give access to masses of information, at least for most people in most parts of the world. But the evidence suggests that, instead, the uses of media by different socioeconomic groups tend to deepen existing knowledge gaps: Those who already command substantial knowledge in an area, will learn relatively more from their media use (see further p. 136). Potential explanations will refer both to an 'early' context (collecting knowledge or information from the media) and to a 'late' context (the knowledge gaps accumulated over time throughout a population): People who already hold some background knowledge will collect information differently, and will come to know even more, than people who know little in advance. And the mechanism has wider implications: Because the accumulation of knowledge through media use facilitates actions and initiatives in *other* social contexts (education, investment), the end result likely is a perpetuation of existing social inequalities (differences in knowledge and wealth). More than describing what individuals do with media, and how media use affects them, then, audience research also offers perspectives on the relationship between media use and the structure of societies.

Media effects: Quantitative traditions

- **Diffusion of innovations**. For technologically mediated communication to take place on any social scale, several preparatory conditions must be met. First, the technology in question must have been invented, developed, disseminated, and marketed at a price manageable for a significant portion of the population in question. A single mobile phone is of little use. At the beginning of the twenty-first century, much of the world's population take for granted that they are able to contact other people anytime and anywhere: If they cannot be reached, *they* present a problem – for *us* (Ling, 2012). (The mobile phone has witnessed the most rapid diffusion globally of any communication technology (ITU, 2018).) Second, the medium needs to be accessible in a cultural or discursive sense: Ordinary users must have come to see the medium as relevant in their own lives, as a meaningful and applicable resource. Research on the diffusion of innovations (Rogers, 2003/1962) has explored this extended and distributed process with reference to media as well as a wide range of other innovations. In countries of the Global South, studies have sought to map the complex interdependencies of new technologies, cultural contexts, and social progress (Kim,

2018). And, long before the current diffusion of digital media, the tradition considered the interplay of mass communication and interpersonal communication (in a two-step flow – Chapter 1, p. 14): The more members of a given community or culture are familiar with a particular event (or innovation), the more people will have learnt about it in conversation with others (Greenberg, 1964). So far, however, the central interest of diffusion studies has been the material availability and accessibility of different media, rather than their discursive or symbolic diffusion (Jensen, 1993). Spanning material and discursive diffusion, a related research tradition has examined how media are 'domesticated,' or embedded in the everyday lives of persons and households (for overview, see Haddon, 2004).

- **Gratifications sought**. One early way of differentiating the classic question of 'effects' – what media do *to* people – was research on their **uses and gratifications** (U&G) – which asks the complementary question of what people do *with* media (Katz, 1959). Departing from early classics (Berelson, 1949; Herzog, 1944), U&G studies became especially influential from the 1960s onward (Blumler & Katz, 1974; Rosengren et al., 1985). Relying on survey methodologies (Chapter 6, p. 161), the tradition has documented the diverse ways in which different media and genres are taken by their users to be sources of information, entertainment, and socialization (Katz et al., 1973). Whereas the original aim was to identify the gratifications that audiences seek from media (gratifications sought), later studies went on to compare this with the experienced outcomes of media use (gratifications obtained – see below, p. 134). In U&G studies of digital media, the research questions have included not only the users' experiences of fictional and factual contents, but also their appreciation of communication with others, specifically through social media (Ancu & Cozma, 2009).

- **Consumption**. The majority of all audience and user studies measure different demographic segments' contact with and consumption of various media, genres, and discourses. In addition to being conditions of other categories of uses and effects, contact and consumption are of evident economic interest in commercial communication systems, specifically to advertisers, but also to the producers and programmers being paid by advertisers for the users' time and attention (Napoli, 2003). Without contact, there could be no communication, no interpretation, no further (economic) effect in the form of purchases and consumption of other goods and services. Media-user contact is documented primarily by quantitative measures, increasingly through 'cookies' and other automated, digitized techniques (see further Chapter 6, p. 181). On top of a steady quantitative mainstream of audience research have come diverse qualitative attempts at exploring the details and nuances of media consumption in everyday contexts, for example, **secondary media use** in parallel with other tasks and chores. As far as advertisers and senders generally are concerned, audiences are notoriously distracted and faithless, which has prompted the introduction of quite imaginative methodologies. One example is a group of studies that have embedded

Image 5.2 Viewing the viewers. Bill Viola, Reverse Television – Portraits of Viewers, 1983, Broadcast television project. Kira Perov © Bill Viola Studio.

Whereas most studies of television viewing (as well as of internet and print media use) employ quantitative measures and partially automated methodologies, other research explores various qualitative aspects of media use, for instance, through interviewing and observations in everyday contexts (Chapter 6, p. 157). Yet another variant of viewer studies has introduced an 'inverted television' in which a camera is embedded in a television set to produce a recording of events in front of the set. The findings indicate that, in many cases, 'television viewing' is secondary to other activities such as household meals, taking care of children, or family quarrels; in other instances, literally nothing is happening, even while the television set is turned on – the room is empty, the viewers absent.

video cameras in television sets to document the viewers' presence in front of, and attention devoted to, the screen – or lack thereof (Image 5.2) (Bechtel et al., 1972; Borzekowski & Robinson, 1999; Schmitt et al., 2003). Other studies have relied on even more fine-grained techniques of eye-tracking, which meticulously register, for example, which elements of single advertisements or advertising breaks viewers will look at, for how long, and in what sequence (Thorson, 1994). (See Chapter 6, p. 171.)

- **Gratifications obtained**. As mentioned, the tradition of uses-and-gratifications research (U&G) has proposed a distinction between what users seek, and what they obtain, from media. One motivation has been to explore the extent to which, and the ways in which, the media experience sought, is shaped by earlier experiences of the same or similar media and genres (Palmgreen & Rayburn, 1985). In practice, however, it has proven difficult to capture that distinction through the standardized surveys preferred by U&G. Media experience holds a range of ambiguous and, sometimes, controversial aspects that call for alternative empirical methodologies. One such technique is the so-called **experience sampling method** (Hektner et al., 2007): Here, participants will rely on a mobile terminal – whether using a dedicated app or responding to text messages from researchers – to register what they are doing at randomly selected times, and how they are feeling in those moments, perhaps while watching television (Kubey & Csikszentmihalyi, 1990).
- **Memory**. One measure of how users are affected by media, is the extent to which they later recall the contents presented (Shapiro, 2008). Focusing on people's memory immediately or soon after media use, studies have employed a variety of experimental techniques and survey methodologies. Perhaps surprisingly, a common finding is that people recall very little of what, after all, they seem to take a continuing interest in, for example, daily news reports. The rate of recall, however, does vary with the respondents' background knowledge, which, in turn, correlates with their educational level and, hence, with social status (on knowledge gaps as a product of media use, see further p. 136). Research indicates, further, that media organizations are able to enhance both basic recall and a deeper understanding of the contents they provide (from current affairs to advertising), for instance, by integrating and balancing the verbal and visual components of messages. But audiovisual media and modalities are not, in and of themselves, more effective communicators than print formats.

Box 5.2 Exercise

Forgetting the media

- Prepare a recording either of a social media feed (e.g., from Instagram or Facebook) or a YouTube session, on your computer or mobile phone.
- Make sure either to scroll some way into the feed, or watch three to five consecutive YouTube videos by following YouTube's recommendations for the next video to watch – and do so together with at least one other person (roommate, friend, family).
- Immediately following this joint viewing, ask the person(s) in question to note down as many elements of the contents as possible. And note down as many elements as you yourself can remember, too.
- Review the recording, and compare the recording of the actual feed / the YouTube videos with the notes that you and the other participant(s) in the exercise had made about the contents. Make an analysis of, and

try to explain, any differences between the recording and the recall with reference both to the feed / videos (their contents and forms) and to the participants (their background and interests). (Your prior knowledge of the purpose of the joint viewing session may explain why – perhaps – you recall more than the other participant(s).)
- If possible, discuss the results of the comparison with the person(s) who watched the feed / videos with you. Ask them to reflect on what they did (not) remember, and why.

- **Agenda-setting**. Compared to recall studies, which focuses on media users' memory for specific items of information, research on the agenda-setting function of media shifts attention to the communication of more complex 'issues,' 'events,' and 'stories,' above all in the domain of politics. The tradition has participated in the general questioning by scholarship, since the Second World War, of the (still widespread) assumption that media will tell people *what* to think, that is, which opinions to hold on particular matters. Research since the early 1960s had suggested that the media rather tell people what to form opinions *about* (Cohen, 1963; Trenaman & McQuail, 1961: 178), and the position received its classic formulation in a study of political communication in a small community in the United States during the 1968 presidential election campaign (McCombs & Shaw, 1972). In methodological terms, studies of agenda-setting have combined content analyses of news media with surveys about their readers, listeners, and viewers (on these methodologies, see further Chapter 6, p. 176 and p. 161), thus identifying and comparing 'media agendas' and 'audience agendas.' Subsequent research has added a third category – 'policy agendas' – with reference to parliamentary debates and legislation taking shape within established political institutions, further exploring their interaction with media and public debate (Dearing & Rogers, 1996). A variety of empirical studies have suggested that the agenda-setting functions of technologically and institutionally distinctive media (print and electronic, commercial and public service organizations) are, nevertheless, broadly similar (Strömbäck & Kiousis, 2010). And recent big-data analyses of online evidence have shown that the media are able to set agendas both for specific issues and for entire policy areas (King et al., 2017).
- **Campaigns**. In response to the accelerating availability of information from both mass and social media, and the intensifying competition for user attention, systematic campaigns promoting both facts and opinions on behalf of a range of private and public interests, have become integral parts of contemporary media and communication environments (Holtzhausen, 2008). Campaigns are typically conducted across multiple media, extending through time, as well. While some of the earliest studies of campaigns centered on propaganda in times of war (Hovland et al., 1953), today the mainstay of research in the area are commercial campaigns for goods, services, and brands, with public information

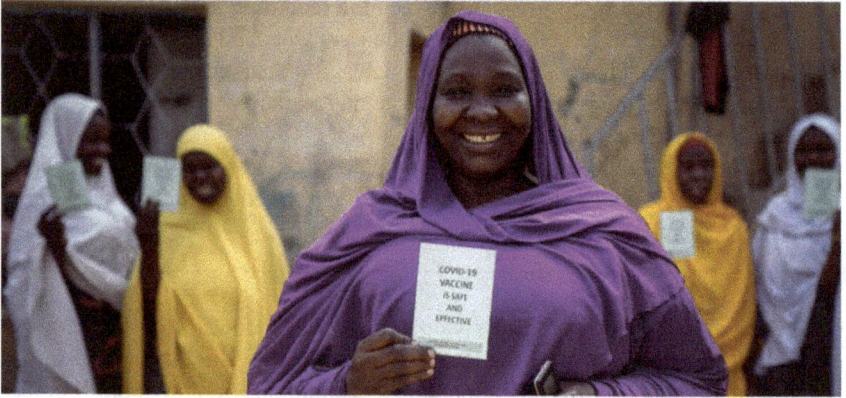

Image 5.3 Communicating for our lives. © UNICEF 2022/Rooftop Productions.

The typical purpose of a campaign (p. 135) is to get people to do par-
ticular kinds of things – and not *to do certain other things. Where commer-*
cial campaigns promote the sales of goods and services, public information
campaigns regarding, for instance, health issues, seek to have target groups
'do the right thing': eat healthy food, stop smoking, start exercising, and much
else. It is the right thing for the individual (a longer and better life), but also for
society (fewer health-related expenses) and humanity (lower risks of epidemics
and pandemics). Campaigns are commonly conducted across several media, in
some cases media of all three degrees (Chapter 1, p. 5). In the aftermath of the
Covid-19 pandemic, national and international health authorities, including the
World Health Organization (WHO), have kept up campaigns to persuade people
to accept vaccines and to take other precautions. The photo represents a woman
alongside her sisters in Kano, Nigeria (media of the first degree), carrying the
printed message (media of the second degree) that the 'Covid-19 vaccine is
safe and effective,' which was communicated globally through a United Nations
website (media of the third degree).

campaigns figuring as poor cousins in the family of campaigns. Although it is,
in fact, quite difficult to determine the specific effects of campaigns, particularly
when it comes to purchases and other material reactions, advertisers and other
campaigners take into account what would happen if they did *not* maintain a
continuous presence in the marketplace of attention (Webster, 2014). A widely
cited motto concerning advertising, commonly attributed to the American mer-
chant John Wanamaker, is: 'Half the money I spend on advertising is wasted; the
trouble is I don't know which half' (http://en.wikipedia.org/wiki/John_Wanama
ker, August 1, 2024). Because of their complexity and variation, campaigns are
examined through a variety of quantitative as well as qualitative methodologies,

adapted to the different stages and contexts of campaigning. Beyond social scientific studies of their effects, campaigns lend themselves to humanistic analyses of their forms and contents as texts and intertextual networks (see further Chapter 2, p. 43).

- **Knowledge gaps**. To a considerable extent, contemporary mass media and social media make the same information available to all socioeconomic segments of various populations. As noted in the introduction to this chapter, one might, therefore, expect communication to increasingly level the differences between more and less knowledgeable individuals and groups. The research tradition on knowledge gaps has argued, in contrast, that media, in fact, tend to consolidate and, even, deepen knowledge gaps (Tichenor et al., 1970). One likely explanation is that persons who are already knowledgeable about various domains and topics, are better able to fit new information into their preexisting cognitive and cultural frameworks; another explanation may be that the same social segments witness more opportunities to act on new information, to exercise influence in and on the social contexts being represented in the media, which may motivate them to process the available information as a resource for later use. Empirical studies have confirmed that different media, including social media, tend to either maintain or deepen knowledge gaps (Lind & Boomgaarden, 2019), including in the case of social media (Li & Cho, 2023). In recent years, research projects and public debate concerning knowledge gaps have pointed to the existence of specific **digital divides** between the top and bottom of contemporary 'information societies,' both within countries and between the Global North and South (see further Chapter 4, p. 111). Such persistent gaps and divides challenge what remains a common assumption underlying policy and marketing regarding digital infrastructures, namely, that the worldwide diffusion of the internet is countering inequality and promoting democratization, locally and globally.
- **Framing**. The concept of 'frames' draws attention to the fact that the many individual items of information afforded by media – which feed users' 'memories' and enter into shared 'agendas' – will be interpreted and understood in the context of much larger, meaningful wholes (Borah, 2011; D'Angelo et al., 2019). The research tradition examining the framing of information, explores how comprehensive worldviews, articulated in narratives and arguments, already inform media contents and communicative practices – which, in turn, maintain and, to an extent, transform the frames or worldviews of users over time (Carey, 1989a). To account for the complex psychological and social processes at work, the field of media and communication research has taken theoretical inspiration from cognitive and experimental psychology as well as from micro-sociology examining everyday interactions (Scheufele, 1999). Empirical media and communication studies have gone on to combine qualitative and quantitative approaches in order to identify the frames at work in users' engagements with media (e.g., Jensen, 1998; Liebes & Katz, 1990; Neuman et al., 1992). The concept of frames, moreover, has facilitated detailed comparisons of the production and reception of media content. On the production side, media practitioners will seek to frame their contents in socially and culturally meaningful ways, keeping

the anticipated audiences in mind (e.g., Ettema & Whitney, 1994; Gans, 1957). On the reception side, media users, equally, rely on frames of interpretation and understanding that are molded and modified through lifetimes and generations, with input from media of all three degrees (e.g., Gamson, 1992; Graber, 1984). Compared to premises guiding other research traditions, that media either tell audiences *what* to think, or what they should form opinions *about*, the tradition studying framing suggests that the media tell audiences *how* to think about topics and themes in society and culture at large (Scheufele, 1999: 19).

• **Cultivation theory**. One of the most ambitious – and contested – approaches to the long-term effects of media has proposed to examine how, in particular, television cultivates or produces specific worldviews among its viewers (Morgan, 2008). The original hypothesis was that, sometime in the second half of the twentieth century, television had acquired such a central position, especially in North American culture, that it constituted a massive symbolic environment, which competed with, distorted, and, in part, replaced the lived reality of its viewers (Gerbner & Gross, 1976). The research tradition has examined that claim through a combination of content analyses and surveys, concluding that 'heavy viewers' are more likely to give 'the television answer' when asked about, for example, the risk of walking down the street or the percentages of different ethnic groups holding various occupations. While cultivation research has continued to attract researchers (Hermann et al., 2021), critics have pointed to three main weaknesses of the tradition. First, quantitative colleagues have questioned the statistical procedures substantiating its results (Hirsch, 1980, 1981), while qualitative scholars have argued that the approach fails to consider television programs as texts, and the viewers as active interpreters of these texts, not least when it comes to the representation of violence in factual and fictional genres, respectively (Newcomb, 1978). Second, studies of television viewing in other countries have not confirmed the findings from the United States (Gunter, 1987). Third, the tradition has given surprisingly little attention to the interrelations between television and other media, despite some research on social media (Hermann et al., 2023). In a historical context where the medium formerly known as television may be disappearing, or will be redefined through digitalization, research centered in the 'cultivation' of worldviews through television probably cannot deliver a sufficiently general theory of media, their effects, and wider social and cultural implications (Williams, 2006).

Media reception: Qualitative traditions

Quantitative effects research traditions are frequently summarized under 'the dominant paradigm' heading; qualitative contributions are commonly referred to as a minor and recent trend. It is true that, within the academic literature, qualitative audience and user studies still represent a minority; and a qualitative tradition was only defined explicitly and as such from the 1980s. However, focus groups and other qualitative interviewing are essential elements of commercially oriented media and communication studies. And some of the traditions bundled under 'the dominant paradigm' have long included qualitative components, not just as 'pilot studies' to be followed by 'real' research (Chapter 6, p. 189), but as scholarly contributions in their own right. One early example was the classic Payne Fund studies in the United States during the 1930s, which examined the effects of film on children and young people (for overview, see Jowett et al., 1996). Another example, comparable in some respects to the Payne Fund project, was the 'mass observation' of visits to the cinema and other aspects of everyday life in England of the 1930s (Richards & Sheridan, 1987).

This section reviews the dedicated qualitative tradition (and its sub-traditions) that has become a notable contribution to audience and user studies in recent decades. While sometimes quite critical of the dominant paradigm, the tradition has positioned itself both as a complement to the quantitative traditions and as a necessary constituent of media and communication research as a field of inquiry.

A characteristic feature of qualitative audience and user research follows from the distinction between **emic** and **etic** analysis (familiar, too, in other social scientific and humanistic research) (Headland et al., 1990; Pike, 1967). Deriving from linguistics, and a frequent reference within the discipline of anthropology, the two concepts indicate different ways of approaching both personal experience of the world and entire cultures – from the 'inside' or the 'outside' – from a native, empathic perspective or from a distanced, analytical perspective. Phonetics (*etic*) describes language from the outside, so to speak, as a continuum of sounds that can be measured and rendered visually on a screen as frequencies. Phonemics (*emic*) approaches language from the inside, as a set of meaningful relations and structures. A person who does not speak Chinese, Spanish, or other languages is perfectly able to record and visualize speech in the given language, but cannot understand or explain the meaning of the sounds. By analogy, studies of the uses and interpretations of media and communication can either refer to concepts and theories that have been predefined by the researchers, or they may rely on the users' own, contextualized understanding. It is emic analysis – the users' own perspectives on media and on themselves as users – that guides qualitative media and communication research.

Reception analysis is the term commonly used to cover qualitative audience and user studies. Despite certain overlaps, reception analysis can be subdivided into three varieties with different primary research questions, which we consider in the following sections.

The social contexts of media use

As shown in Figure 5.1, qualitative and quantitative research traditions are organized around a dividing line – but in one instance, a qualitative and a quantitative tradition are anchored in the same point on that line, namely, the encounter of medium and user, which allows consumption, contact, attention, and perhaps additional effects, to take place. The key difference between the traditions above and below the line follows from their distinctive theoretical conceptions of this 'context,' which further give rise to the choice of different empirical methodologies. Qualitative reception studies, first, approach the context as a preexisting, manifest, and meaningful social setting. The context of use does not appear of out nowhere, nor is it simply the product of the media and communications on offer. Second, the aim of reception studies is to explore, in considerable detail, the human actions and social interactions that unfold in, through, and around the medium as it is being used in context.

Against a background of classic studies dating from the 1930s as well as subsequent uses-and-gratifications research, a renewed interest in media use as part of everyday contexts was signaled by James Lull's studies of **the social uses** of television in American households (Lull, 1980). His aim was, on the one hand, to move beyond individuals' media use – 'user meets medium' – which had been the focus of uses-and-gratifications studies until then. On the other hand, Lull's approach remained centered in the household and families as specific micro contexts. 'Social uses,' in other words, did not include public uses of media, for example, as elements of citizens' political involvement or cultural participation.

Lull's empirical studies, nevertheless, contributed an innovative typology of the meanings and implications of 'watching television.' His analyses identified, first, a number of **structural** uses of television – beyond the experience of factual and fictional representations carried by images and sounds. Not only does television contribute to a shared atmosphere enveloping family life, or to the filling of awkward silences among the members of a household. Television also serves as a concrete resource and practical instrument for marking periods of and transitions within everyday life, for example, children's bedtimes: 'As soon as this program is over, you're going to bed.' Second, television has a variety of **relational** uses, regulating household members' interactions with each other, typically as a source of information and a point of reference for conversation (two-step flows of communication, see further Chapter 1, p. 14). 'Being right' in an argument with others, with reference to facts or opinions supplied by the media, serves to maintain relations of status and power, in families as in other social groupings: 'See what I said?'

Contextual studies have continued exploring the close integration and mutual adaptation of media use and other everyday activities (for overview, see Alasuutari, 1999; Ross & Nightingale, 2003). A majority of studies have centered either on families or on children's media use, despite some research on media use in public spaces and other social contexts (Gauntlett & Hill, 1999; Lemish, 1982). One practical explanation for the emphasis on the microcosms of family and children – and on television – is that these interactions have offered delimited, convenient objects of analysis. In contemporary households, where family members increasingly are able to watch different kinds of content on different devices, some genres – news, films, and popular series – still offer shared points of reference for daily media rituals (Courtois & Nelissen, 2018). To an extent, studies have also looked into the social contexts of use for radio (Moores, 1988), books (Radway, 1984), and films (Gomery, 1992; Stacey, 1994; Stokes & Maltby, 1999), as well as the combined uses of several media by individuals and families (e.g., Barnhurst & Wartella, 1998).

The most common methodology employed by this first variety of reception studies has been **participating observation** (see further Chapter 6, p. 166). Taking inspiration from classic, long-term anthropological fieldwork, the approach has lent itself to capturing distinctive uses and experiences of media both within and between cultures (e.g., Gillespie, 1995). Relying on interviewing to document media use (e.g., Gray, 1992; Morley, 1986), other research has had to depend on informants' recall, verbalization, and likely rationalization of their choices and actions in past contexts. A further limitation of contextual studies has been their lacking, or limited, attention to media contents, which, after all, provide the concrete texts and genres that users will interpret and apply for various purposes in the moment. Lull's (1980) original study, for one, did not highlight the likely different social uses of a fiction series and a football match. A tendency of reception studies, thus, has been for observational studies to concentrate on contexts, with more limited attention to texts, whereas research relying on interviewing has emphasized the **decoding** of media contents (which we take up in the following section).

It should be noted, lastly, that mobile and other digital media have introduced new social conditions for communication and, hence, for the 'observation' of the 'contexts' of media use. For one thing, digital media blur the lines between texts and contexts, whether the physical setting is a living room, a café, a classroom, or some other locality (Image 5.4). Digital texts have become more thoroughly integrated into diverse contextual activities; and texts on digital screens establish contact with other, distant, proliferating contexts. For another thing, digital technologies give access both to new types of data and to new ways of analyzing them – digital data can be both made and found, as we elaborate in Chapter 6.

Decoding media

The largest body of reception studies have examined how individuals with different social and cultural backgrounds, and diverse socioeconomic groups, experience and interpret – 'decode' – the contents of media (for overview, see Livingstone, 1998; Schrøder et al., 2003). Compared to the observational research reviewed in the previous section, which served to supplement established social-scientific approaches, humanistic studies of actual viewers, readers, and other media users were very rare indeed before the 1980s. The 'breakthrough' of decoding studies combined two elements: a theoretical conception of the process of reception as the production of one more 'text' (or, perhaps, several texts) and empirical, comparative analyses of the media texts and the 'user texts' – of the production of meaning and culture in and through the many encounters between media and their users.

To one side, reception analysis derived many of its concepts and theoretical frameworks from the humanities. Niches of literary studies – Umberto Eco's (1987) writings about literature and semiotics, and the German tradition of reception aesthetics (Holub, 1984; Iser, 1978; Jauss, 1982) – had already underlined how literary (and other) texts constitute open structures, which are understood in remarkably varied ways, for instance, in different historical periods and social settings. But literary studies had largely shunned investigations of actual, living, historically and culturally situated readers. The response of reception analysis, to the other side, was to call for sustained empirical research along social-scientific lines that

Image 5.4 Everyday media. Photo by Guvluck from Pexels.

> *Media, among other things, provide resources that people will use to structure their surroundings, indicating boundaries between 'me' and 'others.' Reading a book or newspaper, listening to music, or using a mobile phone is an indirect form of communication: 'I don't want to communicate with you.' Such media use was employed to symbolic effect in the novel (Anne Tyler, 1985) and feature film (Lawrence Kasdan, 1988)* The Accidental Tourist, *in which the main character makes sure to always bring a book on his travels to 'defend himself' against fellow travelers – a piece of advice that he passes on in the travel books that are his occupation.*

would include both texts and receivers as objects of analysis – an integrated form of **audience-cum-content research**.

The agenda-setting publication (Morley, 1980) appeared in the same year as James Lull's equally agenda-setting article (but without previous contact between the two researchers). The point of departure, negatively speaking, was again a critique of the uses-and-gratifications tradition, including its individualistic and functionalistic understanding of the interplay between media users and the social structures embedding them. Positively speaking, Morley's study grew out of the British **cultural studies** tradition, the key inspiration deriving from Stuart Hall's (1973) work, specifically his model of the 'encoding' and 'decoding' of media texts. This model emphasizes *both* that media practitioners (and the social system which they, to an extent, represent) 'prefer' and 'inscribe' particular, ideologically loaded meanings into media texts, *and* that audiences will not necessarily 'extract' and 'accept' those same meanings. In contrast, through a focus-group methodology Morley identified three prototypical decodings (drawing on critical social theory (Parkin, 1971)): a **dominant** decoding (which accepts both the concrete message and the ideological premises of the text in question); a **negotiated** decoding (which agrees to the premises, but questions the message to some degree); and an **oppositional** decoding (which rejects both the message and the premises). Importantly, the configuration of decodings that emerged from the focus groups, aligned with the participants' overall social status as well as with their diverse positions and roles in the workplace, for example, as managers, union representatives, or rank-and-file workers. The further implication was that, depending on their social circumstances, some audience members could be seen to exercise a critique of – and a resistance to – the predominant social relations of power that were being articulated in and advanced by the media, through mundane acts of interpretation.

These and similar findings from a range of studies have led some scholars to highlight – and exaggerate – the 'interpretive power' of media audiences. Eco, for one, described audiences' active and critical engagement with texts as 'semiotic guerilla warfare' (Eco, 1976: 150). In an article published the year after his first book, Morley (1981) himself recognized the limitations, both of the methodology employed in that book and of the critical-political implications of the findings. Beyond the acceptance, negotiation, or rejection of a dominant ideology, the reception, in Morley's case of television news, covers a spectrum of reactions and potential actions, from basic understanding and visual fascination to practical engagement with the issues and agendas of public debate. Later research has gone on to address some of these dimensions of reception, as well as attending to other aspects of user identities than social class, including gender and ethnicity (e.g., Parameswaran, 1999; Park et al., 2006; Press, 1991; Schlesinger et al., 1992). As in the case of the social contexts of media use, television has been the pivotal medium of decoding studies, with particular reference to news and melodramas such as daytime and evening soap operas (e.g., Liebes & Katz, 1990; Livingstone, 1990).

Perhaps the most important contribution of reception analysis to the wider field of media and communication research has been its elaboration of how to integrate the study of media users' **demographic** background with the **discursive** processes of their reception and interpretation of the contents and forms of media. In doing so, reception analysis has moved beyond traditional literary approaches, which have relied on textual interpretation to identify 'the reader in the text,' including the German tradition of reception aesthetics noted earlier and Stanley Fish's (1979) conception of **interpretive communities**. A common assumption of literary approaches to reception has been that texts give rise to different degrees of shared interpretation, but that such patterns of interpretation may be deduced from the texts, without asking the readers.

In a further development, reception analysis has operationalized the link between demographic and discursive categories of analysis with reference to **interpretive repertoires** (Potter & Wetherell, 1987). Rather than assuming that people already belong to, or might be sorted into, delimited communities, the first analytical step becomes one of accounting, in concrete and contextual detail, for the interpretive strategies that persons and social groups variously mobilize in the course of their media use. The next step then confers these strategies with the users' demographic backgrounds, the contents and forms of the texts in question, and the wider historical and cultural context in which discourses and demographics intersect. Empirical studies may, thus, substantiate the prevalence and operation of more or less persistent interpretive communities, both within and across different socioeconomic segments and subcultures. The repertoire approach, moreover, offers an interface between reception analyses and quantitative studies of lifestyles (see Chapter 6,

Image 5.5 Harry Potter across media. Added by Penguinsfan101. Posted in Potter Puppet Pals. List of Harry Potter paradies. User:Lunlovhp. (CC-BY-SA).

Media characters provide resources for social and cultural activities, serving as points of departure for media users to interpret, modify, share, and enact identities and worlds. Harry Potter has maintained an intertextual and cross-media presence, thanks not only to film adaptations of the book series and an abundance of toys, gear, and costumes for sale, but to fan creations as well, exemplified here by the 'Potter Puppet Pals': Harry Potter, Hermione Granger, Ron Weasley, and Professor Dumbledore. In 2022, the twentieth anniversary of the first film – The Philosopher's Stone *– was marked by a television special,* Return to Hogwarts, *streamed on the HBO Max platform.*

p. 164): While departing from different methodologies, the two traditions come together in conceptualizing and examining media users as, at once, demographic and discursive phenomena.

Media in contexts of social action

The third and final variety of reception analysis has focused on the ways in which media and communication enter into and enable *other* social action – beyond their immediate context of use, and beyond the decoding of particular media texts. While fewer in number, this category of studies has been growing along with the diffusion of digital media and mobile practices of communication. Where classic mass media invited research on the decoding of particular programs or articles, and of their local contexts of use, the embedding of digital media into private and public life calls for – requires – renewed attention to communication as a mediator of other human action and social interaction.

Compared to decoding studies, the third form of reception analysis, while recognizing that media offer **representations** *of* reality, emphasizes that media, simultaneously, provide **resources** for acting *in* and *on* reality. The social uses of media point well beyond their functions as sources of information and diversion, to a range of practical applications – from political involvement to personal development. In this respect, the research questions of reception analysis overlap, for example, with those of the agenda-setting and framing traditions: How do media and communication contribute to orienting users' cognitions and actions, beyond the here and now in front of screens and other interfaces, into future contexts and engagements with the institutions and practices that make up societies?

To address such questions, reception analysis has relied on several methodological approaches. A classic example is Janice Radway's (1984) study of women reading print romances. Through a combination of observation, interviewing, and textual analysis, Radway showed how these readers – in addition to producing a rich range of decodings – employed that literature as a sort of self-help literature for navigating their marriages and life in general. At the same time, in and through reading, the women would insist on having 'my own time' in the home, which for many was also their primary place of work, and certainly more than a context of media use. As such, the act of reading came out as more important than the particular romances or decodings: The books, above all, constituted resources for the women to insist on a degree of freedom in their own lives, rather than serving as romanticizing representations of the unattainable lives of others.

A second example is an investigation of the reception of American television news (by one of the authors of this book). News had been (and often still is) examined with reference to issues of objectivity and bias: Does the news provide positive, negative, or neutral representations of political and economic events and issues? This reception study, instead, related news to the viewers' potential practical uses of the information being presented, for instance, as input to their own political deliberations or for tackling their economic circumstances (Jensen, 1986). The findings from a discourse analysis of qualitative interviews with American viewers indicated that they would approach the news genre with an ambiguous or divided consciousness. While arguing, in detail and at length, for the importance of 'keeping up' with current developments in national politics and the economy, the respondents, in fact, associated limited, if any, instrumental value with the news as a resource in their own lives.

Yet another example comes from a study of the place of the internet in everyday communication (by the other author of this book) (Lai, 2021). In a thematic analysis of interviews and diaries, it emerged how women – significantly more than men – would turn to digital media throughout the day to stay in touch with different members of their social networks. Typical examples were either 'phatic' messages (see Chapter 2, p. 53) on social media, in which 'liking' an image, sharing a post, or congratulating someone essentially reaffirmed an emotional bond, or a 'micro-coordination' of the many mundane tasks of everyday life (Ling & Yttri, 2002). Not only did these patterns of communication reproduce a traditional division of labor among women and men when it comes to staying in touch with family and friends: On the internet, such gender-specific socialization may be consolidated, even reinforced, by algorithms inducing users – women as well as men – to do more of the same.

A final instance of media use as performative, is fan cultures, where 'canonic' texts (a feature film, a television series, the songs of a band) deliver the raw materials for subcultural activities (Baym, 2000; Jenkins, 1992). Here, more than the decodings, the subsequent, renewed **encodings** of texts, music, or films often turn out to be quite creative, sometimes the outcome of a collaborative endeavor. In further steps, these productions may be distributed among larger communities of fans, previously via print fanzines, currently via webzines or apps. The reception of media as social and cultural resources enables the production of still more resources.

Media ethnography?

Since the 1980s, the challenge of describing and documenting highly differentiated and widely distributed contexts of media use, has entailed methodological debate. 'Ethnography' presented itself, early on, as one potential, popular solution – recalling the practice of anthropological fieldwork in which the researcher's long-term interaction in and with a localized community allows for an in-depth accounting of cultural practices such as media use, as they relate to the rest of community life (Schrøder et al., 2003: 57–102). In an early contribution to these debates, Radway (1988) argued *against* research departing from the media, and *for* studies centering on their users as members of existing social and cultural communities. Users, arguably, precede media, empirically as well as theoretically.

Although Radway's (1984) own work on women reading romances had delivered an exemplary case of such an approach, her book represented the exception rather than the rule in early reception studies. Instead, there was a manifest tendency to refer to research relying on a range of qualitative methodologies, including interviewing, as 'doing ethnography.' And the tendency attracted criticism, since published studies appeared not to live up to criteria of data collection, analysis, and documentation that had been standard practice in anthropology and related fields for decades (e.g., Schensul & LeCompte, 1999). As James Lull (1988: 242) commented: " 'ethnography' has become an abused buzz-word in our field."

With the digitalization of media and communicative practices, the challenges of studying media use as part of – and across – social contexts have multiplied. The question remains whether ethnography, in fact, represents a distinctive methodology, compared to other qualitative and multi-method approaches (Jensen & Jankowski, 1991; Lindlof & Taylor, 2019). Chapter 6 elaborates on some of the theoretical as well as practical considerations when designing qualitative (and quantitative) research projects. For now, Figure 5.2 summarizes one response to the question that early debates on media or audience 'ethnographies' had raised: How could and should the relationship between media and their users be conceptualized theoretically and investigated empirically?

For most research questions, it is neither relevant nor possible to empirically describe the total life circumstances of an entire community or population without running the risk of 'data death' – all media, all use contexts, and all social and cultural characteristics of users would have to be included. An alternative is to apply a comprehensive theoretical perspective while recognizing the practical need to sample or select specific media, genres, texts, contexts, and users for further empirical examination. Figure 5.2, accordingly, lays out two categories of research questions.

To the left in Figure 5.2, the question is how the same medium (or genre or text) is approached and interpreted by several different audiences or user groups, typically addressed through comparisons of their decodings. To the right, the question is how a socially and culturally distinctive audience or user group makes use of several different media, typically in studies of media as they enter into an

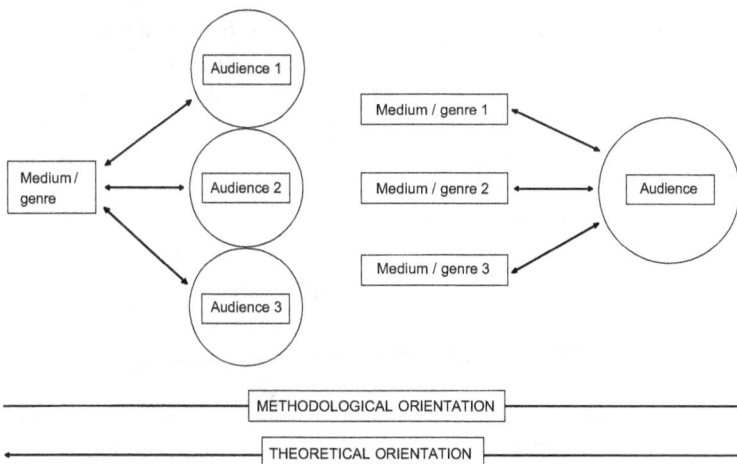

Figure 5.2 Two varieties of reception study.

Image 5.6 Schools and media. Monkey Business Images/ Shutterstock.

Media are an integral part of the upbringing and socialization of children and young people. Although much effects research has been driven by concern over what the media might do *to young audiences, it is as important to ask what children and young people themselves* do with *media (Katz, 1959). Media are resources of formal education as well as informal learning; media are common denominators for both these processes across school, home, and leisure activities.*

immediate use context or a wider context of social action. In both instances, the media constitute the methodological focus: What difference do *media* and *communication* (not other objects, events, or interactions) make in individual lives and social life? Answers will emphasize *either* the characteristic uses and interpretations of selected media (genres, texts) by several different user groups *or* one group of users, their uses and interpretations of multiple media, genres, and texts across contexts.

The arrows at the bottom of Figure 5.2 suggest a final point regarding both categories of research questions. Methodologically speaking, meaning flows from the media into society – the empirical analyses center attention, respectively, on the difference that a single medium (genre, text) makes for several user groups, and the difference that a full media diet or repertoire (Hasebrink & Domeyer, 2012) makes for a single user group. Theoretically speaking, however, meaning flows from society into the media – their distinctive institutional role is to circulate meaning in society. To appreciate and account for the full process of communication, it is more helpful to be standing in society looking into the media, rather than to be standing inside the media peering into society.

Box 5.3 Theories at issue

Echo chambers and filter bubbles?

Renewed interest in the potential effects specifically of digital media on individuals and societies has marked the beginning of a fifth phase in the history of effects research (p. 129). A key issue for research and public debate has become how the internet socializes its users to become participants in shared – or separate – realities. Two overlapping concepts have signaled an underlying concern: *Echo chambers* (Sunstein, 2007), first, refer generally to situations in which groups of people will only receive information from others holding attitudes and values similar to their own – so that they likely are confirmed in the opinions they already hold regarding public issues and agendas. *Filter bubbles* (Pariser, 2011), second, focus attention on the internet, which, through algorithmic feedback from and to users, is said to curate particular messages for particular people – who may, thus, end up living in finely filtered bubbles. Beyond a segmentation of the general public into multiple, separate publics, this might promote polarized, extreme positions – conspiracy theories at odds with scientific evidence, common sense, or both. The concern has been especially pronounced in the case of political democracy because, to participate in the public sphere (Chapter 4, p. 100), citizens need shared premises to be in a position to debate their disagreements, search for compromises, and arrive at decisions for the future.

The two concepts – echo chambers and filter bubbles – have been linked, in public and policy debate, to additional notions of **misinformation, disinformation**, and **'fake news'** circulating at national as well as international levels (Kapantai et al., 2021). As emphasized from Chapter 1 onward, media and communication deliver more than representations *of* the world – they constitute resources for individuals, groups, entire societies, and, indeed, humankind to act *in* and *on* the world as their shared habitat. If local and global community is not nourished by a consensus of facts, and by procedures for resolving doubts and disagreements about the facts, the end result, more than segmentation and polarization, could be fragmentation and dissolution – anarchy.

Media and communication research, however, has not supported the pessimistic and, sometimes, dystopian implications of the two hypotheses – echo chambers and filter bubbles, as accentuated by misinformation, disinformation, and fake news. First, empirical studies find that both media users generally and persons who get their news primarily from the internet, tend to be exposed to a considerable variety of facts and opinions (Bakshy et al., 2015; Bruns, 2019b; Fletcher & Nielsen, 2017; Hosseinmardi et al., 2021). Second, as highlighted throughout this chapter, the path of technologically mediated information into attitudes and toward social actions is complicated: So far, there is no strong scientific evidence that misinformation or disinformation specifically leads people to think or do particular kinds of things (Lazer et al., 2018). Studies, rather, have suggested a positive contribution from digital media and communication to citizens' political knowledge and democratic participation (for overview, see Lorenz-Spreen et al., 2023)

There is, in short, a remarkable dissonance between widespread public perceptions and scholarly findings concerning (this type of) media effects. As always, further studies may begin to validate (or further invalidate) public perceptions. But research should also ask the antecedent question of how and why the existence of echo chambers and filter bubbles came to be taken for granted in so much political and public debate (and in a great deal of journalism and commentary, as well). 'Shooting the messenger' is a set expression suggesting that when people receive bad news, they will blame the sender – even if the messenger likely has little or no responsibility for unwelcome news. In a historical moment when both media and opinion polls register growing segmentation and polarization of public debate within nations, and intensifying tensions between nations and world regions, it is only natural to search for explanations. Here, one explanation suggesting itself is the media and their modes of communicating about public issues, rather than the forbiddingly complex ideological and institutional processes that are summed up in public issues.

The search for explanations is a fundamental feature of human cognition and communication, as it is of research about media and communication. Chapter 7 returns to some of the ways in which the interpretations and explanations offered by the present field of research are fed back into public debate and other communication about media and society (under the heading 'double hermeneutics,' p. 214).

Box 5.4 Exercise

My world, your world, our world?

One long-term impact of media use is a comprehensive and updated understanding of the world in which media users find themselves – they become, and remain, socialized into a particular society and a particular world. But different individuals are socialized differently, in part because of the media they use and the communicative practices they engage in. The exercise illustrates how different understandings of the world may relate to media use and communication, specifically the ways in which, and the extent to which, the participants' 'worlds' can be seen to differ.

1. Select two to three people from your networks who are *the least* like yourself (because of their education, political or cultural inclinations, age, etc.)

2. Ask the people you selected to indicate – and indicate for yourself:
   a. The two most important events or issues in *your own country* over the past year.
   b. The two most important events or issues in *the world* over the past year.
   c. The five most important media in *their* – and in *your* – media use on a weekly basis.
3. Compare the results – and try to explain any (lack of) correlations between (different) media uses and (different) perceptions of the world.

The exercise can be extended to include, for instance, a reading group, a class, or an entire educational program.

Socialization, institutionalization, and media

Whether through qualitative or quantitative methodologies, a special challenge relates to the study of long-term effects – the 'late' contexts of the encounters between media and users, as laid out in Figure 5.1 (p. 130). For one thing, it is often difficult or impossible to collect relevant and valid data across longer time periods. For another thing, the conjunctures of media with developments in people's lives over years – or decades – are so complex that a single specific source of any (lack of) change typically cannot be identified. Long-term effects can be characterized, however, with reference to two general processes – socialization and institutionalization: Media and communication contribute to the socialization of individuals, and to the maintenance and modification of social institutions. Selected aspects of these processes may, then, serve as theoretically motivated **indicators** that can be examined further in empirical studies.

Media and communication evidently contribute to the socialization of individuals; the difficulty is in specifying the nature and scope of this first process. A distinction is commonly made between **primary** and **secondary** socialization. First, the site of the primary care for and upbringing of children traditionally has been families – where stories are told, knowledge is passed on, and unique little persons take shape. Second, the ongoing qualification and integration of young people as well as adults into society is accomplished by a range of institutional agents: schools, religious communities, social organizations, and media of all kinds, from children's television to mobile phones.

In quantitative terms, people particularly in the Global North spend ever more time on media and communication. Qualitatively speaking, historically changing media and other agents of socialization increasingly offer essential facts about, and standards for, being human and performing roles in social contexts (Beck et al., 1994). And, as a sequence of 'new' media that have been integrated into the lives of children and young people, in school and anywhere else, primary and secondary socialization have been converging. This, in sum, is the lesson of a long line of classic studies, from the Payne Fund project of the 1930s (Jowett et al., 1996)

(p. 139), through analyses of young viewers during the introduction of television (Himmelweit et al., 1958; Schramm et al., 1961), to more recent studies of 'kids online' (Livingstone & Haddon, 2009). The blurring of the traditional boundaries between primary and secondary socialization is paralleled and reinforced by ongoing reconfigurations of the 'private' and 'public' domains of contemporary social life: Media and communication crisscross life stages and social contexts of interaction.

Chapter 6 details one influential research tradition that addresses the relationship between socialization and media use (p. 164): Studies of **lifestyles** and, more generally, the **life forms** of different social classes and cultural formations, first, produce snapshots of the general condition and distribution of socialization in a given society. Second, the analytical methodologies of such studies allow for a recording over time of changing values and consumption patterns, as they inform the ongoing process of socialization. In addition to being of evident commercial interest – who is interested in buying what, and why? – the findings of the tradition hold further insights into the formation and transformation of individual identities and social structures, with media use as, at once, an end product and an input to the process as it unfolds.

Like socialization, **institutionalization** represents a 'late' **context** of media-user encounters. The theory of social structuration (Chapter 1, p. 20) suggests how the interaction of social agents and social structures result *both* in the maintenance of social institutions *and* in their modification, however minimal or modest in each instance. And media and communication literally mediate – orient and guide – these interactions. Four traditions of research provide indicators of the place of media in the institutionalization of society:

- *Introduction of new media.* When a new medium is introduced – to an entire community or a particular user segment – this presents a unique opportunity to examine the consequences, for political democracy, for public participation in cultural activities, and for social life generally. The context is an 'experimental,' but naturally occurring situation with a well-defined 'before' and 'after' (on experimental methodologies, see further Chapter 6, p. 169). Especially television, which was introduced at a historical time when media and communication research itself was taking shape and developing theoretical frameworks and empirical infrastructures for large-scale projects, has been examined in this perspective. At the time of writing, mobile media have become key objects of analysis (and topics inviting student projects): Mobile communication is socializing users and institutionalizing societies, in different world regions, in historically and culturally distinctive ways (for overview, see Ling et al., 2020).
- *Public events.* Media coverage of major national and international events delivers indicators of how local and global communities communicate about common concerns. What motivates and justifies a national ceremony? What characterizes a political scandal? How do media users engage with the events and the media coverage of ceremonies and scandals? Such questions have been

addressed, not least, by the research tradition on **media events**, which Chapter 7 takes up (p. 196).

- *Institutional practices.* Chapter 4 reviewed media as a unique social institution. Through media, and with the participation of their users, the ends and means of other institutions are articulated and debated in public. Users, too, are institutionalized in and through the algorithms and related procedures by which the social uses of digital media are recorded – yielding measures and interpretations that are fed back to and, in turn, inform and orient the operation of these media. (See further Box 5.5 analyzing 'Users in systems,' p. 153.)

- *Cultures.* Cultures, lastly, can be understood and studied as the cumulative outcome of innumerable communications. Since the invention of writing, communications have been fixated and documented in increasingly granular detail, in shifting technologies and genres of interaction, and as carriers of worldviews and guides regarding the users' present, with practical implications for the future of current and coming human cohorts. Comparative studies of cultures depend on, and offer insights into, the common yet historically and contextually variable practice of communication (Kim, 2018). Cultures are the products of years, decades, and centuries of communication, which, literally, inform the agents and structures of society, here and now, as well. Chapter 7 – the final one of this book – returns to the concept of *culture* in the singular, and to *cultures* in the plural, to assess the place of communication in the long-term development of societies. First, however, Chapter 6 presents the main methodologies for empirical studies of communication, which, in conjunction with the theories reviewed in the other chapters of the book, are necessary conditions of accounting for – interpreting and explaining – the interdependence of media and society.

Box 5.5 Analysis

Users in systems

In Chapter 4, it was commented that institutions are normally understood as the general, abstract, impersonal building blocks of the structure of society: the legal system, the political system, the educational system, and so forth. But institutions are, simultaneously, the sum of all the concrete actions that living social agents undertake: pronouncing verdicts; casting votes; giving and taking lessons; and much else. Individual users and their interactions with media, equally, make up an institution to the extent that they are described, measured, and interpreted. The initial purpose is to gauge who is 'supplying' attention for various media, genres, and texts – because this attention is 'demanded' by companies and corporations advertising their wares through the media (Chapter 3, p. 74). Over time, descriptions, measurements, and interpretations have been standardized so that, at any given time, systems for analyzing the uses and users of media are in place, coordinated with the systems carrying commercial and other communications. And as media and communication systems change – from print via electronic to digital formats – the systems for analyzing users change with them: Users today are being institutionalized through rather different means than over the course of the twentieth century.

Studies of who reads, listens to, and watches what, have traditionally been conducted by polling institutes and marketing agencies and through dedicated panels, on behalf of media, advertisers, and other stakeholders, historically with a special focus on one-to-many or mass communication. The digitalization of media and communicative practices has made it ever more important, in addition, to document streams of one-to-one and many-to-many communication, in parallel and intertwined with one-to-many communication. Most important, a significant proportion of all these streams of communication are now being documented 'automatically,' because all users (not just panels and samples of people, as happened in the past) continuously communicate many-to-one, too, into the system (Chapter 2, p. 56). The consequences are far-reaching – for media, advertisers, and users.

Figure 5.3 illustrates the streams within a digital communication system, with special reference to one-to-many and many-to-one communication. From left to right, media, first, communicate to their users (Communication$_1$). The system, second, registers the presence and actions of the users – who perform metacommunication right to left, into the system. The media, third, continuously process the data they receive from users via the system, adjusting their communication accordingly (Communication$_2$). In later rounds of interaction, sequences of adjustments will follow (Communication$_n$), with reference to more metacommunication, and to additional data deriving from the users' one-to-one and many-to-many communication across multiple systems.

The mechanism that is summarized in Figure 5.3, entails the registration and analysis of users' communicative practices, not as separate activities

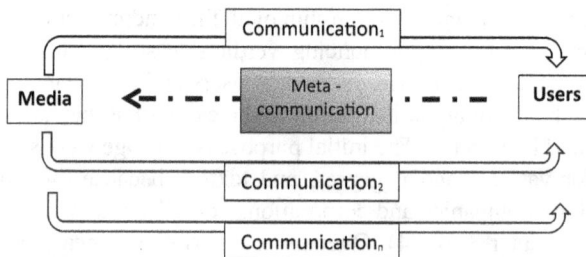

Figure 5.3 A model of metacommunication as feedback.

assigned to external collaborators, but as an internal, integrated activity of the business of being a medium – in collaboration with the platforms that media and advertisers alike depend on. What was once two institutions – a media institution and an institution monitoring flows of communication and attention – have become entangled, technologically and institutionally, with implications for other economic, political, and cultural institutions. And the users, who used to perform two social roles – as consumers of media (in public) and as (anonymous) informants responding to polling institutes and marketing agencies – have come to occupy an ambiguous, less-than-transparent position: In and of their communication with the media, they metacommunicate data into the media, which shapes future communications by media as well as other social interests – to themselves and others like them.

The introduction to this chapter noted that the 'users' of media are, at once, 'recipients' and 'consumers' in a 'market,' as well as 'citizens' and, potentially, 'senders' in a 'public sphere.' It is the interrelation of these classic constituents of communication that is being reconfigured in digital communication systems, returning equally classic normative issues to research agendas (Chapter 4, p. 107). It remains of clear social interest to ask who is in a position to communicate what to whom, but also, and as importantly, who ends up knowing what about whom, as an effect of metacommunication: Produced, in part, by communication, knowledge is a source of power and control. Both these questions and their interrelations – who communicates what, and who knows what – appropriately, have recently risen to the top of national and international agendas of research and public debate (for overview, see Flew, 2021; Jensen & Helles, 2023).

The further entanglement (or not) of the media institution and the institution analyzing media and communicative practices, will be an outcome of the specific political and economic conditions for digitalization that societies in different world regions are currently instituting, through collaboration, contestation, and conflict. Chapter 4 described aspects of that long-term process under a heading of convergence (p. 117), but convergence extends well beyond both media and media studies: Whereas this book centers on media, the streams of communication and metacommunication, data and metadata, already have acquired, and are acquiring, a widening range of more or less legitimate uses across public and private domains. It is for this reason that it is incumbent on media and communication research to look beyond media systems to communication systems as infrastructures circumscribing what was formerly known as 'the media' (Chapter 3, p. 91).

6 Methods about media

"You know my method…"

…says Sherlock Holmes, time and again, in Sir Arthur Conan Doyle's stories featuring the master detective (https://sherlock-holm.es, August 1, 2024). When solving crime mysteries, Holmes has an extraordinary ability to infer, from small and seemingly irrelevant details, who is the guilty person. But he also insists, again repeatedly, that we must never draw final conclusions before all the necessary evidence has been collected and assessed. Bright ideas of who did what, must be tested systematically – methodically.

The two professions of detective and researcher have a number of features in common, which has inspired books and articles on how the two endeavors may learn from each other – even one volume entitled *You Know My Method* (Sebeok & Umiker-Sebeok, 1980), which compares Sherlock Holmes with the American pragmatist philosopher Charles Sanders Peirce. The affinity relates to the use of a 'method,' but also to 'you know' – the recognition *that* one is relying on a particular method, and that *others* using the same method would arrive at the same results. It is a common assumption that research should be objective, not subjective; the last section of this chapter returns to that notion and to related issues regarding the nature of scientific methods and their appropriate uses.

By way of introduction, suffice it to note that research on media and society relies on a whole range of methods, first to collect documentation – **data** – and next to draw conclusions – **inferences** – about their implications. Through methods, two (or more) subjects consider what is objectively (or may be) the case regarding particular aspects of media and moments of communication. And, just as a detective's conclusion can have life-changing consequences for the parties in a criminal case, so the findings of media and communication studies may carry substantial implications for the media and society. Therefore: Know your method!

The first section of the chapter reviews some of the most common methods of social-scientific and humanistic scholarship, elaborating and exemplifying their relevance for research questions within the field of media and communication studies. In the middle section, we highlight a distinctive set of digital methodologies, which

DOI: 10.4324/9781032655109-6

have become increasingly important in recent years: To examine media and communication in the context of ongoing society-wide and worldwide digitalization, it has become essential to also digitalize *research about* media and society. The last section of the chapter ties the knots of the various methods as they relate to the theories and themes covered in the rest of the book: Which kinds of knowledge are produced through which theories and methods? And how does all this knowledge contribute to better understanding, interpreting, explaining, and, perhaps, reforming media and communicative practices as they currently exist in and impact society?

Figure 6.1 lists six methods for examining the diverse interrelations and interactions between media and society. Along the vertical dimension, we distinguish three categories of evidence that empirical studies draw on: What people *say* (speech or verbal language); what people *do* (actions or behavior); and the texts, documents, and other sources that people *produce*, and which later – sometimes much later – lend themselves to further analysis. On the horizontal dimension, these materials can either be 'counted' through **quantitative** methods or 'interpreted' through **qualitative** methods of analysis. On both dimensions, such formulations provide brief characterizations of important prototypes in the toolbox of research. The following sections elaborate on each prototype. Throughout the chapter, it should be kept in mind both that qualitative studies, similarly, require documentation and systematic examination of the objects of analysis, and that quantitative research, equally, entails interpretation of the meaning of the numbers it generates (see further the analysis Box 6.3 on 'Quant and/or qual?', p. 178).

Interviewing – individually and in groups

One of the most widely used methods for collecting data, within media and communication research, and generally in the social sciences and humanities, is interviewing. The commonsensical motivation is that "the best way to find out what the people think about something is to ask them" (Bower, 1973: vi). But, on second thought, things are not quite that simple: People may not say what they mean, nor do they always mean what they say. It is not that interview respondents will be lying or trying to deceive interviewers. The point is that no human being – be it interviewees or researchers – has full insight into what they 'mean' and 'say,'

	Qualitative	Quantitative
Speech/verbal language	interviewing	surveys
Action/behavior	participating observation	experiments
Texts/documents	discourse analysis	content analysis

Figure 6.1 Six prototypical methods of empirical media and communication research.

and why. Neither thought nor language is transparent to the person thinking and speaking (see further Chapter 2 on 'the hermeneutics of suspicion,' p. 31). An interview is a form of communication that gradually articulates what people think and mean. To arrive at an understanding of an interview (and of any other form of communication), analysis and interpretation of the words being spoken are of the essence (for overview, see Kvale & Brinkmann, 2015).

The premise of qualitative interview studies, then, is that the answers do not deliver direct representations of people's thoughts or opinions. Interviews, instead, amount to negotiations in which, step by step, turn upon turn, an interviewer and a interviewee formulate viewpoints and insights: Unlike many everyday conversations, it is a "conversation with a purpose" (Burgess, 1982b: 107). As such, qualitative interviewing generates nuanced insights, for instance, into the thinking that went into content being produced by television journalists or online influencers; what different users took away from that content; and what users were thinking as they commented on or shared the content. All interviews, therefore, require analysis – interviewing produces data, not findings, let alone conclusions. Once an interview has been completed, the interesting, rewarding, hard work of analyzing the data is about to begin. **Data collection** and **data analysis** constitute interrelated but distinctive activities. (Tools for qualitative data analysis include discourse analysis (see p. 173), as applied in studies of media content, too.)

Media and communication research employs four main types of qualitative interviewing (all of which may be conducted either offline or online). Where the first two occur between a researcher and a single interviewee, the last two engage several other people in communication.

Individual interviewing

- *Respondent interviews*. In the first type of individual interviewing, the interviewee is considered representative of particular social categories, such as young gamers or older internet users. Although the participants in qualitative interview studies are not statistically representative of the wider population, as members of the category in question they are in a position to express – 'represent' – characteristic perspectives on media, their uses, and their implications. Respondent interviews are commonly applied in studies of media use, for instance, to uncover the surprisingly diverse interpretations of and user responses to the 'same' media content.
- *Informant interviews*. Compared to respondents, who represent specific social and cultural groups, informants serve as sources about and points of access to social and cultural domains, typically media organizations or user segments that might otherwise be difficult to engage in conversation, for example, fan cultures or disadvantaged groups (Atkinson & Flint, 2001). The premise is that such informants will be well placed, insightful, and reliable when it comes to perspectives on and conditions within the given social group or setting. While informant interviews are less common than respondent interviews in media

Image 6.1 Focus group. Patrick van Katwijk / Contributor / Getty Images.

Focus groups are widely applied as a method of data collection, both within media and communication studies and in other academic inquiry into people's opinions and preferences; as part of the introduction and promotion of new products and services; as well as in political life and by civil society organizations. Communication among the participants in a focus group is recorded, as sound and, perhaps, video, for subsequent analysis and assessment. In some cases, manuscript writers, advertisers, and other stakeholders will attend focus groups to gain firsthand impressions of the viewpoints expressed and the interactions among participants – as observers of the interactions, hidden behind a one-way mirror.

and communication research, they are of special interest for studies of the institutions and organizations variously originating and enabling communication, from national media of record to global tech companies.

Group interviewing

- *Naturalistic group interviews*. To capture what normally happens in a particular social setting, some interview studies will rely on naturally occurring groups, focusing either on the sending or on the receiving side of communication. The topic might be households' uses of apps and search engines to pinpoint bargain offers. Or studies may address the design of apps and websites, including the trade-offs between technical and aesthetic features as designers develop these artifacts; in such production studies, interviews are typically combined with observation of the collaborative processes of construction as they unfold (on observation, see further p. 166).

- *Constituted group interviews*. The last variety of qualitative interviewing combines aspects of the naturalistic and respondent modes. It convenes a small number of people with predefined background characteristics, and initiates realistic conversations and group dynamics, which serve to articulate the participants' perspectives on the media and communicative practices in question. Most often, projects will aim for relatively homogeneous groups in the interest of a trustful and comfortable dialogue. One example (actually in the borderlands of naturalistic and constituted interviewing) is a classic study of how the American television series *Dallas* was experienced and discussed when it was originally broadcast (and widely debated) in many different countries around the world: In each location, a sample of households were asked to invite couples from other households to watch and talk about the program together (Liebes & Katz, 1990). The most common approaches, however, have been **group interviews** and so-called **focus groups** (Image 6.1) (for overview, see Barbour, 2007; Stewart & Shamdasani, 2015). In both these instances, people who typically do not know each other beforehand, are brought together to assess, for instance, an advertising campaign, its contents as well as its form of expression. Whereas, in group interviews, interviewers will assume an active role in the conversation, a key purpose of focus groups is to have participants themselves express and negotiate a range of viewpoints on the matter at hand. Originating from classic sociology (Merton, 1987; Merton & Kendall, 1955), today focus groups are employed, not least, in commercial settings. (For a critique of the 'commercialization' of the focus group methodology, see Morrison, 1998.)

Interviews as interactions

Across the different varieties of qualitative interviewing, it is important to anticipate and design the preferred structure of the interaction as a whole. This entails three types of considerations:

- *Duration*. Interviews range from brief conversations to hour-long and repeated dialogues regarding the place of media and communication in the lives of respondents and informants. The choice depends, for any given inquiry, on its purpose. Even though long interactions are not ends in themselves, time is often a decisive factor if an interview is to accomplish its purpose of **exploring** – carefully inquiring into – people's lived realities.
- *Structure*. Perhaps the greatest challenge of conducting qualitative interviews is to maintain, at once, structure and flexibility – which takes a good deal of practice: Interviewing is both an art and a craft. Qualitative interviews can be very open, akin to informal everyday conversations, if the primary purpose is

exploratory. But, in many instances, **semi-structured** interviewing serves to address a number of predetermined topics, sometimes relying on set formulations in a specified order in order to register, for example, media users' interpretations of selected aspects of a television series or an advertising campaign. Regardless of the preferred structure of the interview, it is the researchers' responsibility, first to motivate, and later to maintain this structure – to avoid wasting the respondents' (and their own) time.

- *Depth.* Especially individual qualitative interviewing is sometimes referred to as 'depth interviewing.' Here, it is imperative that researchers conduct themselves in an empathetic and responsible manner: As researchers of human communication, we are dealing with persons who have the right to define for themselves what they would like to communicate about, and with whom. The task of qualitative interviewing is to bring out respondents' uses of concepts and terminologies for further examination, not to transgress their boundaries, and never ever to move into varieties of therapeutic interviewing. (On ethical aspects of planning interview studies and other empirical projects, see further p. 191.)

Surveys – offline and online

Where qualitative interviewing seeks depth, survey interviewing prioritizes breadth. The dictionary definition of 'survey' is 'overview.' And survey studies are, indeed, the method of choice for arriving at a general understanding of the uses of different media and communication services by different socioeconomic groups – this is one reason why surveys are, without question, the most commonly applied method within media and communication research. A survey typically documents the communication habits of specific social segments and/or their opinions or attitudes toward particular media, genres, and texts. At the same time, survey analyses will confer media uses with the **demographics** of the groups in question, that is, typically gender, age, and social status: Who is consuming which media, when, and to what extent? How do patterns of consumption vary for men and women, young and old, persons in either advantaged or disadvantaged social positions? And how do different user groups assess the given supply of, as well as their own experiences of and gratifications from, media and communication?

Yet another reason for the popularity of survey research is that it provides important instruments in planning the production of media content and evaluating its consumption. This is especially true for commercial media and advertisers, who will want to know both how many and who, specifically, is spending their money or their attention (or both) on the supply on offer. For the same commercial reasons, a large proportion of such studies are confidential, and are never published, or are only made available to scholars and interested publics with delay. The sponsors of the research, thus, are paying for the production of a particular type and set of knowledge, but also for having this knowledge kept from other interested parties. Beyond the commercial sector of media and communication, it is of significant interest for society at large, as represented through the institutions of political democracy,

Image 6.2 Data in the bank. © European Union 2024. Courtesy of Eurostat.

Surveys are undertaken continuously, nationally and internationally, about people's attitudes and actions regarding all kinds of human endeavors. Many studies have specific commercial or political motivations – who is interested in buying what, and in voting for whom? But other research represents comprehensive and regularly repeated analyses, for instance, of media use, its variations across different social and cultural groups, and its development over time. One example is national and regional statistics covering communication and other cultural practices. In the European Union, such evidence is coordinated through the Eurostat agency, enabling comparisons both between countries and across time. And some of the data is made available online so that students, researchers, and other interested parties may download and further process the data to address specific questions, in this case "private households' expenditure on culture."

to monitor developments in the public's uses of media, through surveys and other methods, to consider appropriate forms and levels of economic, legal, and technological regulation. (On the practical applications of media and communication research, see Chapter 7, p. 217.)

Survey research is typified by a number of standard elements and concepts (see further Clark et al., 2021; Deacon et al., 2021):

- *Population and sample.* To make the analysis of evidence manageable, studies rarely examine an entire **population** regarding their media uses and communicative practices, relying instead on a subset of individuals – a **sample**. The aim typically is to identify a representative sample, selected according to a principle of statistical randomness. Depending on the community or country in question, samples of 1,000 to 1,500 persons are commonly used to cover the population of interest.
- *Instrument.* The classic means of collecting survey data is standardized questions and answers. The practical instrument used to be mail-order questionnaires and conversations either face-to-face or over the phone. But with the wide diffusion of the internet, it has become not just convenient, but scientifically defensible to collect responses via **online surveys**: The online population – the portion of a national population with access to the internet – increasingly resembles the population in its entirety, particularly in the Global North. It is, moreover, possible to weigh online samples and the panels that polling institutes and marketing agencies rely on, departing from baselines deriving from national statistical agencies (Salganik, 2018).
- *Description and analysis.* Surveys normally serve one of two purposes. On the one hand, studies can simply **describe** how media uses and communication patterns relate to different media, genres, times of day, and so on, and how these uses vary across different segments of the population in question. On the other hand, research may seek to establish through analysis, and hence **explain**, various interrelations, typically departing from one or more predefined **hypotheses**. The 'effect' of an advertising campaign, for instance, can be examined by comparing what the sample knew about the specific product or service before and after they were exposed to the campaign through different media and platforms. Here, studies will refer to two types of **variables**: The **independent** variable is the campaign, the dependent **variable** is the awareness of the product or service – the awareness depends on the campaign. Several other conditions likely affect the impact of communication, including the users' demographic features and their wider media use. In survey studies, these conditions are treated, similarly, as variables that interact with other variables, resulting in additional measurements and correlations.

Of the many different kinds of surveys being conducted on a regular basis, one category is of special interest for media and communication research, namely, **segment analysis**. This approach throws light on people's media uses and communicative practices as they relate to attitudes and, more generally, **lifestyles** – the members of different 'segments' or portions of a population can be seen to share distinctive lifestyles, which, further, relate to their social status. Segmentation surveys depart from sets of questions addressing the respondents' fundamental values, supplemented by demographic information and more specific questions about social domains such as media and communication. The responses are subjected to so-called **correspondence analysis** (Greenacre, 2016), which yields a 'map' of values, their interrelations, and their correlation with, for example, the respondents' media use. And the position of individual respondents on this map follows from their combined responses to the questions concerning values and media uses. In this way, the map can be read as, at once, a manifestation of each respondent's self-perception and as a representation of how different perceptions of self and society relate to each other.

Lifestyle maps enter into both academic studies and commercial research and development by media and other organizations, and they feature in public debate about the present state and potential future development of society and culture. Figure 6.2 is taken from a study of the population of Flanders, Belgium, in the European Union, regarding their disposition toward and participation in different forms of culture (Roose et al., 2012). The two dimensions of analysis displayed in the figure together served to map distinctive sets of cultural practices: Along the horizontal axis, the left side appears to emphasize active involvement (indicated by +) in things like going to the movies and traveling, while practices on the

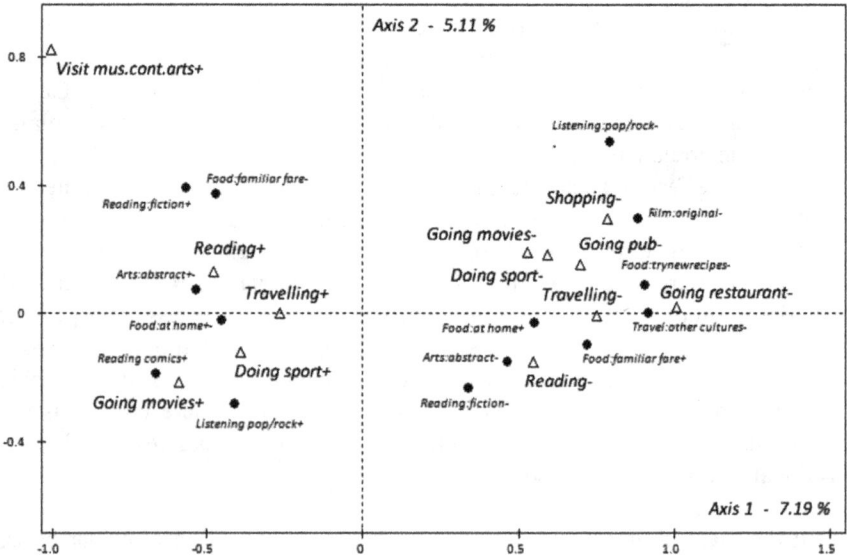

Figure 6.2 Mapping lifestyles.

Source: Roose et al. (2012: 501).

left side suggest a rather more passive or sedentary lifestyle in these respects (indicated by –), including preparing familiar kinds of food at home (+). Along the vertical axis, the upper segment may go for relatively more highbrow forms of culture, such as visiting (+) contemporary art museums, and *not* listening [–] to pop/rock, which the lower segment does turn to (+), in addition to consuming, for example, comics (+). And each of the four quadrants invites further interpretation of how different cultural preferences and practices come together in the lives of various social segments: Answers to this question are of great commercial interest for advertising and marketing, which helps explain the rise, during the twentieth and twenty-first centuries, of global analytics industries measuring and monetizing media uses and other cultural and communicative practices around the world.

Both quantitative surveying and qualitative interviewing take as their point of departure what people *say* about their media uses and communicative practices. In comparison, the following two methods – observation and experiment – focus on what people *do* in contexts involving media and communication. Again, this is *not* to suggest that these other methods allow researchers to immediately infer the meanings and implications of what people do with media – all methods depend on analysis and interpretation of the data or evidence collected. Nevertheless, observations and experiments offer insight into other aspects of media and communication than interviewing, surveys, or textual analysis. Choices of methods are a matter of sometimes-one, sometimes-another – both-and, not either-or.

Box 6.1 Exercise

What's your lifestyle?

Media uses and communicative practices are part of wider lifestyles, which further depend on the economic and cultural circumstances of different individuals. This exercise explores the relationship between lifestyles and communications.

- Start by reviewing the lifestyle segments of the four quadrants laid out in Figure 6.2. Would you place yourself in any of them?
- Next, search the internet for comparable lifestyle maps from companies operating in your national and cultural context. Which segments are identified here? Which segment would you say you belong to?
- Go on to search the internet for available statistics on the patterns of media use in your national and cultural context. In some settings, lifestyles and media uses are reported together; if not, it may be possible to assess the likely media uses for different lifestyle segments, departing from your own media use and communicative practices as well as those of family, friends, and acquaintances.

Compare your findings with those of others in your study group (or in the class you are taking), and discuss potential explanations for your findings – and any explanations for the statistics and other evidence that is (not) available online for your context.

Observation and ethnography

'What's really going on here?' This question informs a great variety of studies in which researchers will spend (shorter or longer) periods of time in a particular location – a television station, a software company, a household, a waiting room, or another setting – to investigate either media production or media use in context. In these settings, observers are a position to explore practices and conditions that the persons being observed – whether producers or users of contents and devices – may be unaware of, and which, therefore, do not lend themselves to interviewing and surveying. Depending on the particular domains and research questions, combinations of observation with interviewing and analyses of either media contents or organizational documents, help secure broader and deeper documentation of what, in fact, is going on in these social contexts (Schrøder et al., 2003: 57–102).

Several different terminologies have been used to refer to observational approaches. The discipline of **anthropology** has traditionally spoken of **participant observation** with reference to extended stays in and engagements with a 'foreign' culture (increasingly also portions of one's 'own' culture). Within media and communication research, in most cases it is more appropriate to refer to **participating observation**, as undertaken in other social sciences and humanities, too. The term suggests the possibility of combining varying degrees of both 'observation' and 'participation,' over long or short periods of time (Hammersley & Atkinson, 2019). Even observers striving for distance and neutrality can never fully turn themselves into the proverbial fly on the wall: Those present, like it or not, can both see and hear the observers. Conversely, researchers cannot be full participants in events while accomplishing the scholarly purpose of their observations. Instead, the purposes and domains of inquiry motivate specific, deliberate degrees of observation and participation, to be followed by analysis of and reflections on the strengths and weaknesses of the resulting insights.

Research relying on participating observation entails three main requirements. First, the several stages of entering, engaging with, and returning from the research setting must be documented, with care and in detail. Second, the resulting data are to be analyzed and assessed in light of the entire process, including unanticipated difficulties. And third, the subsequent process of interpretation should include sustained reflection on the kinds of inferences and conclusions that the fieldwork does (not) allow for.

For the first stage of documenting the process of observation, it is helpful to distinguish three types of **field notes**:

- *Substantive notes* – descriptions of the context being observed
- *Logistical notes* – documentation of the circumstances in which those descriptions were collected as data
- *Reflexive notes* – preliminary analyses and interpretations of the data collected (adapted from Burgess, 1982a).

Pen and paper remain extremely practical instruments for observational research, even if mobile phones and other digital media afford new means of documentation in sound and image beyond traditional textual formats. Further resources count maps and other drawings of the location being observed, along with documents and other artifacts that researchers may be able to bring back with them for later analysis (with permission from the persons present and authorities in charge of the scene).

An important consideration is which analytical and interpretive activities should be undertaken while still in the field, and which activities are best left for a later

Image 6.3 Media use in public spaces. Photo by John Morgan on Flickr, CC BY 2.0, 2012.

People use media in the presence of others and in full public view. Because of their media use, they may be physically present but mentally absent, perhaps taking turns observing their screens and communicating with those around them. To document the diverse communicative interactions unfolding among persons, and between humans and machines, researchers need to simultaneously observe and participate in the social contexts being studied (Humphreys, 2005; Humphreys & Hardeman, 2021).

stage. A rule of thumb is to concentrate on 'what' (substance) and 'how' (logistics) in the field, and to turn attention to 'why' (reflection) in the later stages of a project. For participating observation, researchers are themselves the primary 'instruments' of data collection, with limited overview and capacity for reflection in the heat of moment. The point is not to divorce theorizing from the empirical field, only that reflections can be carried wider and deeper with some distance from the field. As already emphasized, interview responses are not direct representations, of a person's thinking or of reality, and the same limitation applies to field notes: They offer selective documentation calling for analysis and interpretation to establish 'what was really happening.' Field notes are, literally, working documents – the beginning, not the end of observational studies.

Participating observation can be quite difficult and demanding in terms of both time and effort – but when it succeeds, it yields unique insights. The findings provide what the anthropologist Clifford Geertz (1973) termed **thick descriptions** of social life (with inspiration from the philosopher Gilbert Ryle (1971: 465–496)). 'Thick,' highly detailed descriptions of social settings are often necessary conditions for establishing the meanings and implications of what people either do or say, for instance, when using irony or local jargon. Instead of spreading resources thinly across wider fields – typically addressing predefined questions (as exemplified by surveys, p. 161) – thick description prioritizes in-depth and lengthy inquiry into delimited contexts, where both the articulation of relevant questions and the identification of potential answers are key components of the research process. This strategy of gradually clarifying questions and exploring answers - in both cases grounded in the participants' own perspectives on their lives and circumstances, and relying on multiple methods – is also referred to as **ethnography**. As explained in Chapter 5 (p. 146), however, it is important to recognize a distinction between the classic ethnographies of anthropology deploying participant observation, and the more focused and usually short-term studies of media use and other communicative practices.

Employed for studies of media production as well as media use, participating observation has made a special contribution to the understanding of media organizations, as observed from the inside. A good example is a set of international studies of how news comes to be produced (e.g., Gans, 1979; Golding & Elliott, 1979; Tuchman, 1978). Also today, individual news media and journalists are routinely criticized for being biased – for slanting 'the news' according of their personal attitudes and preferred opinions. By observing (and interviewing) journalists and editors to better understand the circumstances of daily news work, this research tradition has established that it is, above all and despite exceptions around the globe, time constraints, economic demands, and other structural conditions that explain the selection and presentation of news, not ideologies advocated and promoted by either the journalist or the news organization. It is, of course, evidently true – unavoidable – that some items of information rather than others will be chosen, combined, and configured as news. But it is the social structures, rather than the individual agents, that decide which events and topics turn out as 'news.'

Experiments – in the lab and in the field

Both observations and experiments direct attention to what people can be seen to be *doing* in specific settings and conditions, whether during or after media use. But the two methods differ in one important respect: For participating observations, researchers, in a sense, wait around for something to happen whereas, in experiments, they make things happen: If *we* do this to participants, then what will *they* do?

Associated, not least, with natural and medical sciences, experimental methods are also part of the toolbox of media and communication research. This introduces a contested terminology: If this media content is the **stimulus**, then what is the audience or user **response**? The aim, in short, is to establish manifest, causal relationships between media and users, in carefully controlled, experimental conditions (for overview, see Ørmen, 2021: 265–269).

The paradigmatic studies within the field of media and communication research examined children, and were conducted by Albert Bandura and his colleagues from the early 1960s, at first relying on live role models, later referring to representations of individuals' actions in films (Bandura et al., 1963). The upshot of their findings was that children who had witnessed violent behavior, appeared later to imitate the violence in their play. A key element of the experimental setup was a Bobo doll – a doll that an adult role model would hit and kick, and which children participating in the experiment were later given an opportunity to play with – and hit and kick.

The basic arrangement of such experiments involves an **experimental group** and a **control group**, in this case two different groups of children. Where the first group was exposed to violent media content, the second group was shown 'neutral' content. Subsequently, both groups were placed in settings where they could choose to behave aggressively toward the doll. And, indeed, the studies found a statistically significant difference between the two groups, so that children in the experimental group could be seen to mimic or reproduce the role models' physical and verbal aggression toward the doll to a considerable extent. The role models' violence was the stimulus, the children's violence the response. Technologically mediated violence, in short, could and, perhaps, would make people violent in the real world.

Before attempting to evaluate the strengths and weaknesses of experimental approaches, it is important to specify the underlying logic – which differs from that of other quantitative (as well as qualitative) approaches. Compared to survey studies, experiments work with smaller, nonrepresentative samples. Instead, participants are assigned to the two groups in an experiment according to a principle of statistical randomness (in Bandura's case, though, the assignment of children to the two groups had been guided by teachers' assessments of their aggressiveness in school life). The background to experimental media and communication studies is long-standing psychological research traditions, which take as their premise that the fundamental cognitive and affective processes guiding human behavior, will be identical across different (all) individuals. Social and cultural variations, accordingly, can be treated as secondary. The central focus, then, becomes the specific 'stimulus' of the experiment and its contribution to any differences observed between the 'responses' of the two groups.

Experiments come in many variations and operate at different levels of ambition. The classic setup involves a **pretest** and a **posttest**. Participants are assigned randomly to the experimental group and the control group, each of which is exposed to a distinctive stimulus or experience. And both groups will be tested both before and after exposure, thus measuring any difference or 'effect' on what the participants know, think, or do. Even in this basic format, however, it might be questioned whether the experiment, in fact, measures what it is designed to measure. This is because the pretest may influence how participants conduct themselves, both during and after the 'treatment' or exposure: Perhaps the pretest 'reveals' the point of the experiment, or the participants are given an opportunity to 'rehearse' relevant competences for the posttest.

A solution to this problem is the so-called **Solomon four-group design**. Here, the four groups comprise two experimental groups and two control groups: One experimental group and one control group only take the posttest; the other two groups respond to the pretest as well as the posttest. Through this procedure, it becomes possible to assess any impact of the pretest on the outcome of the posttest. (A less welcome result is the higher cost in terms of time and money – which helps explain why the more complex experimental research designs are comparatively rare, at least in media and communication studies.)

Not surprisingly, the 'clinical' flavor of experiments, when applied to human communication, has engendered skepticism and criticism. A primary concern has been that experimental research designs tend to divorce media use from its social and cultural contexts. For one thing, participants in experiments are exposed to media and their contents in artificial settings, or 'laboratories' (even if the setup does not feature buzzing machinery and technicians in white coats). For another thing, the stimulus has commonly been 'manipulated,' adapted to the purpose of the specific experiment, so that participants may be exposed, for example, to brief sequences of violent action extracted from much longer episodes of a television series.

In fairness, though, critiques of experimental media and communication studies may end up being too categorical, suggesting that experiments, in and of themselves, reduce human beings to organisms that might be expected to respond to media stimuli according to a simple repertoire of biological and behavioral regularities. In his classic studies, Bandura (1963), for one, did not lay claim to strong conclusions or sweeping statements regarding children's (or adults') reactions to representations of violence generally. Instead, he showed how people *may* learn to act violently from media. Experimental methods help identify some of the conditions under which media can lead to certain kinds of effects on some of their human users.

Experiments, moreover, are regularly conducted outside laboratory settings. **Field experiments** retain the random assignment of participants to two groups whose members are exposed to different materials and experiences, typically

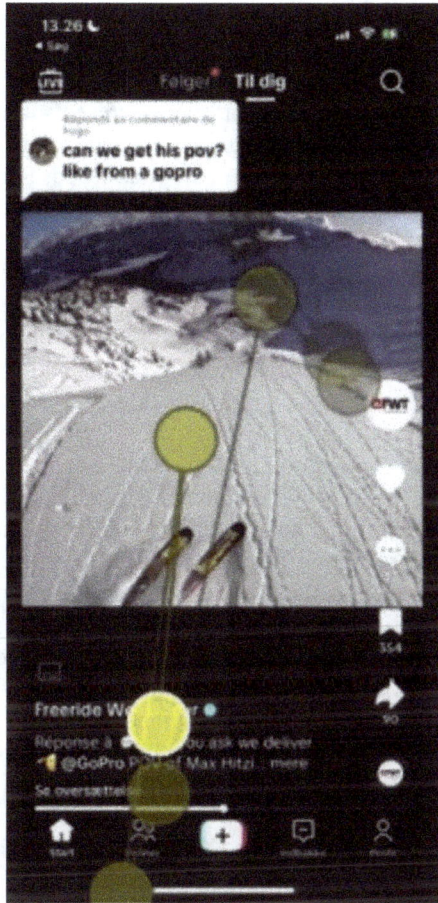

Image 6.4 Eye tracking. Marquart, F. (2024). *Social media use on mobile devices – Visual attention to TikTok posts* [Ongoing research project]. Department of Communication, University of Copenhagen.

*The purpose of experiments that rely on **eye tracking**, is to examine, in minute detail, how a user's gaze moves between and across the diverse elements of book pages, newspaper layouts, and screen interfaces – headlines, photos, graphics, images, letters, words, sentences. The equipment allows for the identification of where users stay for a while, as suggested by the video about skiing on TikTok with markers of where the user focuses their attention. Both movements and focal points bear witness to what appears to interest users, but also where they may 'get stuck' in seeking information and otherwise interacting with the communication system in question. By varying formal features of the medium, and by recruiting participants with different social backgrounds and skills, eye-tracking experiments begin to suggest potential changes, both in the specific design of the medium for particular target groups, and for enhancing their general media 'literacy.'*

two types of media content or two versions of a communication service. At its simplest, this approach is known as **A/B testing**: Media organizations will try out several different versions of what amounts, essentially, to the same product, before deciding which one may serve its strategy best. In **natural experiments**, the experimental condition simply presents itself as a lucky strike, so to speak: Studies may compare two groups that either have or do not yet have access to a new communication service being launched. For example, Western users first encountered TikTok in 2017, whereas its Chinese equivalent, Douyin, had premiered in 2016.

Digital media have provided new opportunities for experimental studies, because of the ease of varying – programming – both their forms and their contents. Experiments are particularly suited for examining, in detail and depth, the encounters and interactions between digital media and their users, up close to the interface: What happens to the reception and response if we modify (ever so slightly) the structure of the interface, its texts and images, and their configurations in narrative or instructional formats? Such questions are central to the field of **human–computer interaction** (HCI) (Jacko, 2012), which overlaps with, and increasingly informs, the field of media and communication research. One topic of HCI is **interaction design**: Through experiments addressing the design of interfaces as well as the systems behind the screens, it becomes possible to reshape interactions with digital communication systems for different user groups and contexts of application. Importantly, these contexts extend far beyond the private lives of citizens and consumers – which have been primary centers of attention in media and communication studies – to their working lives on the job: Media are indispensable tools enabling collaboration as well as communication, as examined in research on **computer-supported cooperative work** (CSCW).

Box 6.2 Exercise

24 hours with media

Prepare a documentation of your own media use for 24 hours, on an ordinary day. Consider, in advance, at least the following points:

- Ask yourself what could be interesting questions to address, and select a few of these.
- How will you structure your self-observation, and the collection and documentation of data: in time periods (how long); with reference to the places where you use media; or according to different media and genres?
- To what extent will you be able to produce either a 'quantitative' registration of your media consumption or a 'qualitative' description of your interactions with and interpretations of media?

- Will you document your media uses and communicative encounters through notes on paper and/or a form of recording?
- How might you go on to analyze, interpret, and explain the resulting data?

As part of a group or class project, the exercise may refer to a specific theoretical framework and rely on an elaborated 'methodology' (see further p. 188), perhaps combining qualitative and quantitative approaches and recruiting a wider sample of participants.

Textual analysis, discourse analysis, and source criticism

Chapter 2 already presented several conceptions of and approaches to **textual analysis,** with special reference to the texts that make up the contents or messages of media. The present chapter situates textual analysis in the context of other **empirical methods,** all of which afford instruments for collecting and analyzing data and documentation about human communicative practices, their elements, structures, and consequences. Sometimes, authors will contrast 'textual analysis' and 'empirical methods' – but that is an unhelpful, even misleading conception of what textual analysis is and does. Textual analyses are empirical; they simply rely on a different category of empirical materials or data than, for example, experiments and focus groups. For in-depth studies of film classics such as *Citizen Kane* (Orson Welles, 1941) or *The Matrix* (Lana and Lilly Wachowski, 1999), the empirical data are the films as such, with analyses addressing their forms, contents, and potential interpretations. But if the research question is which interpretations actual users make of the films – or how the production and distribution of films has been organized, then and now – it is essential to turn to other methods.

Media texts are an instance of what is sometimes referred to as 'unobtrusive measures' (Webb et al., 2000): measurements that do not affect the communication or other objects of analysis being examined. Media give rise to a great variety of texts, not just feature films and computer games ('contents'), but also textual 'data' in the wider sense, including the memorandum about an upcoming advertising campaign and the government white paper anticipating new legislation about digital platforms. One advantage of such data is they already exist and are there to be found, having been produced in and of the operation of media in society. There is, accordingly, no need for researchers to engage and 'interfere' with the production of precisely this kind of data – which might, after all, have an 'effect' on the object of analysis (say, an advertising agency or a policy office) and, hence, on the understanding of how advertisements and policies come to be designed and implemented.

The corresponding disadvantage is that unobtrusive measures typically relate less directly to the specific research questions of media and communication studies, compared to data from, for instance, depth interviewing or surveys. This is because unobtrusive research is making **secondary use** of data: The data originate from separate institutional and practical contexts, which means that their relevance as well as their quality – as data reflecting on the scholarly business at hand – may be difficult to assess. Current media and communication research here comes face-to-face with classic challenges of **source criticism** as developed over the centuries within historical sciences (for overview, see Alvesson & Sköldberg, 2018: 134–146). First, a distinction has traditionally been made between **relics** (or remnants) and **narratives**: Early mobile phones can still be found, picked up, and examined (relics), but to appreciate how they were originally developed, looked upon, and used in practice, it is necessary, in addition, to consult, for example, contemporary user manuals and advertising for mobile devices and services. Second, either **firsthand** or **secondhand** sources (or both) may be available: The technicians developing the hardware and software for mobile communication at the time and the designers of the associated advertising campaigns, will be both more knowledgeable and more dependable than younger colleagues who may have heard or read about their accomplishments. A third and final distinction is made between **primary** and **secondary** sources: Primary sources provide the first available testimony or evidence in the matter (even if they do not represent either a firsthand source or *the* first source – which may have been lost in the meantime), whereas secondary sources build on and commonly rework primary sources. In the example of mobile phones, primary sources would include the (likely older) producers and users of some of the first mobile phones as well as early cases of advertising for devices and services. For students doing a project on the development of mobile media and communication, a likely first stop is *Wikipedia* (http://en.wikipedia.org/wiki/Mobile_phone, August 1, 2024) – which is a secondary source (but, at least in this case, a solid resource). From there, students can (and should) start working their way back from *Wikipedia* (including its helpful notes and references), toward the various primary and firsthand sources, typically technical and product information, government reports, and original scholarly works. In this way, students can begin to address questions such as how bulky, heavy, and expensive mobile phones once were, and how many (or few) were in a position to call or text each other in that recent past.

Compared to textual analysis, which examines texts *in the media*, and source criticism, which centers on documents *around the media*, **discourse analysis** lends itself to research on both categories of texts, and then some. As elaborated in Chapter 2 (p. 50), discourse analysis supports detailed studies of terminologies, arguments, implicit premises, narrative structures, and more – as they enter into media contents, but also everyday conversations and communications unfolding deep within private companies and public institutions. Chapter 2, further, illustrated how discourse analyses contribute critical perspectives on the ideologies or dominant **discourses** that are the sum total of many discursive details – what Roland Barthes referred to as **mythologies**.

Discourse analysis serves as a method of media and communication studies in two main respects. On the one hand, its objects of analysis are the many different discourses that are produced in, for, and around the media as organizations and social institutions. These discourses belong to four main categories:

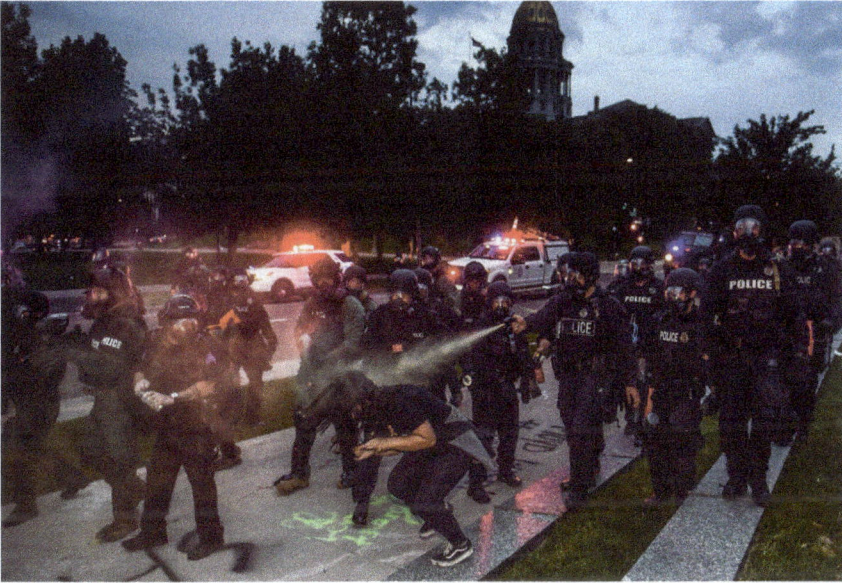

Image 6.5 Source media. Michael Ciaglo/ Stringer/ Getty Images.

When journalists collect information, for instance, at press conferences, they rely on so-called **source media** *(Ericson et al., 1987: 41), including sound recordings, scribbled notes, and reports provided by the organizations behind press conferences. Source media constitute a 'raw material' for news articles, radio updates, and television coverage. With the development of digital and mobile media,* **user-generated content,** *too, has come to serve as source media, documenting crimes such as the murder of George Floyd by the American police officer Derek Chauvin in Minneapolis, USA, May 25, 2020, followed by protests and confrontations between citizens and police, here a Black woman being peppersprayed by police in protective gear. Both professional and amateur source media, next, become resources for research to study in order to better understand how media and their users record, process, and act on events in the context of wider social movements such as #BlackLivesMatter.*

- *Media discourses*: the texts, images, and sounds that the media originate and circulate in society
- *Production discourses*: manuscripts, documents, conversations, and other means of preparing and supporting media organizations' activities and communicative practices
- *Audience discourses*: media users' own communications, which serve to interpret and further process the contents afforded by the media

- *Context discourses*: frames of reference for understanding and approaching media, their contents, and their social uses, for example, the cinema as a social and cultural forum (Gomery, 1992), and households as sites of individual and collective television viewing (Spigel, 1992).

On the other hand, discourse analysis performs the role of qualitative **data analysis** (Jensen, 2021d: 298–306). Qualitative data collection methods – interviewing and observation – are textual engines, producing large and complex sets of data. But, compared to quantitative data analysis, there have developed many fewer well-defined approaches to and procedures for the analysis of qualitative data. Discourse analysis offers a systematics of organizing qualitative evidence and substantiating the steps from empirical documentation to theoretical interpretation. Qualitative data analyses result in **meta-discourses** – discourses about discourses – which variously analyze (divide) and synthesize (unite) the elements of data sets into meaningful and consequential configurations. Like analyses of media discourses, discourse analyses of other varieties of qualitative data undertake stepwise interpretations of the collected evidence within a hermeneutic circle (Chapter 2, p. 33).

One example of discourse analysis as data analysis, combined with source criticism, was John Durham Peters's classic volume on the history of the very idea of communication (Peters, 1999): What, indeed, is the meaning of 'communication,' and how has this familiar phenomenon been understood at different times throughout history? Among other sources, Peters relied on statements from people who had been instrumental in developing the techniques of radio transmission in the second half of the 1800s. Further analyses showed that a characteristic feature of their vocabularies was a set of analogies to, and comparisons between, radio and telepathy – mind reading (Peters, 1999: 104–108). The technicians in question were hardly 'superstitious' in a literal sense, but the analogies provided them with frameworks for grasping what presented itself (at the time) as a radically new form of communication, enabling humans to 'hear voices' at a distance. More recent examples of shifting interpretations of the interrelations between technologies and realities have been 1990s notions of a separate 'cyberspace' – an idea coined in the world of fiction (Gibson, 1984), whence it was imported into technical environments developing the software behind this new social space (Stone, 1991: 98) – and its reassertion, in projections of the early 2020s, that online and offline worlds would converge in a metaverse (Ball, 2022).

Content analysis

Content analysis might be thought to denote simply the analysis of content. In fact, 'content analysis' covers a specific approach to content, namely, the quantitative equivalent of qualitative text and discourse analyses. (A brief introduction can be found in Deacon et al. (2021); a more detailed presentation is given by Krippendorff (2018).) The method describes, counts, and correlates the constituents of large sets of media texts and communicative interactions. Comparable to surveys of media use, its primary purpose is to offer overviews and broad characterizations of the contents of various media, genres, and discourses, for instance, how fiction series on television associate particular ethnic groups with the roles of either good or bad guys, and how news media cover major political figures in an electoral campaign or over an election period. A common additional purpose is to assess whether and how media present precise mirrors of reality, or perhaps a hall of mirrors. Media regularly reflect reality in surprising and contestable ways, calling for systematic analyses to support personal reflection and collective deliberation among their users.

An early classic of content analysis was Leo Löwenthal's (1961/1941) study of the representation of 'idols' in popular magazines in the United States during the first half of the twentieth century. Idols were defined as individuals who were considered sufficiently important (by the magazines) as participants in and contributors to society that they deserved special notice through biographical articles and portraits addressed to mass audiences. Through quantitative content analysis, Löwenthal identified a shift, across the decades, in terms of the social sectors with which these idols were primarily associated. Whereas, around 1900, as much as 46% of the portraits covered political leaders, business tycoons, and scholars, by 1940 their share had dropped to 25%. The focus had shifted, instead, to movie actors, entertainers, and athletes. Furthermore, the portraits were taking an increased interest in the private lives of those selected for coverage, including their romantic affairs and styles of dressing. Based on these findings, Löwenthal concluded that the interest of the media had shifted from 'idols of production' to 'idols of consumption.' And he took that change to reflect a more fundamental transformation of the values guiding (American) society: As indicators of the good life, consumption and private life had taken over from production and public life. The question remained, of course, to what extent the media could be said to originate, motivate, and legitimate, rather than merely passing on, these values to the public.

Content, however, is not what it used to be. Media use today is so much more than reading portraits of the rich and famous on paper. Traditionally, content analyses have centered on the fixed entities carrying information through mass media: A book, a newspaper, a magazine, a film, and a radio or television program hold a set of manifest components waiting to be counted and tabulated. In digital media and communication, in comparison, content is broken up into bits, shared, and put back together again, in multiple steps and sequences. Users, similarly, enjoy enhanced degrees of freedom when selecting and combining components of content for themselves. Even the content being pushed to users, as individuals and groups, is, in part, a product of their own earlier pulls: The results people receive from Google's search engine (a form of content) bear witness to countless earlier searches (by themselves and others), which have been registered, analyzed, and applied through recursive tweaking of the search engine.

Consequently, even more methods are needed, not to replace, but to supplement tried and true approaches. To bring out similarities as well as differences, the next section begins by summarizing the six prototypical methods reviewed so far in this chapter, before comparing and contrasting these with a repertoire of digital methods that is still in the making.

Box 6.3 Methods at issue

Quant and/or qual?

The other chapters in this book have taken up 'theories at issue' – different and sometimes conflicting ways of interpreting and explaining the relationship between media and society. In the case of methods, too, research is ripe with contested premises and procedures for conducting empirical studies. The most basic and frequently referenced divide separates, on the one hand, research traditions that consider quantitative and qualitative studies of equal relevance and value, and, on the other hand, traditions that defer to quantitative work as 'real' science, while assigning little, even no, scientific value to qualitative work.

The background to the qual-quant distinction is the long history of different sciences emerging and establishing themselves across the centuries, which, in brief summary, resulted in a distinction between 'hard' sciences examining nature and 'soft' sciences exploring human cultures (for overview, see Kjørup, 2001): Where nature lends itself to precise measurement, explanation, and prediction, the meanings that humans ascribe to themselves and others call for interpretation – and generate many *different* interpretations (see Chapter 2, p. 30 on hermeneutics). As the social sciences were separated from the humanities in the decades around 1900, debates followed regarding the appropriate and preferable profile of social science: Should studies of society and culture shape themselves in the image of the natural sciences, seeking law-like regularities through quantitative descriptions pointing toward formal models and theories? Or should the social sciences still take their cue from humanistic, qualitative, interpretive approaches to human beings and their meaningful interactions in variable historical and cultural circumstances? Or might there be a golden mean accommodating and, in some respects, combining the two legacies? Debate on these questions has continued ever since, including within media and communication research, and without resulting in any stable consensus, even while a majority of publications in the field have tended to be quantitative (Walter et al., 2018).

Today, media and communication research is home to two main positions regarding the place of qualitative and quantitative approaches in empirical inquiry. To one side, a common viewpoint is that while both may be needed, 'some methods are more equal than others': Quantitative research is designated as the primary source of the gradual accumulation of justified or established knowledge, for instance, concerning the mechanisms of media economy or the strength of various media effects. Qualitative studies, in comparison, are said to deliver **supplements**, regarding topics such as the lifestyles and forms of everyday life being affected by media economies and media effects. In this perspective, a common argument is that qualitative approaches deliver preliminary or pilot studies (see further p. 189), among other things preparing and testing, through qualitative interviewing and focus groups, the questions that will be later be addressed, through surveys, to a representative sample of the population in question. This first position sometimes signals an affiliation with 'hard' sciences by referring to media and communication studies as a 'science' rather than merely 'research' (Berger et al., 2009).

To the other side, a substantial number of media and communication scholars argue that qualitative studies provide not just supplements but **complements**, that is, necessary constituents of and contributions to a rounded understanding of media institutions, media texts, and media uses (Jensen, 2021b). Their reasoning is that research must first ask *what* is to be investigated, and *why*, before deciding *how* to conduct investigations. Some media uses and media effects, for example, lend themselves primarily to qualitative inquiry: Chapter 5 reviewed several research traditions (appearing 'below the line' in Figure 5.1, p. 130) focusing on aspects of everyday media use that would have been difficult or impossible to capture through quantitative approaches. This second position recognizes that it is, indeed, possible to accumulate knowledge about various interrelations of media and society. But it simultaneously insists that, to serve this end, both qualitative and quantitative approaches are necessary – and neither is sufficient. They are 'different but equal': Quantitative and qualitative approaches deliver complementary insights into different aspects of media production and media use, media economy and media effects. Chapter 7 returns to the place of quant and qual in private and public social institutions – in production and planning by commercial media organizations, and in the monitoring of media uses and communicative practices by public agencies.

Data – lost, found, and made

A common feature of the first four methods – interviewing, surveys, observations, and experiments – is that they all 'make' their own data: Data is produced at the researchers' initiative and request. The last two methods, in comparison, work with already existing data, which researchers can be said to 'find': sources, documents, texts (Jensen, 2012). Admittedly, also with this second group of methods, scholars will collect data according to specified purposes, necessarily selecting some data for further examination. But, as the reviews of the six methods have suggested, there is, nevertheless, a categorical difference between made and found data: If you have not yet watched the first episode of a new fiction series from (one of) your national television station(s), you are likely to find it available for streaming online – and you may go ahead and analyze it. But if you do not conduct interviews or surveys with samples of viewers right away, very soon it will be too late to assess

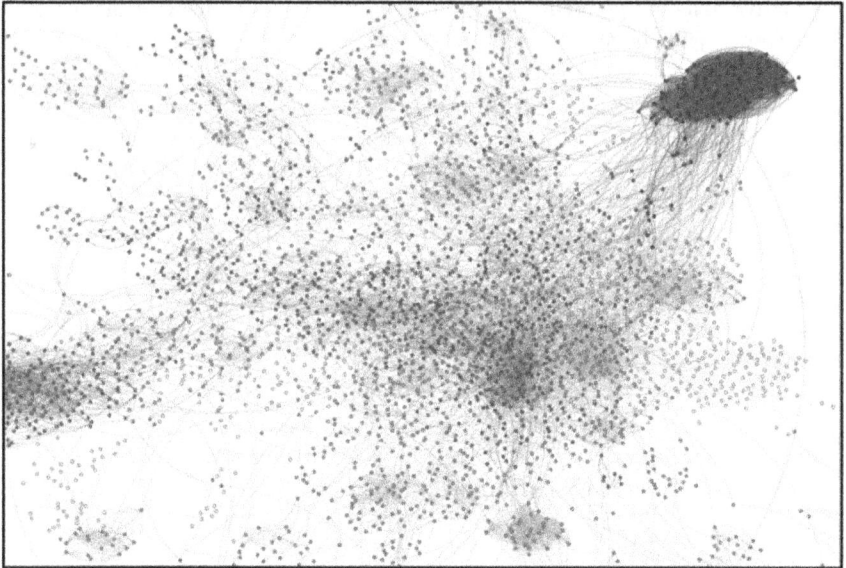

Image 6.6 Social network analysis. Courtesy of Rasmus Helles.

Digital media in general, and social media in particular, are sources of very large data sets – 'big data' – about their uses and users in social contexts. One way of making sense of all these data is social network analyses (SNAs). Findings from SNAs are visualized in graphs such as this one, which depicts overlaps among persons who are members of one or more Facebook groups dedicated to 3,891 different television shows. To the left is an overview of the entire network (without titles of the television shows); to the right the graph focuses on the most popular shows (with titles). 'Popularity,' in the present context, means that these Facebook groups have the most links to other groups dedicated to other shows. But, in fact, those shows in the network that are especially popular (many overlaps between their memberships) coincide with the shows that have the most viewers overall (the size of their memberships). So, even without access to the actual number of viewers (ratings) for the individual series, the viewers' behavior on social media bears witness to the popularity of the series on television, at least to the extent that the most popular television shows on Facebook (which presumably are watched by many of the same persons) also have many shared users. At the same time, the present SNA brings out how particularly popular shows make up an 'island' in the network, probably because the groups devoted to other shows represent more special interests and, hence, have fewer members.

the size of the audience for that first episode, and how viewers interpreted and evaluated the series when it premiered. Then the relevant data will be lost – gone forever – just as most human communications throughout the history of the world have vanished into thin air (Peters, 1999).

The data that researchers 'find' include, first of all, the lower cells shown in Figure 6.1 – texts and documents. They are studied, as indicated here and in Chapter 2, through 'old' methods – source criticism, textual analysis, and content analysis. But, by applying 'new' methods to 'new,' digital media, it becomes possible to find new varieties of data, and in large numbers: 'big data' (Image 6.6) (Mayer-Schönberger & Cukier, 2013). This is because digital media, to an extent, auto-record *how* they are being used, *as* they are being used. Chapter 2 introduced this peculiarity of digital communication systems with reference to their production of **metadata** ('information about information') and processes of **metacommunication** ('communication about communication'). Digital data bear witness, for example, to where specific elements of specific communicative interactions originated, who else paid attention to the elements and the interactions, and who went on to communicate further about some of them with particular others. Sooner or later, students and scholars need digital methods to examine digital data in digital media.

Digital methods for digital media

Richard Rogers (2013), who directs the interdisciplinary Digital Methods Initiative at the University of Amsterdam in The Netherlands, has suggested that digital

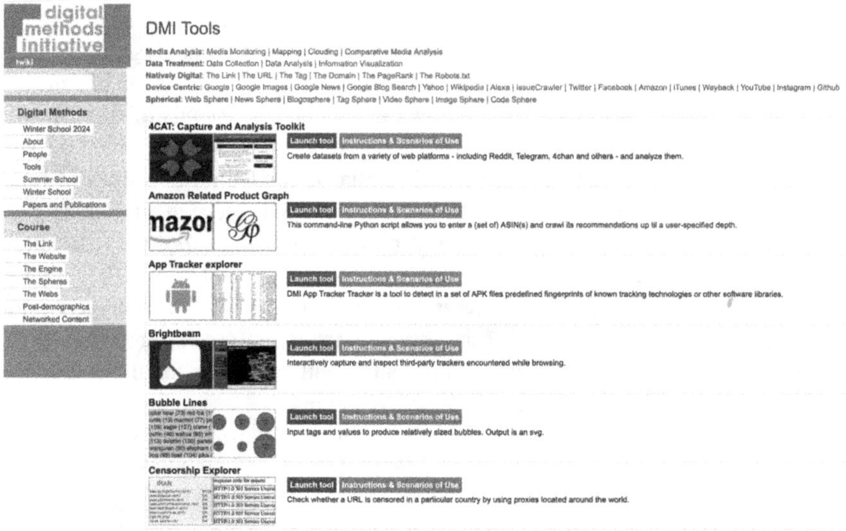

Image 6.7 Digital tools. © Digital Methods Initiative, 2024.

Scholars who develop digital methods often choose to share these tools with others to support further research. The Digital Methods Initiative (abbreviated DMI in this portion of the website of the research group) lists and links to various tools in their database, which is available at this address: https://wiki. digitalmethods.net/Dmi/ToolDatabase.

methods are 'the methods of the medium': Digital methods take advantage of distinctive communicative affordances (Chapter 3, p. 64) of the technologies behind digital media to study those same media. By reverse-engineering selected elements and processes of digital devices (laptops, smartwatches) and platforms (TikTok, Instagram, Spotify), research is in a position to study (some of) the social and cultural phenomena that unfold on and through these devices and platforms. Numerous studies, not least of Facebook, have collected and analyzed data about social networks, hashtags, likes, shares, and more, to identify trends in public debate (Venturini & Munk, 2021) and developments within online business models (Nieborg & Helmond, 2019). Other studies of smartphones and apps have taken advantage of the technological infrastructures of mobile communication to document how user data are shared with third parties, not just with the business behind the app itself (Pybus & Coté, 2021). And maps of so-called hyperlink networks have both described how, and helped explain why, specific web pages link to each other (Brügger et al., 2020).

Digital methods lend themselves to both quantitative and qualitative analyses – and to multi-method combinations. A **quantitative** study of how Facebook relays information to and among users of the service, included no fewer than 253,238,367 unique users, 75,888,466 URLs (addresses on the internet), and 1,168,633,941 relations between a user and a URL (Bakshy et al., 2012). The findings, not surprisingly, showed that Facebook has contributed to accelerating the exchange of information: People share information more often, and they do so more quickly, if they receive the information from their online contacts. But the analyses also threw new light on a classic research question, namely, the relative value of 'strong' ties (family, close friends) and 'weak' ties (acquaintances, friends of friends), for instance, when individuals are looking for a new job (Granovetter, 1973). Even though specific strong ties did have a substantial influence on the flows of relevant information, nevertheless, it was the sum of weak ties, in particular, that accounted for the accelerated exchange of new information. The Facebook study was an example of **social network analysis** (Freeman, 2004), which explores how different individuals and groups in society, but also organizations, communities, and entire countries make up interrelated networks (see further Image 6.6). Communication is a necessary, though not a sufficient, condition for all these social networks both to take shape and to operate over time.

Qualitative research, too, can 'find' relevant data that have been registered in and through the operation of digital media. Especially for observational and ethnographic studies (see further p. 166), researchers are able, first, to participate in and, later, to observe their interactions with the field (Pink et al., 2016). Moreover, several types of digital data can be combined, for example, in research on online gaming: recordings of the gameplay, of interviews with players residing in different parts of a country or around the world, and of the ongoing interaction among the participants in a game through messaging applications (Thorhauge, 2007). And recordings of gaming as well as of other media and genres can inform subsequent individual interviewing or focus groups: Why did you do *this* at *that* particular point of the game? Why did your debate about *this* particular political issue develop into *such* a heated argument?

One illustrative qualitative study centered on **communities** on the internet, combining several methods to consider several media (Baym, 2000). The title of the book reporting the project – *Tune In, Log On* – suggested the focus of the project: the experience of watching television, specifically American soap operas, and entering into discussions about these programs with other fans as members of an online community. The methods included an online survey, detailed analyses of a large archive of posts to the newsgroup in question, as well as the researcher's own participation in discussing (and watching) the television programs over several years. Through this combination, the study integrated textual analyses of 'dead' texts from an archive – which were once 'living' engagements with the series and with other fans – with several other methods.

Finally, digital methods provide special opportunities for combining quantitative and qualitative research, again because of the enabling technologies. On the one hand, the same bits of 'found' data can be analyzed qualitatively and locally as they relate to specific users and contexts; on the other hand, the same data may enter into larger datasets, scaling the analysis to address wider sociodemographic groups or institutional settings. Advocates of digital methods, further, have highlighted the possibilities of moving back and forth between micro and macro perspectives on the same communicative and social phenomena through so-called 'quali-quantitative' approaches (Venturini & Latour, 2010). For example, studies of hashtags may consider both an entire social movement mobilizing people around a current issue such as #metoo, and the participants' engagement with the issue in individual posts reflecting their own life circumstances.

Returning to Figure 6.1 (p. 157), we categorize digital data – along with the texts and documents in the lower cells – as evidence that somebody left behind, and which can be retrieved for later inquiry. But, as suggested by the examples reviewed here, the traditional distinction between qualitative and quantitative approaches is less clear than suggested by the dichotomous columns of Figure 6.1. Scholarship is still in the process of developing and refining new, digital methods and assessing their potential combinations with the six old, analog methods.

In conclusion, we caution that digital methods are, indeed, 'methods of the medium,' for better, but also for worse. When the objects and the methods of analysis increasingly converge (Marres, 2017), research is conditioned *both* by the general features of digital technologies, including all the things that digital systems will *not* register by default, *and* the design and implementation of specific apps and websites according to particular business models. It follows that, within the available systems supporting communication *and* communication studies, some research questions can (not) be posed, and some empirical research designs can (not) be pursued. And, of course, research on digital media and communication depends, in the end, on access to data: The tech companies that own so much of the data relevant for research, have proven increasingly unwilling to cooperate with academic and independent scholars (Bruns, 2019).

Box 6.4 Exercise

The walkthrough method

A useful method for characterizing the affordances (Chapter 3, p. 64) of different media and genres – from web pages to games – is to 'walk through' their elements. This exercise gives insight into selected apps, their technical features, and their anticipated uses in the context of everyday life and social networks (for an elaboration of the method, see Light et al., 2018).

Start by choosing an app that you know of, but do not use regularly. Next, walk through the app as follows:

The technical walkthrough

First, complete three basic steps, each involving a few questions:

1. **Registration and entry**: How does one download the app, and how does one register to become a user?
2. **Everyday use**: What purposes might the app serve, in which contexts?
3. **App suspension, closure, and leaving**: How does one uninstall the app, and how does one close a user profile?

The technical walkthrough, moreover, involves descriptions of how interfaces will guide users through apps by the placement of menus and buttons; how certain actions are encouraged or even necessitated by filling in required fields or pop-up menus; how the presence *or absence* of specific choices within menus, perhaps in sequences, both enable and constrain use; and how the colors, fonts, and sizes of interface elements contribute to the user experience as a whole.

The environment of expected use

From the technical walkthrough, it becomes possible to assess which uses of the app its developers and owners consider likely and preferable. Describe the following three aspects of the probable embedding of the app in users' everyday lives and in society at large:

1. **Vision**: The visions of apps cover their purposes, target audiences, and potential uses, typically summed up in the characterizations provided by app stores. For example, Tinder is presented as a platform facilitating dating by two individuals, which suggests monogamous relationships as a social norm. Other dating apps reflect alternative perspectives on intimate relationships, in which dating several different partners at the same time is considered (equally) normal.

2. **Operating model**: Income may be generated through payments from users, either for the app as such or for services offered within the app: Examples include Spotify's premium model, which allows for listening without commercial breaks. Many apps, however, offer their services in return for user data, which can be sold to advertisers and other interested parties and stakeholders.

3. **Governance**: The governance of an app consists in the app provider's administration and regulation of user activities, so as to support its vision and operating (business) model. The concrete approach to governance appears from internal guidelines and rules for using the app (the so-called Terms of Service – ToS), determining who may use the app, and what they may do with it. Governance is enacted, further, through technical means, when, for example, Instagram relies on a particular script to track and delete images with total or partial representations of female nipples (representations of male nipples are allowed).

The exercise can be extended to include comparative analyses of different categories of apps, or of the app version and the web version of the same service.

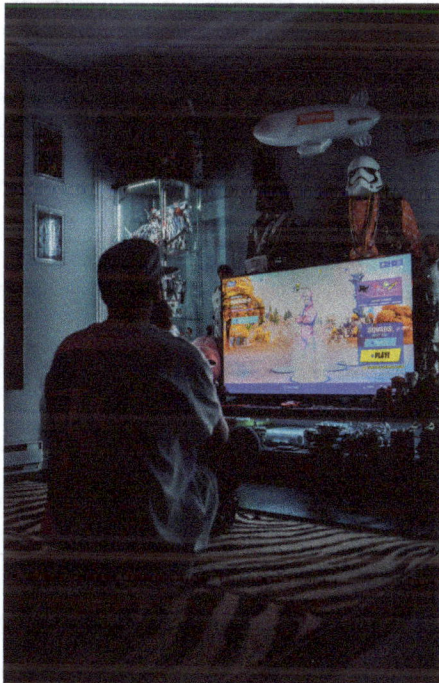

Image 6.8 Fortnite. Photo by Erik Mclean on Unsplash.

> *Video gaming is a prominent example of communication that moves across technological platforms, and which, in doing so, establishes and relates social contexts. As we complete this book,* Fortnite *is the most widely used online game globally. In one variant of the game, up to 100 players will fight to survive, and to become the last person standing. The game can (and should) be studied on screen, but also behind the screen – among producers and programmers – as well as among the many users in front of local screens.*

Methods, theories, and theory of science

The introduction to this chapter briefly noted that the specific methods reviewed so far, raise general questions concerning the status and relevance of research – the nature of science and scholarship. Rounding out the chapter, we are now ready to revisit those questions. The concluding box presenting "Ten rules for conducting empirical studies" offers advice and recommendations regarding the planning, conduct, and completion of student projects.

Figure 6.3 (Jensen, 2021b: 333) lays out six levels of doing research about media and communication. Earlier sections of the chapter have focused on two of these levels: data collection and data analysis. This final section returns to their interrelations with the other four levels and to their place within the figure as a whole. Throughout the section, the accounts of levels rely on the same example – the distinction between fact and fiction, as observed both in   the genres of media content and in the procedures of research. While findings from scientific research may, from time to time, appear abstract or far-fetched, they refer to facts in the real world, and the insights have practical consequences – for people's understanding of the world and for their interactions with others in and about the world.

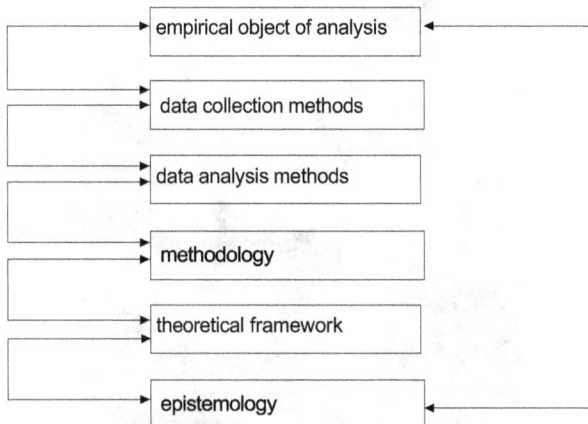

Figure 6.3 Six levels of empirical research.

Objects of analysis

Media texts, media organizations, media executives, media users, and more – all are potential objects of analysis, in themselves and as they relate to each other. The reference to 'objects' does not imply that researchers are always, or even mostly, in a position to precisely identify, from the outset, the individuals, artifacts, or interactions to be analyzed. Scholarship is a trial-and-error business, proceeding according to preliminary definitions and through continuous reflection. What empirical studies nevertheless *can* do, is to formulate delimited research questions, for example, regarding communication as an experience, an event, or a social mechanism, lending purpose, orientation, and a proposed trajectory to the process of inquiry. The point of departure is a **description** of **categories** of objects to be examined in further, empirical detail – and those objects may be subjects: persons and groups of people.

In the media as in other social domains, a cognitive, affective, and performative divide separates **fact** from **fiction**. It is essential to recognize, for instance, whether physical fighting occurs in the street, on the evening news, or in the context of a crime series. And yet, it is sometimes difficult to draw that line – a famous example is a 1938 radio play about an invasion from Mars, which was taken as factual news reports by a considerable number of U.S. listeners, creating a panic among segments of the American population (Cantril, 1940). For analytical purposes, as well, the distinction is not always clear-cut: Factual and fictional genres rely on similar means of expression and representation – think of documentaries and action movies. To appreciate similarities as well as differences between fact and fiction, then, research questions must specify whether the objects of analysis are their distinctive forms of expression and representation, their references to the real world, or the users' experience of the interfaces between representation and reality.

Data collection methods

Depending, next, on their focus on either senders, messages, or receivers, data collection methods prepare different insights into the boundary between fact and fiction. Production studies, for example, **document** the distinctive working routines of journalists compared to those of film directors and YouTube influencers, via observations and through interviewing, complemented perhaps by marketing materials reflecting the factual and fictional ingredients of the finished products. Content studies will either qualitatively **identify**, through textual studies, the narrative and other discursive conventions of newscasts, feature films, and advertisements, or quantitatively **measure**, through content analysis, the relative proportion of fact and fiction (and, by implication, 'enlightenment' compared to 'entertainment') in the menus of different radio and television stations and systems. And, for audience and user studies, beyond surveys mapping the demand for factual and fictional supply, experiments may manipulate the images and sounds of news, commercials, and other genres to bring out the discursive details that explain why some narrative wholes come to be interpreted as fiction, others as fact.

Data analysis methods

Data analysis methods, as noted, largely follow from the data collection methods chosen. Quantitative and qualitative methods of collecting and analyzing data go together: Although it is possible to perform statistical analyses of the answers to a limited number of in-depth interviews or focus groups, for instance, to detect patterns in participants' vocabularies, quantitative data analyses are employed, above all, in the context of survey research (and of experiments as well as in content analyses). Conversely, textual and discourse analysis are the methods of choice for exploring the details and nuances of in-depth interviews, observational notes, and the diverse genres of media content. As already suggested, some data are 'made' while others are 'found' – finding is a mode of collecting. And when data are found, the analysis may already have been begun in and through the act of encountering data: One example was the analysis in Chapter 2 of the cover of *Paris-Match* (p. 40), which immediately prompted a series of critical questions for Barthes.

In delineating fact and fiction, data analyses address two types of questions. First, studies may seek to establish their **occurrence** and **recurrence** according to established definitions, for instance, measuring the relative proportion of factual and fictional genres on YouTube (content analysis), or the differences and similarities between music channels and science channels on YouTube (discourse analysis). Second, beyond research questions regarding the quantities supplied by media and demanded by users, fact and fiction invite investigation of the **experience** of their distinctive features. There are, for example, fundamental differences in how children and adults experience factual and fictional modes of representing reality (small children do not distinguish the two). If data are collected through focus groups with children and adults, subsequent data analysis will look into their respective **categorizations** of 'reality.' And if data collection relies on experiments, data analysis may establish dependencies – **correlations** – between characteristic forms of representation and their categorization, as either fact or fiction, by different age groups.

Methodologies

Methodologies can be understood as plans of action guiding the conducting of particular projects. Often, *methodologies* incorporate multiple *methods*, and may be grounded in one or several specific theories (covered in the next section). Methodologies are also referred to as research designs: You design a piece of research by first considering **what** will be studied, and **why**, before settling on the **how** – the methods through which it will be carried out. Scholarship is typically governed by one or more relatively general **research questions** concerning an object of analysis or domain of inquiry, in some cases also by more specific **hypotheses** regarding the expected findings. Once the questions have been posed (and the hypotheses specified), researchers will go on to select particular methods, assess the time and resources available, and lay out the logistics and schedules of the constituent activities. It is also at the level of methodology that decisions regarding the application of qualitative or quantitative methods, or some combination of these, is arrived at.

Regarding the differences and similarities between fact and fiction, we already exemplified common research questions and approaches relating to media production, media texts, and media use: Methodologies may focus on the prominence of fact and fiction in the output of individual media or particular sectors of cultural industries; on fact and fiction as distinctive forms of aesthetic expression and representation; or on users' definitions and decodings of fact, fiction, and reality. And different methodologies represent variable scopes and ambitions: The purpose may be to test a preliminary set of survey questions or analytical content categories through **pilot studies**. Or individual studies may enter into large-scale collaborative and **comparative** investigations, for instance, of the distribution of factual and fictional genres in the programming of national television stations during the 1950s and 2020s, respectively.

Theories

In common parlance, science and scholarship are associated, above all, with 'theories' – theories can be defined as configurations of concepts that enable researchers (and readers of their publications) to understand, interpret, and explain the status and relevance of the findings and insights deriving from the analysis of data. Theories may be expressed in ordinary language as well as in graphic models and mathematical formulae. Whether formally or informally articulated, theories afford frames of reference that make sense of – lend meaning to – the data at hand and, by implication, to the domains of reality that have been singled out for further inquiry. Whereas empirical data and reality domains are concrete, theories are **general**, lending themselves to many different cases of fact and fiction.

Theories enter into the practice of research in two respects: Empirical projects may contribute to either **theory development** or **theory testing** (or to the generation and testing of more specific hypotheses). Most likely, previous studies will have produced one or more conceptions of and hypotheses about the age at which children begin to distinguish between (what adults consider) fact and fiction. Next, those hypotheses (informed, in addition, by more general theories deriving from developmental psychology) will be tested through experiments involving children in different age brackets. In other domains of media and communication, new concepts and models, or entirely new theories, may be called for, for example, when reality presents itself in unfamiliar shapes and forms: Is cyberspace or the metaverse fiction, or fact, or a third category of reality? Whereas these last questions do not translate into straightforward hypotheses, the process of arriving at a range of potential answers may nevertheless contribute to clarifying and specifying scientific and public understanding of historically shifting objects of analysis.

Theory of science

The top level in Figure 6.3 is theory of science – theories addressing what constitutes and qualifies as science in the first place, and how science can and should be undertaken. Related terms will refer to **meta-theory** – theory about the-ories – and **epistemology** – theory of knowledge, or how to justify what (we think) we know. In fact, the figure might have been turned upside down, placing theory of science at the bottom of the structure. That would, indeed, have been in line with a classic and still common understanding, that specialized theories and spe-cific studies must be grounded in one solid, universal, even eternal foundation – an understanding which has increasingly come to be contested, especially in social and human sciences such as media and communication research. The very con-testation of such a foundation – and of any foundation – suggests the open-ended nature of science and scholarship, in theory as in practice.

For present purposes, the arrows in Figure 6.3 serve to highlight the interrelations and interdependences of the six levels. Methods of data collection and methods of data analysis go together; the choice of particular methods is justified through methodology; and theory is required to account for the meaning and relevance of the diverse empirical data – represented by words, images, and numbers – that methods and methodology generate. And theory of science, in its turn, weighs mul-tiple and potentially conflicting theories with reference to the domain of inquiry (*what*) and the purpose(s) of inquiry (*why*): Why, after all, do people engage in science and scholarship?

Science and scholarship serve to verify and falsify knowledge *about* the world, and to justify individual as well as collective actions *in* and *on* the world: Theory informs practice; theory has consequences. This last point is suggested by the arrow relating theory of science back to the objects of analysis – reality. Empirical investigations are driven by interests in the real world – knowledge interests (see further Chapter 7, p. 217). Media and communication research has three distinctive, if overlapping purposes:

- *Interpret*. Beyond describing the place of media in society, media and commu-nication research interprets both the meaning of specific media texts and the wider implications of media for social developments across historical time and cultural space. While this purpose may be most manifest in qualitative studies of media texts and media uses, surveys, experiments, and content analyses, too, lead on to interpretations of their findings and implications. Before (quantitative and qualitative) data will speak to us, we need to ask questions of them.
- *Explain*. A further ambition of the field is to explain how media come to carry specific contents, why there is such a thing as media and communication in the first place, why people communicate in and through media as they do, and which effects different media may have on individuals and societies. Explanatory approaches are most commonly associated with quantitative studies, which rely on representative samples of populations or experimental designs to estab-lish correlations, such as those between patterns of media use and media users' socioeconomic background. However, also qualitative studies, for example, of the institutions and infrastructures of communication seek to uncover how the contents and services on offer follow from or depend on media economy and media law.

- *Change.* Finally, research may propose to change – and, arguably, improve – media as they currently operate. Such instrumental purposes are especially manifest in the many small and large research projects undertaken by, or on behalf of, commercial companies and, to an extent, public institutions. The aim might be to have consumers buy more candy (advertising campaign) or, conversely, to have them eat less candy (public health campaign). Traditional academic research, as well, may engage in studies designed to change the objects of analysis. **Action research** (Bradbury, 2015; Greenwood & Levin, 2007) is a distinctive tradition in which investigations are planned in collaboration with particular social agents or interests that have a practical interest – and therefore a knowledge interest – in interpreting, explaining, and changing, for instance, the conditions under which they communicate. One example is activist or nongovernmental organizations (NGOs) involving researchers to improve the coherence and consistency of their internal and external communications (see further Chapter 3, p. 91).

The extended process of empirical inquiry that this chapter has covered, itself constitutes communication. Throughout data collection, data analysis, theory development, and the publication and dissemination of findings, researchers engage as subjects in communication with other subjects about selected, shared objects of analysis. At the end of inquiry, they cannot claim 'objectivity' for their findings in an absolute sense, nor are the findings 'subjective.' Science and scholarship produce **intersubjective** insights – which are the outcome of sequences of communicative interactions involving respondents and informants, other scholars and ourselves – through notes and drafts. And communication goes on, as other researchers (re)interpret earlier findings and design new studies. Through practice and reflection, students become able to master this complex process, so that they may interpret, explain, and perhaps change media and communicative practices in their current forms. Chapter 7, the final one of this volume, sums up the relationship between media and society, and elaborates on the place of media and communication research in social life.

Box 6.5 Analysis

Ten rules for conducting empirical projects

1. First, make sure to ascertain the rules and procedures in your social and cultural context and academic institution regarding a preparatory *review* of research involving human subjects.
2. Always treat the people under study as *people*. They are neither things nor texts. A standard procedure for ensuring their rights and preventing harm is informed consent.
3. Exercise *caution* and *concretion*. Be prepared to give up a question (or an entire study) if, in context, it violates the ethical, cultural, or personal limits of the people involved. Be prepared to explain in detail the relevance of any question to informants and others.

4. Practice *reflexivity*. The analysis of (conscientiously collected and concrete) data begins in the empirical field. In qualitative as well as quantitative projects, supplementary evidence and notes will support both the respectful use of respondents' contributions and the explanatory value of later interpretations.
5. Safeguard the *anonymity* of people and the *confidentiality* of information throughout the research process.
6. Be honest about the *sources of ideas* informing a study and the *contributions of peers* in developing and conducting it.
7. A research report includes accounts both of *process and outcome*, and of *successes and failures* in each respect.
8. Two key requirements of a research report are a systematic *documentation* of evidence and an explication of the bases of theoretical *inference*.
9. Explore several different *publication formats*, including a means of *feedback* to the people contributing to a study.
10. Consider *what's next* – further research, the social relevance of findings, and the possible unanticipated consequences of the research.

7   Media in society

Institutions to think with

Each of the previous chapters in this book has focused on a specific aspect of the interrelations and interchanges between media and society: Media as social institutions; media users as agents in everyday and social life; and the signs and discourses that carry communications between humans, between humans and machines, and among different kinds and degrees of media. At several points, we have highlighted how society manifests itself *inside* the media, just as their users act *in* and *on* society – increasingly through or with reference to media. The preceding chapter introduced the empirical methods that provide necessary resources for substantiating inferences and conclusions about media institutions, media texts, and media uses, as well as for motivating practical ways of organizing and politically regulating media. This final chapter returns to the big picture, summarizing some general theoretical perspectives and normative issues at the interface between media and society.

In the following sections, we first explore the relationship between media and culture: Media represent a unique institution carrying culture as a unifying force of society, but media also deliver means of reflecting on and criticizing the structure of society and the state of culture as we find them. We further elaborate on how analog as well as digital media constitute – produce – specific social relations and interactions, including so-called media events and mobile contexts. And we take stock of current media and communication environments with reference to the emerging Internet of Things (IoT). In the IoT, information and communication flow in ever more steps; people 'act' in indirect and, typically, less than explicit or conscious ways; and the IoT can – should perhaps – be understood as a fourth degree of media (on the first three degrees, see Chapter 1, p. 5).

We end the chapter and the book by considering the contributions of media and communication research to contemporary societies. Scientific research amounts to thinking, more than once, about the present, and looking ahead to the future. And when findings and insights are published, they communicate to and with the rest of society about what is the case, and what ought to be done. Media and

DOI: 10.4324/9781032655109-7

communication research examines a critical local and global infrastructure, and as such it contributes – like media institutions – to maintaining as well as transforming society.

Media and communication enable individuals to stay updated on events and issues in the world, to reflect on appropriate reactions, and to understand one's own place and role in the context of others and society as such. Commercial enterprises, political parties, and popular movements, likewise, rely on media to keep tabs on the world around them, to position themselves, and to act in social contexts. And countries and international organizations, equally, monitor the world through diverse sources and channels to inform their deliberations and decisions on behalf of larger communities. Media are **institutions to think with** at all levels of society.

Modern societies are typified, not least, by their complex, technology-enhanced media and communication infrastructures. But the use of media of different degrees 'to think with' is common to all historical periods and cultures. In his research on 'foreign' cultures, the anthropologist Claude Lévi-Strauss (1991/1962) noticed that the communities he visited and studied would frequently refer to specific things – stones, plants, or animals – as points of departure for joint reflection and deliberation on political, religious, and existential issues. Especially animals appeared to provide resources for people to address questions of who or what they are – as individuals and as groups – where they come from, and where they fit into a larger scheme of things.

Lévi-Strauss (1991/1962) described such things as **objects to think with**. In the case of animals, the point was not so much that they were 'good to eat,' but rather that they were 'good to think with' (p. 89). Beyond their physiology and biochemical makeup, certain animals could be assigned particular roles, functions, or meanings that amounted to cultural conventions with social consequences. In other societies and cultures, the exact same animals might be understood in entirely different ways. Assessments of whether animals are good to eat, equally, represent conventions. And the two kinds of conventions are commonly related: Pork, for one, is considered impure in the perspective of the world religions of Islam and Judaism.

In more mundane terms, food tells stories about the people eating it, and about the societies in which it is being eaten. Toward the end of the twentieth century, for example, turkey, which traditionally has been associated with Thanksgiving and Christmas in the United States and the United Kingdom, became popular in European countries, too, partly in light of public information campaigns suggesting that lean meat is healthy meat. During the same period, the single market of the European Union, along with wider processes of globalization, contributed to the rising popularity of wine in historically beer-drinking Northern Europe, followed by a renaissance there for beers produced by local as well as far-away microbreweries. And in response to higher beef prices after the Russian invasion of Ukraine in 2022 (Chapter 1, p. 4), some European markets experienced a growing demand for horse meat. We become the food we eat, and the media we consume – following long, interwoven processes of a physical, mental, and cultural nature.

Compared to 'objects to think with,' media depend on technological resources, economic markets, and complex organizations before they can be used to think with (see further Chapter 3). And media are **programmable**, also when it comes to non-digital media. Books can deliver either fiction or fact; television institutions broadcast and stream classic films as well as the latest reality series. Whereas animals, plants, and stones lend themselves to variable degrees of modification, so that they become media carrying meaning, the potential range and scope of expression and, hence, their information value, are normally limited.

These bounds to the depth and breadth of communication were broken, first by speech and subsequently by a historical sequence of technologies, with revolutionary consequences for culture and society. Animals, plants, and stones are different *kinds* of objects than humans, analog, and digital media – which, in the terminology of this book, constitute different *degrees* of media. News media, feature films, and social media all afford highly differentiated and

Image 7.1 Libraries and media. Photo by Calvin Uy on Unsplash.

Throughout history, societies have developed diverse institutions for preserving knowledge about the past, and communicating about this knowledge, so that citizens may think about the present and plan for the future. In addition to 'media' as commonly understood, classic instances are libraries, archives, museums, schools, and universities. Today, libraries are, at once, places where people read and check out books, and digital hubs enhancing the uses of printed materials through access to online archives and communication services.

specialized registers of expression, content, and use: They are institutions to think with, which enable both reflections *of* society in text, image, and sound, and reflections *on* society by their users. And when media reflect, and reflect on, selected events in society in particularly elaborate ways, they give rise to 'media events'.

Box 7.1 Analysis

Media events

Some contemporary events are commonly referred to as 'media events.' The term typically suggests something less than authentic, that is, events created either by the media themselves or by people seeking to attract attention from the media. That sort of skepticism concerning media as witnesses to important events in the world, motivated the first substantial analysis of media events: a 1961 book by Daniel Boorstin (1961), who referred to them as **pseudo events**. According to Boorstin, pseudo events follow from pressures on people to create an **image** for themselves if they are to attract attention or gain a voice in a public sphere hosting ever more voices and offers of information and entertainment.

Other scholars have countered such positions, holding instead that media events are not symptoms of either cultural or political decline that is the media's 'fault.' One early study suggesting an alternative position examined the return to the United States from Korea of the war hero General Douglas MacArthur, during the Korean War (1950–1953) (Lang & Lang, 1953). A key argument, for this and several other studies, has been that, in many cases, media are necessary conditions for events to come to the attention of the general public, or even a substantial group of people. In other words, the medium is not an irrelevant addition distorting the event 'as such'; on the contrary, media and communication are conditions of existence for events involving more than a few people within sight and hearing range. In a certain sense, then, all significant events in society and the world *are* media events.

This last understanding – that media are constitutive elements of important events, and that media events are relevant contributions to social life – was elaborated by Daniel Dayan and Elihu Katz (1992). Their studies focused on the coverage of momentous events that bring together an entire country or even the whole world. According to their classic definition, media events have four distinctive features: They interrupt daily routines, they represent preplanned activities, media will cover these activities in live transmissions, and the media events perform social ceremonies or rituals (see Chapter 1, p. 4), which convene a public around an event (Image 7.2). This definition led the authors to identify three categories of media events:

Image 7.2 Public reaction after the death of Queen Elizabeth II, 2022. Anthony Kwan / Stringer/ Getty Images.

The death of the British princess Diana in a car crash in 1997, became a media event (belonging to Dayan and Katz's (1992) category of Coronations). And the event has had a long afterlife: Many people alive today still remember the incident, and it is regularly referred to in media and recycled, for instance, in the television series The Crown *(Peter Morgan, 2016–2023) as a personalized, emotionalized anchoring of the longer story of a monarchy and a nation. The 1997 event unfolded in the media, but it also generated great public empathy and engagement across borders, virtually via websites (before the coming of smartphones and apps) and physically through flowers and candles at Buckingham Palace in London and at British embassies around the world. And when Queen Elizabeth II's passing in 2022, once again, produced seas of flowers, at Buckingham Palace and elsewhere, the event invited comparison – and renewed criticism of the fact that, after Diana's passing in 1997, it took several days for the Queen to return from Scotland to London, to visit the flower memorials, and to address the nation on television. (On intertextuality, see further Chapter 2, p. 43.)*

- *Conquests* (achievements pushing boundaries, for instance, the first human landing on the Moon in 1969)
- *Contests* (competitions such as the Olympic Games, but also television hearings investigating political scandals)

- *Coronations* (literal coronations of kings and queens as well as state funerals, but also cultural events such as the Academy Awards show in Hollywood).

It is, of course, debatable whether the three categories really capture the decisive interactions between the media and the various events that could be said to mark important developments in society. For one thing, the three categories reflect the authors' primary ambition of analyzing cross-cultural or universal phenomena. As a result, the categories are less sensitive to the diverse structural and cultural circumstances of media and their representations of the world in different countries and regions of the globe. For another thing, the three categories de-emphasize events that may be less spectacular, but which over time carry crucial consequences – from pivotal compromises in national and international politics, to dubious investments in the financial sector of the kind which, in 2008, elicited the worst world economic crisis since 1929.

Nevertheless, Dayan and Katz's (1992) studies reaffirmed the important point that, for the most part, the media themselves do not 'invent' events. And political spin doctors and commercial campaigns, after all, only exert so much influence on media agendas. Instead, media and communication environments represent a shared social condition. We should ask, not how political, economic, or cultural events might unfold if there were *no* media, but how *specific* media contribute to the representation and circulation of events in society, including those that are not public ceremonies. Media exist *in* society; they shape and are shaped *by* society.

The very idea of 'media events' has been changing along with media and societies (for overview, see Ytreberg, 2022). In a study following up on the classic volume (Dayan & Katz, 1992), one of the authors concluded that a different category of media events – disasters, wars, and terrorism – had come to increasingly divide rather than unite societies (Katz & Liebes, 2007) (see further Mitu & Poulakidakos, 2016; Skey, 2021; Sonnevend, 2018). While such events may interfere with daily routines, they are rarely planned, nor are they typically covered live, and they do not join people in meaningful rituals. The shift may be explained by a growing number of conflicts at national and international levels; or by more extensive as well as intensive media coverage of conflicts; or, most likely, a combination of these developments across media and society.

A final point is that, because of the changing place of media in social infrastructures, media events are not what they used to be. With a greatly enhanced supply of media and communication services and 24/7 availability directed at increasingly specialized audiences, it has become less attractive for media to allocate substantial resources to the coverage of a relatively small number of events for everybody – with major sporting events as one exception. Media still contribute to people holding opinions *about* particular things (agenda-setting), and *how* these opinions are articulated (framing) (see further Chapter 5, p. 135). But in media and communication environments where both media producers and media users are "always on" together (Baron, 2008), the occasional drip of media events is being replaced by continuous flows of information and communication.

Box 7.2 Exercise

Media events

Media events come in many different shapes and forms – parliamentary elections, Mars landings, Tour de France competitions, natural disasters such as floods, social disasters such as migrants drowning in the Mediterranean, and more. Choose three examples of 'media events' from recent years, including one centered in your country of residence and another of a global nature. Describe each event and its connection to media with reference to the following aspects:

- Do the events belong, in whole or in part, to the three categories stipulated by Dayan and Katz (p. 197)? If not, do some of the other factors mentioned in the previous section on media events help to account for the coverage of the event?
- To what extent did media coverage of one or more of the events you selected qualify as a 'pseudo-event'?
- In which respects did the event lead to personal reflection and/or public deliberation of the kind referred to as time-out culture (p. 199), and in what ways did reflection and deliberation feed back into time-in culture?

Time-in culture and time-out culture

Chapter 1 briefly noted how communication, slowly but surely, accumulates as culture, and how the cultures accumulated, next, deliver backgrounds to and frames for ever more communication – about the past, the present, and the future. Throughout the intervening chapters, we have approached culture as meaning or, to be precise, *meanings* in the plural, which are produced, negotiated, and circulated through all of the media available at a given historical time. Culture lends coherence to society, its many institutions, and its diverse practices. And culture brings together the inhabitants, members, or citizens of communities and countries, at least as common frames of understanding enabling further communication. But culture is, simultaneously, a site of struggle: Chapter 2 referred to the divide between high culture and popular culture, which the modern mass media have, variously, disseminated and debated. We are now in a position to further specify that divide, and next to bridge the divide with reference to a set of theoretical concepts that facilitate more nuanced analyses of communication as it produces and maintains culture in variable forms.

Media are, today, self-evident sources of meaning and culture. Culture resides in media texts, in the minds of their users, and throughout society whenever meaningful exchanges take place. The three-way interaction of texts, users, and societies has motivated many theories and much debate concerning the very idea of culture. As mentioned in Chapter 2, it remains a common viewpoint that media and communication are not part of culture, even the opposite of culture: banal entertainments in contrast to sophisticated arts. Already during the 1950s, an overview of scholarship had identified 164 different definitions of culture (Kroeber & Kluckhohn, 1952); a comparable review of the concept of communication later noted 249 definitions (Anderson, 1996), a good number of these overlapping with the concept of culture.

And yet, two primary concepts of culture inform both research and public debate. Culture can be understood, first, as **representations** of reality, typified by literature, arts, and other high-cultural forms of expression, and emphasizing aesthetic considerations. The premise is that artworks contain privileged insight into the human condition, its challenges and rewards. Here, culture centers on the beautiful as well as the true and the good – a famous formulation from 1869 by the English cultural critic Matthew Arnold noted that culture is "the best that has been thought and said in the world."

The second concept of culture includes all forms of human expression and social interaction, incorporating everyday doings and beings, as well – **practice**. A later English (actually, Welsh) cultural theorist, Raymond Williams (1975/1958), defined culture as "a whole way of life" (p. 18). Emphasizing the interrelation of culture with everyday practical matters, Williams insisted that all classes or segments of society have culture. One implication was that popular culture and media of all kinds (and degrees) belong in the large tent of culture, and within the study of culture, too. Another implication was that non-Western cultures are to be recognized and researched along similar lines, in principle if not always in practice. Scholars, accordingly, should study both 'foreign' cultures and their 'own' cultures as complex wholes, interwoven with the rest of society, and through multiple methods beyond aesthetic studies of texts and artworks.

In research as in public debate, the two concepts of culture are still often pitted against each other, suggesting absolute boundaries between aesthetic scholarship and social science, and leading to heated debates over the status and relevance of elite and popular culture. The two positions bear witness to distinctive and, frequently, deeply held sympathies of a scientific, political, and personal nature. But dialogue between the positions, about culture as it is practiced in and around media of all kinds and degrees, is still possible. Chapter 1 referred to media and communications as, at once, aesthetically articulated **products** and **processes**

Image 7.3 Time-out – in sports and in media. Rawpixel.com/ Shutterstock.

Sports – in stadiums, arenas, and media – allow humans to live out and live through basic emotions related to winning and losing, conflict and community. In some sports such as rugby, a time-out provides a time to think, during which players and coaches together consider next steps within the time-in of the game. Media, similarly, offer their users opportunities to reflect – on their own identities, their relations with others, and on society at large – before moving on with other everyday games.

unfolding in social contexts (p. 3). That duality – rather than dualism – is captured by two complementary conceptions of culture.

The duality of culture can be illustrated through an analogy from the world of sports. Basketball and (American) football, for instance, feature what is known as a **time-out** (Image 7.3). When coaches wish to confer on tactics with their teams, they request a time-out, which pauses the game for a short while. Once the break is over, the **time-in** of the game resumes. But, even while it temporarily suspends the game, enabling reflection and conversation, the time-out occurs *within* – and it addresses – the time-in of the game. The two times, and the associated social and mental spaces, are inextricable parts of the game as a whole. Similarly, the media (and other cultural institutions such as theaters and museums) may serve as a time-out from everyday obligations and concerns. But media use still unfolds within the time-in of everyday life; the contents and uses of media revolve around events

Time-in		Time-out
Integrated meaning production	← →	Separate meaning production
Social routine	← →	Creative construction
The ordinary	← →	The extraordinary
Resource	← →	Account
Action	← →	Representation

Figure 7.1 Dimensions of time-in and time-out culture.

and topics arising from society and the world. Following moments of reflection in interaction with media, their users are ready, so to speak, to reenter the games and struggles of personal and social existence.

It should be underlined that time-out culture and time-in culture do *not* represent separate practices, discourses, or institutions in society. Time-out culture is embedded within time-in culture. The experience of media is framed and anticipated by everyday experience; media contents and uses refer back to everyday concerns. Time-in culture does not equal an exclusive or narrow orientation toward practical purposes; time-out culture does not entail entirely abstract considerations of what could, in principle, be said and done. And the integration of digital media and communication into the pores of everyday life is resulting in a further blurring of the time-out and time-in aspects of culture.

For analytical purposes, however, it is helpful to distinguish the two aspects of culture on several dimensions. Figure 7.1 lays out five key dimensions. The arrows highlight the premise that the dimensions refer to scales or degrees, rather than mutually exclusive concepts and phenomena.

Culture may be more or less **integrated** or **separate** as it informs and orients media users' various other activities and engagements. Culture, accordingly, may be part of a set **routine** or a more **creative** expression, perhaps an innovative solution to a familiar problem, prompted by media use. The meaning being produced in and through media use, accordingly, may be experienced as relatively **ordinary** or **extraordinary**, compared to the media users' assumptions and expectations. Depending on the purpose of media use and the specific meaning being produced, culture may thus provide either **resources** – information with concrete use value, for example, the date of a parliamentary election – or **accounts** such as news, opinion, and debate regarding the platforms of the political parties running in an election, which subsequently may lead into personal reflections and communications with others. Lastly, culture-as-resource will commonly be associated by users with particular types of **actions** – voting, debating, working for a political party – whereas culture-as-account offers **representations**, affording access to (actual or imagined) universes: news from parliament or the next episode of the television series *Borgen* set in a parliament (see further Chapter 2, p. 45).

Chapter 2 examined the signs and texts that are the discursive vehicles of communication. When signs and texts are combined and accumulated in pro-liferating configurations, they emerge as culture: The whole is more than the sum of the parts. And, beginning with handwriting, the cultural whole has been fixated through historically shifting media: Each medium has been instrumental in circumscribing societies and inscribing cultures. By retracing signs and texts throughout diverse communicative processes, we are now ready, in the next section, first to sum up the place of media in contemporary cultures and societies, and next to begin addressing and assessing what that place could and ought to be in the future. Most people already take for granted that media have become mobile, so that we may communicate with others anywhere and anytime. With the Internet of Things (IoT), "things" have started communicating in unprece-dented ways.

Signs and texts in society

Chapter 2 covered the texts that are the vehicles of communication and, hence, of culture; subsequent chapters have elaborated on the place of media users and media institutions in processes of communication and, hence, in society. The following sections specify the interrelations between the texts, the communicative processes, and society as a whole. Texts circulate *through* media and *in* society. Signs, texts, and communications contribute to the ongoing production and maintenance of society.

From signs and discourses to hypertexts and media environments

- *Discourses and discursive elements.* All communication consists in discourses – social uses of signs in contexts. A single sign or discursive element – the heading of an advertisement or the anchor's choice of words as she introduces a news story – may determine *how* the rest of that advertisement or news story is understood and, perhaps, translated into action. And the context of such min-imal components of communication may decide *whether* the information in question is understood in the first place and remembered at a later point in time. Experimental studies have suggested that Facebook updates are recalled more easily than comparable sentences in books, presumably because the personal nature of many contacts and interactions in the Facebook setting heightens users' attention to the information on offer (Mickes et al., 2013).
- *Single texts.* Compared to aesthetic analyses of novels or paintings, studies of (mass) media texts have typically emphasized general or recurring elem-ents and features. The premise has been that these texts follow standardized formats as delivered by Hollywood and other 'dream factories.' But, in some instances, a particular media content – a single text – acquires a special stature in a culture or society along the lines of unique artworks. Chapter 6 referred to

the 1938 radio broadcast that frightened (some) listeners in American cities (p. 187). Additional examples of distinctive single texts include television series blazing new trails, such as *Dallas* and *Dynasty* (Gripsrud, 1995); reality television shows like the *Big Brother* and *Got Talent* shows in several countries (Hill, 2005); viral video such as *Chocolate Rain* and *Keyboard Cat* (Burgess, 2008); and memes exemplified by *Success Kid* (2007) and *Barbenheimer* (2023).

- *Genres*. Chapter 2 drew attention to genre as an important level of analysis regarding the interplay of media and society: Genres carry, at once, the communicative forms and the social functions of communication. On the one hand, media production and media use constitute social actions that, through the distinctive features of genres, relate media texts to meaningful aspects of social life and human existence. When watching, respectively, sports, news, and a new fiction series on television, people participate in culture and society, but in very different ways – which producers have anticipated and articulated. Genres entail informal contracts between senders and receivers. On the other hand, media use may invite further social actions – physical exercise, political involvement, or debate on where one's national culture is heading. Genres are modes of address: They invite and promote specific types of individual reflection and interaction with others.

- *Media*. The premise of this book is that media have three aspects (Chapter 1, p. 9): Media are material technologies; they carry discursive forms of expression and interaction; and they make up social institutions. Media technologies enable the distribution of – and communication about – new as well as old information, fact and fiction, increasingly across time and space. Consequently, media have become ever more central social institutions – which leads economic, political, and cultural agents to (try to) influence the organization and operation of these institutions in accordance with their own interests, in both the short and the long term. Nevertheless, each medium holds specific and delimited affordances (Chapter 3, p. 64), even as media are adapted over time to ongoing social developments.

- *Flow*. Electronic media – radio and television – introduced a distinctive set of affordances that differed in fundamental ways from the forms of communication and culture that had remained dominant for centuries. The cultural theorist Raymond Williams (1974) summed up these affordances in the concept of flow, with special reference to the media landscape of the United States. His point was that – rather than presenting finished works or texts, each representing a particular genre – electronic media delivered continuous flows or streams of content, normally comprising multiple genres, including, not least, advertising at regular intervals. And flows are planned and managed according to carefully devised strategies. Traditionally, commercial radio and television stations have put a premium on retaining their viewers and listeners, each in *their* flow, for as long as possible, minimally until the next commercial break: The flow must go on. And public service channels have followed suit because they compete for the same audience in the same marketplace for the same attention. Of course, users may choose to change the channel and buy into the flows of other channels. (The next section returns to the different perspectives of senders and receivers on flows, and to the continued relevance of the concept of flow in digital media and communication environments.)

- *Hypertexts.* Hypertexts amount to collections and configurations of texts that are related through hyperlinks, internally among words, sentences, images, paragraphs, and sections, externally with further texts. Indeed, the basic principle of digital communication systems is **hypertextuality**, which can be thought of as programmed, automated **intertextuality** (Chapter 2, p. 43): Users do not have to establish the connections between the texts in their own minds – a click on a text leads to another text. The standard example is the World Wide Web, which represents the largest hypertext in the world. Compared to the flows of radio and television, hypertexts provide many more opportunities for users to select and combine diverse items of information in sequence, and fast, too. Hypertexts, moreover, offer users readily accessible means of producing and distributing their own information. Although the basic idea of hypertexts was familiar from written and printed media (Bolter, 1991), in the form of tables of contents, notes, and indexes, digital technologies have integrated signs and texts into networks, with many more options of further extending, revising, and updating hypertexts.

- *Media environments.* In a final analytical step, the set of media that is available in a particular social setting at a particular historical time, can be understood as a media and communication environment – a cultural environment analogous to the natural environment of living conditions for human and other species. Virtual worlds of signs and texts, similarly, enable and constrain what humans can be and do, as individuals and collectives, in a present and future perspective: Communication and culture are sources of visions and alternatives. Here and now, older forms of communication and culture can teach us lessons, as we navigate changing media environments – as media users and as students and scholars. To begin to conceptualize and analyze digital and mobile media, and the emerging IoT, it is helpful to start from two antecedents: printed works and electronic flows.

From flowing to surfing to swiping...

Traditional television and radio, then, differ from print communication and culture insofar as they present continuous streams of messages – flows (Williams, 1974). Compared to reading a newspaper over breakfast or spending Sunday afternoon on the couch reading a novel, watching television toward the end of the twentieth century – when Williams was writing about flow – was an activity typically covering multiple programs: People could be said to watch 'television,' not this or that single 'program.' And as more satellite and cable channels were added, the activity could go on: The flow never stopped.

Williams (1974), however, missed a small, significant detail when he devised the concept of flow to better comprehend (American) television (and radio). Three different categories of flow are at work in broadcasting (Jensen, 1994):

- *Channel flows*. The broadcasts of individual channels or stations present continuous streams. Importantly, these streams include both commercial breaks and preannouncements for upcoming programs, logos, and other elements filling in the 'blanks' between the 'real' programs. In an economic sense, the programs provide 'bait' designed to keep viewers and listeners hooked until the next commercial break (Chapter 3, p. 74).
- *Super flows*. All channel flows in a particular geographical area or 'market,' together, make up a wider universe of programming and content. Within that universe, channels will compete for viewers (and listeners), who are at liberty to pick and choose and change the channels.
- *Viewer flows*. Viewer flows, finally, are the outcomes of the various choices and changes that particular users or households perform within a given time period. Over time, viewer flows represent communication patterns – diets of users' pickings from media menus.

Figure 7.2 lays out the interrelations between the three categories of flow. The figure highlights the dynamic of traditional television viewing (and radio listening), which is still a common cultural practice in most of the world. As far as the channels are concerned, their aim in life is to build and maintain large audiences over time (and through the commercial breaks in the flows), competing with other channels for the users' time and attention. In the users' perspective, the various channel flows present a range of options, within a relatively fixed and familiar structure. In sum, super flows represent a range of potential experiences and insights, as subsets of wider media and communication environments.

Along with the digitalization of media environments, flow television (and flow radio) are being transformed, as well. Increasingly, users are in a position to choose, both *when* they access particular programs, and *how* they access them – identical programs are available through mobile and stationary sets and devices. And yet, the concept of flow(s) still provides a useful analytical category when it comes to accounting for the interrelations of media, users, and contexts in digital media and communication environments.

First of all, streaming services such as Netflix have established a different kind of channel flow by different means, via functionalities such as autoplay between the episodes of a series, recommendations for other titles ('Because you watched Film A, you may also like Film B'), and 'popular' or 'Top 10' categories on the starting page. In this way, users may feel well served, so well that they will keep on paying for their subscription (or keep on watching, in one of the 12 countries where Netflix Basic with Ads was introduced in 2022).

Second, there are, in fact, basic similarities between broadcast flows and digital flows. Where the users of television and radio used to go with the flow, from program to program, the internet (at first, the World Wide Web) introduced

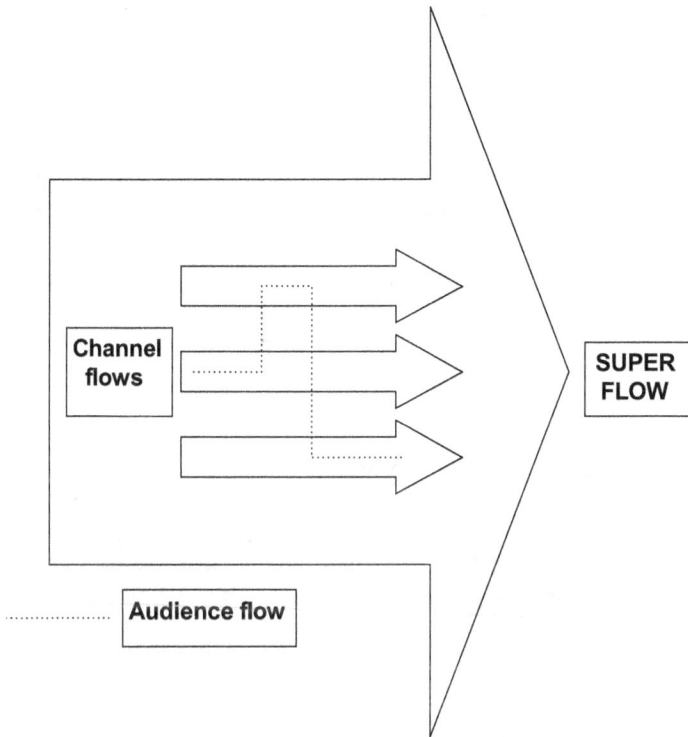

Figure 7.2 Three flows of media use.

the possibility of 'surfing' between a dramatically increased number of 'channels' or websites, with many additional subsites. And, through the windows interfaces that became standard, users gained access to multiple websites, simultaneously or instantaneously with a click. In a further step, the mobile interfaces of smartphones direct users toward and into apps, which can be changed by 'swiping.'

In all three instances – radio-television, web, and mobile communication – comparable sets of structures and functions can be summarized in three generic categories of flow:

• *Information flows*. Television and radio channels, web pages, and apps all offer streams of information, which someone – 'the media' and many other institutions and organizations in society – makes available and accessible, and which users (perhaps) spend time and attention on. The information on offer likely generates more communication, online and offline, one-to-one and many-to-many. And both the information on offer and the subsequent communications point toward other actions, by individuals as well as groups, in small and large matters.

- *User flows*. The users of digital communication systems, then, are much more than recipients of information flows – they participate in communication and act in society. They act, in and of their media use here and now, as well as at later times in other private and public contexts. It is communication that joins all these social contexts across time and space – contexts that, importantly, may be either imagined or material. Chapter 2 emphasized how 'contexts' are *both* texts carrying discursive meaning *and* actual locations in society. And mobile media and communication have made it necessary to develop one more concept of flow to capture mobile contexts – context flows.
- *Context flows*. In common parlance, 'contexts' refer to places where people do certain things – carry out their jobs, go to school, hold parties, visit family, and much else. People move between contexts. But contexts move, too: In the living room, on the train, or in the street – smartphone in hand – we establish contact both with others and with contexts in which communication may unfold (Kakihara & Sørensen, 2002). In mundane interactions, people will make a preliminary arrangement to meet up in *about* this place to go out at *about* this time. In public matters, mobile media have afforded new resources for organizing demonstrations and other political and cultural manifestations (Jenkins, 2006; Rheingold, 2002): Through mobile communications, the participants can regroup, and those who stayed at home so far, can be mobilized to join the rest of the street in action.

Box 7.3 Analysis

What's mobile about mobile communication?

The terminology of 'mobile media' and 'mobile communication' might suggest that earlier variants of media and communication were not mobile. But that is not the case. Instead, we should ask what, indeed, **mobility** entails as it applies to various media: What and who is on the move in (mobile) communication (Jensen, 2013)?

Until the introduction of the telegraph in the nineteenth century, and of radio and television in the twentieth century, communication and physical transportation were inseparable (Carey, 1989a: 15). For communication to occur across time and space, something literally had to move (or be moved): Human beings, manuscripts, printed books, magazines, newspapers. In the long evolutionary and historical perspectives of human communication, media of the first degree – humans, with or without manuscripts and similar materials in their baggage – had been mobile for millennia. In a much shorter, but still quite long perspective, print media had been mobile for centuries: Knowledge, news, and entertainments had been distributed over borders and across continents, at first to tiny elites, later to large publics. And for decades, image and sound have circulated around the world, asynchronously in the case of film exhibition and music recorded on discs and tapes,

---

synchronously through television and radio, at first broadcast over the air and, with time, through cable and satellite systems, too.

What is new about 'mobile communication' can be spelled out by distinguishing three kinds of mobility (Kakihara & Sørensen, 2002):

- *Spatial mobility*. Humans move about in and across spaces; so does this book (in its print version), when it is carried between homes, libraries, and educational institutions. Mobile phones have developed into personal lines of connection between the many private and public spaces of everyday life and reality as such – which is why most people will do their utmost to never leave behind their phone in one of these spaces.
- *Temporal mobility*. Time, similarly, is movable or flexible in the context of communication: People can choose between an asynchronous text message or a synchronous voice call to partners and grandmothers, depending on purpose and context. Many people can contact their family doctor by email – but if it is urgent, people will dial 911 or the national equivalent. And, of course, several such activities can be coordinated *simultaneously* through mobile phones.
- *Contextual mobility*. Lastly, entire contexts became mobile with the introduction of contemporary mobile media: Mobile communication establishes contexts in which we can act at a distance – order commodities online, but also make or change appointments for meetings and other obligations to occur in physical space. Mobile contexts come and go.

The concept of contextual mobility, in particular, serves to clarify the distinctive affordances of mobile media. Both mobile devices and their users are, evidently, mobile in space. And mobile communication has lent new degrees of flexibility to people administering their time on the job, at home, and in other contexts. But it is the contact between and among *both* sets of users *and* sets of information, crisscrossing time and space, which makes mobile communication a historically unique category of interaction. Mobile communication produces and transports contexts around society. One context leads on to another context – as part of ongoing communications and other social interactions in three and more steps. In this way, mobile media and communication are making a new kind of contribution to the ongoing structuration of society across both space and time (see further Chapter 4, p. 97).

...to feedback and into surveillance

The interplay between the innumerable small signs of communication and the structure of society is a continuous and contingent process. The digitalization of media and societies has added a new category of signs to the domains being studied by media and communication research. Chapter 2 introduced the concept of metacommunication through metadata (p. 54), and Chapter 5 elaborated how users thus deliver **feedback** into the system, mostly without an awareness or any detailed knowledge of what later happens to *their* signs and texts (Figure 5.3, p. 154).

Feedback is commonly taken as a positive term: In schools and universities, students are given feedback on their assignment so that they may improve their knowledge and skills; as part of political governance, public hearings provide citizens and communities with opportunities to provide feedback that may qualify legislation or social planning in progress. But feedback can be also be turned against its sources. Research and public debate on surveillance via the internet, which have both grown significantly since the 2010s (Zuboff, 2019), have identified a whole range of challenges and risks that follow from the processing and recycling of users' many-to-one communication into the system. Beyond criminal hacking and classic espionage, the very collection and analysis of data and metadata within interlinked systems present profound ethical and political issues: **Media systems** are embedded in more comprehensive **communication systems** with potentials for commercial as well as governmental abuse (see further Chapter 3, p. 91). In fact, the embedding of ever more aspects of social life and reality writ large into communication systems suggests the coming of a fourth degree of media.

Box 7.4 Analysis

Giving data – and gaining a stake in data

European legislation concerning personal data (the General Data Protection regulation, GDPR, from 2018) empowers all citizens of the European Union to request downloading the data that digital platforms and similar entities collect about them (Araujo et al., 2022; Boeschoten et al., 2022). This regulation allows users to gain insight into the digital traces they leave behind. But users may choose, in addition, to donate their data to research, notably for studies looking into and beyond the analytical practices of commercial companies, thus contributing to more nuanced and rich understandings of human actions and social interactions in digitalized societies.

Such **data donations** started out as activists' attempt at documenting the strategies of big tech players, for instance, the advertising associated with Google search results and the algorithmically generated recommendations for things to attend to on Facebook (Ben-David, 2020). A variety of research projects have examined additional players and platforms. For instance, data donations from iPhone users, in the form of screenshots of the function registering their screen time, have been employed in studies of mobile and app use (Ohme & Araujo, 2022). The relationship between social media use and mental health has been explored through data donations from Instagram users (Driel et al., 2022). And further screenshots of smartphone screens have served to document the extent to which advertisers and other so-called third parties get access to personal user data through apps (Lai & Flensburg, 2020).

Like other empirical methods, data donations present ethical issues and a need to establish best practices. In developing software for data donation (Boeschoten et al., 2022), advocates of this strategy have pointed to three main principles. First, as always, research must safeguard the data donor's identity and privacy. The recommendation, therefore, is that data donors themselves download their data and, in the process, decide what (not) to donate. Second, as a general rule, studies should minimize the amount of data collected, hence minimizing the risk of abuse. And third, again as a standard practice, the recipients of data donations should secure informed consent from participants (Ohme & Araujo, 2022). One further way of recognizing and appreciating the participants' contribution, is to inquire what needs the project in question might serve for them, for example, by demonstrating how their data are being used by digital communication systems, and helping them decipher the data that they had downloaded for the study in question (Prainsack, 2019).

At the time of writing, data donations deliver empirical materials that are not just interesting and valuable, but necessary constituents of research on digital media and communication. The relevant data are, to a large extent, unavailable to independent researchers because of their commercial value: They remain hidden in black-boxed communication systems and walled-garden business models.

In a wider political perspective, the question is who owns the data that users produce, alone and together. The immediate answer is straightforward: Data are owned by platforms and other digital enterprises, because users signed up for this arrangement (that is, they clicked to accept the Terms of Service). But the European Union, for one, has passed legislation reinstating users' right to their own data. There are, moreover, initiatives emerging in different regions of the world that propose to organize the collection and monetization of user data in alternative institutional structures. Such initiatives recall the cooperative principle, familiar in some countries from farming and the bulk buying of household goods at a discount to be shared by the community. A unique feature of data – compared to physical goods – is that they are non-rivalrous and can be (re)used over and over again in new constellations. In this way, donating and sharing them does not consume them. In collaboration with other users and donors, people may make money on their own data, while at the same time passing along these same data to researchers at no expense to either party.

Media of the fourth degree

Digital media of the third degree bring together all previously known media on the same technological platform. But the ongoing digitalization of society suggests further developments in which media are no longer – or not only – separate devices with interfaces providing access to information and communication with others. Information and communicative capabilities can be embedded in other objects, structures, and processes that human beings either find or make (for overview, see Bunz & Meikle, 2018; Greenfield, 2006; Gunkel, 2020). Although the terminology in the area is not entirely settled yet, two terms in the English language bring out the key points: Media of the fourth degree may become both ubiquitous (present everywhere) and pervasive (present in everything, literally every thing).

The originator of the terminology of ubiquitous computing (or ubicomp), Mark Weiser (1991), described the technology and practice by way of a contrast to virtual reality (VR), where users – through goggles, gloves, and other interface components – experience entering a different world. VR offers, so to speak, the whole **world in a medium**. Ubicomp, in comparison, approaches the whole **world as a medium**. The whole world is (to an extent) programmable through the right, pervasive deployment of sensors, processors, and minimal interfaces, which communicate information from "things" to digital machines and their human users. This is the basic idea behind the prospective IoT. Visions for the future also include hardware that operates not on silicon chips, but at the level of atoms (Munakata, 2007), and on interfaces fitted to users' skin, so-called on-skin computing (Steimle, 2022).

So far, the IoT has lent itself to a range of practical applications as part of public and private infrastructures. At a macrosocial level, public agencies are able to monitor traffic on roads and railroads to avoid accidents and backed-up lines of cars and passengers. In industrial production, the IoT facilitates the control of production lines, from the delivery of raw materials to the shipping of finished goods. And while private consumers are still at work or in school, they can turn on their washers and dryers, perhaps when electricity is cheap, as registered through apps, so that their clothes will be ready to pass from washer to dryer, or to be folded, when they return home – perhaps following an adjustment of sounds and lights in the household via personal digital assistants such as Alexa and Siri.

An enhanced internet has already arrived with the latest generation of **artificial intelligence**, specifically the so-called large language models (LLMs) exemplified by ChatGPT (2022), which are trained on large sets of digital data and metadata, and serve as "assistants" for humans to talk to before they make up their minds and go on to act on many different things. Likely to be embedded into things digital as well as non-digital, LLMs can change search and navigation of the World Wide Web; the production of film, television, and other media contents; and text processing programs for writing books such as this (for overview, see Guzman et al., 2023).

In all of the instances mentioned so far, the 'things' of a wider IoT are cultural or human-made. In subsequent stages, 'things' may come to include natural objects, structures, and processes at physical, chemical, or biological levels of reality: Through the IoT, these constituents of reality are rendered as information flows, and once they intersect with user flows, they generate context flows. And, when these flows are registered and documented, surveillance is taken to a new

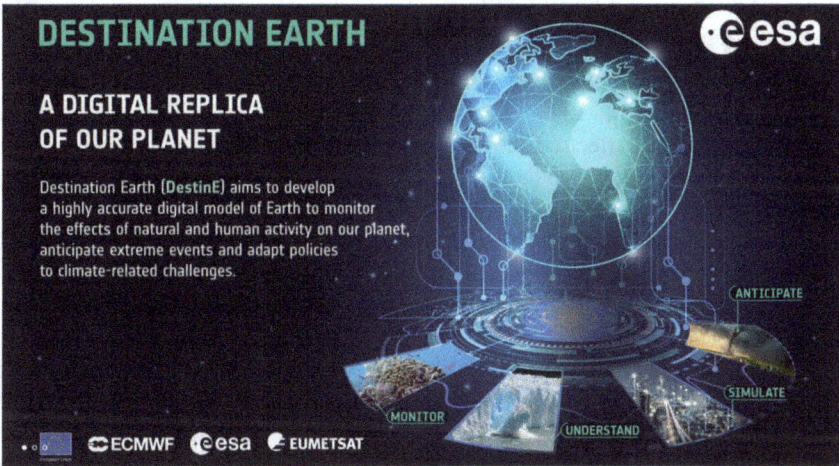

Image 7.4 Media in nature. Courtesy of the European Space Agency – ESA, 2024.

The Internet of Things (IoT) already connects things that are human-made: Through the IoT, and at a distance, people can program, turn on, and turn off household appliances and industrial production lines. Parts of our natural environment, as well, can be designed as media with sensors, processors, and inputs and outputs of information. Destination Earth (DE) is an initiative of the European Union where the aim is to produce highly detailed representations of Earth in its entirety, in order to monitor how natural processes as well as human activities affect the climate and the environment. DE is a so-called digital double (Savage, 2022), which relays information about the state of the planet, so that its human inhabitants, as recipients and citizens, may act accordingly.

degree, presenting heightened ethical and political dilemmas. Image 7.4 describes an experiment in extremely fine-grained documentation of humans' metabolism with nature, which conditions the livelihood of humankind in the future: Should human beings, for example, accept the registration of some or all aspects of their environmental footprints – per year, decade, or lifetime – at the level of individuals or a collective of some sort: the household, the community, the nation-state, the world region?

Media and communication research can contribute to specifying and clarifying – interpreting – these dilemmas, before we act as individuals and societies. Chapter 2 reviewed the tradition of hermeneutics: the theory and practice of interpreting texts, media, and societies (p. 30). The next section takes a further step down the path of interpretation with reference to the *double* hermeneutics that media and communication studies perform.

The double hermeneutics of media and communication research

The introduction to this chapter referred to media as 'institutions to think with.' Through media and communication, humans are in a position to reflect on ends and means, in their own lives and in the perspective of society as a whole. And, once in a while, people will reflect on the media themselves: Are they delivering reliable and relevant information? Do they support communication in public, by the public, and for the public? Do they empower users as citizens to deliberate and act in an enlightened manner? Media and communication research addresses such questions in a systematic fashion, outlining a range of potential answers. Media and communication research is an institution in society that thinks about – interprets – another institution: the media.

The term **double hermeneutics** was introduced by the British sociologist Anthony Giddens (1979: chap. 7), to characterize the social sciences and humanities – which have contributed most of the theories and analytical approaches that are employed in contemporary media and communication research. A distinctive feature of these disciplines and fields is that they interpret a reality that the people being interviewed, observed, or studied by other means, have themselves *already* interpreted. And when researchers interpret people's *own* interpretations, and later feed *their* reinterpretations back to the same people and communities, these people and communities sometimes come to understand themselves and important aspects of their social and cultural contexts differently – and sometimes they go on to act accordingly. Karl Marx, for example, reinterpreted the mechanisms underlying national and international economies, inspiring social revolution by the inhabitants of a number of countries. Sigmund Freud, in his turn, identified the existence of 'the unconscious,' which today is common background knowledge for many people in the world when they seek to interpret why (perhaps) others treat them inappropriately. Natural sciences, in a sense, also interpret nature, but their interpretations do not change the makeup and mechanisms of nature, its plants, and its animals.

Media and communication research, thus, interprets the interpretations that media have of the world, and the interpretations that media users have of the media as well as of the world. The raw material of studies is always already interpretations. And the output, equally, consists in interpretations – of how media institutions and communicative practices work, but also how they *could*, and perhaps *ought* to, work. Here, a hermeneutics of suspicion (Chapter 2, p. 31) is applied not only to texts, but to entire media and societies. Giddens (1979) himself emphasized how an important potential of double hermeneutics is challenging established interpretations and endorsements of existing social institutions, practices, and discourses.

Media and communication research offers interpretations and reinterpretations of the operation of media and communication in the context of society and the world. Findings and insights are communicated back to society in scientific journal articles and academic books, but also through consultancies, government reports, white papers, and press coverage. And because media are more or less constantly in the public eye, studies regularly attract (positive and negative) attention from other social institutions and stakeholders: businesses, political interest groups, cultural institutions, and others. Evidence and conclusions represent resources, both for administering media as they currently operate, and as input to critiques and proposals for reform. In all of these respects, media and communication research participates in a double hermeneutics regarding media and communication systems, in the borderlands of science and politics, and of theory and practice.

Box 7.5 Theory

Five types of theory

There is reason to challenge the commonly accepted divide between theory and practice – between abstract and, sometimes, far-fetched reflections on the nature and potential of human communication, and the business at hand concerning the media that be. As the statement quoted in Chapter 1 from one of the founders of media and communication research in the United States, Kurt Lewin, noted: "nothing is as practical as a good theory" (Lewin, 1945: 129).

A theory can be understood as a generalized understanding of the elements and processes of (a particular segment of) reality, often with additional reference to how humans may approach and act on reality to accomplish particular ends. A further defining feature of theories is that they lend themselves to recycling. That is, they apply equally well to many different instances of the categories of objects, events, and contexts they serve to interpret or explain. When, for example, in 1936 Alan M. Turing (1965/1936) published the principles of digital computing, he presented a theory that was – and still is – valid for all computers. The theory works in practice, for laptops as well as smartphones, and whether devices are used for emailing, gaming, or dating. The proof of the theory is the fact that the computers work.

Theories are only general in certain respects, however. Turing's theory did not address, for instance, interchanges between computers in a network. And it gave no clue as to what might be the social consequences of this or that design of either digital devices or networks. Theories, then, are extremely practical, but only within the specific domains and levels of reality to which they apply. For the same reason, research projects frequently draw on multiple theories, increasingly also on approaches and insights from multiple disciplines and fields. One example is the development and maintenance of healthcare systems, which depend, in a critical and existential sense, on computer systems that can be used by healthcare professionals and patients: To design, implement, and improve these systems over time, hospitals, clinics, and public agencies must rely on the expertise of programmers and medical doctors as well as communication professionals.

The interdependencies of theory and practice can be laid out with reference to the many meanings of the term 'theory.' The media and communications field distinguishes five types of theory (McQuail & Deuze, 2020: 16–18). They bear witness both to the interdisciplinary nature of the field – incorporating elements from social sciences, humanities, and, to an extent, technical sciences – and to the origin of the field in the mundane practice of communication:

- *Scientific theory.* The reference here is to social-scientific theory, and to elements deriving from technical sciences, which together have provided conceptual frameworks for the study, not least, of media institutions and their potential effects on users.
- *Cultural theory.* Alongside social sciences, the humanities have been the other primary source of theories and methods informing media studies, focusing on their contents and forms, and on the place of media and communication in everyday life and wider cultures.
- *Normative theory.* Political and ethical considerations concerning media and communication as means of achieving important social ends, have guided a smaller substream of inquiry, conducted in parallel with theoretical and empirical investigations. However, normative issues, as also articulated in public and intellectual debate, to an extent inform and, sometimes, define broader research agendas. (See further Chapter 4, p. 107, on normative media theories.)
- *Operational theory.* Journalists and other media practitioners are guided in their daily work by explicit professional codes and implicit practical rules of thumb. Both varieties of operational theory are, to an extent, informed by normative and scientific theory.
- *Everyday theory.* Lastly, media users, too, are guided by a variety of practical assumptions regarding the nature of media, the communications unfolding through and around media, and the interests which media and communication serve for individuals and communities. In this sense, all humans are theoreticians – even while their theories are shaped by different and unequal social circumstances and educational levels, and remain subject to continuous updating through double hermeneutics (p. 214).

Media and communication research in society

Like media and communicative practices, media and communication research is situated *in* society. Media and communication studies are signs of their times. And when researchers examine selected aspects of media and communication, both the selections and the approaches bear witness to interests, not merely in the sense that it might be interesting to learn more about these aspects, but in the more fundamental sense that all science and scholarship is driven by purposes – interests in

Image 7.5 Word cloud of *Media and Society.*

One way of representing the relationship between the various concepts that inform texts about particular social domains, are so-called word clouds, tag clouds, or wordles. Through size, color, and font, the visual representation indicates how central various concepts are, and how they relate to each other. As such, word clouds provide a quick overview of the worldview implicit, for example, in websites – or in analyses of websites. Word clouds thus express theories – web designers' operational theories or analysts' scientific theories (p. 216). This word cloud suggests the worldview of this book (Image 7.5).

knowing particular kinds of things. This premise was summarized in the concept of **knowledge interests** by Jürgen Habermas (1971), who distinguished three types:

* *Control through prediction.* Especially within natural and technical sciences, it is an essential purpose to be able to predict events in physical reality, for instance, a chemical reaction or the load-carrying capacity of a bridge. But the approach may be transferred to media and communication, for example, when opinion polls are conducted to predict the outcome of an election campaign; when a website monitors the number of visitors to document its traffic to advertisers; or when social media apply algorithms to anticipate which products, posts, or recommendations will be most relevant for targeting various user groups.

- *Contemplative understanding.* 'Contemplation' implies introverted reflection, perhaps in front of an artwork in a museum or at home with an e-book. The approach is central to humanistic studies of arts and culture as works and texts. Media, equally, give rise to contemplation: empathetic interpretation of a film or emotional release in playing a video game.
- *Emancipation through critique.* To Habermas, this is the distinctive knowledge interest of social sciences. By documenting, for instance, unequal access to the internet and other media, nationally and globally, and by identifying potential solutions to the inequalities, social science may contribute to emancipation, that is, to realizing the capabilities or potentials of individuals, groups, and societies. 'Critique,' in this context, does not necessarily entail an assertion that something is 'not good enough,' but rather suggests that 'it could be different.' As importantly, critique does not pursue researchers' personal viewpoints or convictions, but is guided by specific theoretical frameworks and analytical methodologies.

The three knowledge interests are examples of what one of the founders of the discipline of sociology, Max Weber, referred to as **ideal types**: abstract descriptions of key characteristics of distinctive forms of analysis. Accordingly, they occur in many variations and combinations in concrete studies. But an essential point is that researchers *always* hold knowledge interests, and that they should be aware of, and explicate to others, *which* knowledge interest a given study is pursuing. Habermas, further, suggested that natural-scientific or 'technical' knowledge interests have had a tendency, in the practice of research, to displace or detract from the emancipatory potential of social-scientific research. When departing from technical knowledge interests instead, studies merely seek to predict individuals' actions and social trends to make interventions such as economic policies as efficient as possible. This conflict – between critique and control – is typically rooted in different evaluations of the current state of society (and media) that are themselves in conflict: Should society be administered as it is, or should it be criticized and changed? (See further Box 7.6 on administrative and critical research, p. 221.)

As a social institution with a range of participants and purposes, media and communication research pursues multiple knowledge interests. That is reflected in the types of organizations that carry out studies and projects. Figure 7.3 lays out four main types, which differ in several respects: financing, organizational structure, time frame, and the anticipated use of findings.

In media and communication research as well as among media, a first dividing line separates commercial media from public service media (see further Chapter 4, p. 111). Second, Figure 7.3 distinguishes between the research units of private media companies and university departments. In classic university scholarship as well as in public service organizations, research-based knowledge has traditionally been considered a **public good** (Samuelson, 1954), which, similar to air and water, is (and ought to be) available to everybody. In contrast to this, knowledge can be considered a **commodity**, for instance, the findings from a pilot test (Chapter 6, p. 189) of a planned advertising campaign, which are to be kept from competitors. In this last case, the knowledge is valuable, not only because it may improve the

	Commercial company	University department	Independent research institute	Documentation center
Funding	Income from clients	Public or private funding	Commercial income and/or public funding	Commercial income and/or public funding
Organization of research activity	Management hierarchy	Autonomous researchers within (degree of) collegial government	Board of trustees and management hierarchy	Board of trustees and management hierarchy
Time frames	Days to years	Years to decades	Days to decades	Years to centuries
Anticipated uses of results	Strategic planning and product development	Description and critique of past and present media forms	Descriptive as well as proactive analyses	Description and documentation of media and communication institutions, contents, and uses
Examples	Marketing sections; Advertising agencies; Consultancies	Media studies departments; Schools of communication	Research bureaus and ad hoc centers; Thinktanks	Archives with proprietary and/or public (museum) access

Figure 7.3 Types of media and communication research organizations.

advertising campaign, but also because it remains secret to all but the company commissioning the study. Whereas research is conducted continuously by commercial as well as academic organizations, there is little question that the number of commercial projects is much greater than the number of academic projects – the exact numbers are difficult to assess, not least because the commercial sector, for competitive reasons, rarely presents its findings in public.

The research entities of public service media occupy an intermediate position because the media they serve compete with commercial media in the same marketplace of attention (Chapter 3, p. 82). More generally, media and communication research today is characterized by hybrids of financing and organizational structure. In a global perspective, university departments increasingly depend on external funding from private foundations to undertake research projects. Academic studies, moreover, are funded, in part, by commercial media, which, like public agencies, outsource analyses to universities, partly to ensure their scientific quality, partly to lend credibility and legitimacy to the findings when they are presented to policymakers and publics.

The third variety of organizations – independent research institutes – were part of international media and communication research from the outset. A famous early instance in the United States was Paul F. Lazarsfeld's Bureau of Applied Social Research, which later served as a model for comparable institutes in other countries. Beyond descriptive reports and white papers, research institutes also undertake 'proactive' projects, that is, projects preparing the premises and empirical evidence for investments in the private sector or legislation in the public sector.

The fourth and final type – documentation centers – have traditionally been associated with the collections and archives covering historical legacies and the arts, rather than with modern media and popular culture, with the exception of film, which has been serviced and promoted by film institutes in many countries. With the digitalization of media and societies, such centers have been gaining added importance, both as departments of media conglomerates and tech giants, and as private-public partnerships. In addition to archives of content in image, sound, and text, the documentation of hardware, software, and user data (employing digital methods – Chapter 6, p. 181) represents a strategic resource for product development, in-house research, and innovation generally.

A striking feature of Figure 7.3 is the very different time frames of the various organizations. Where commercial projects are typically short term (days to years), academic analyses commonly hold ambitions of producing general knowledge of lasting value (years to decades), with independent research institutes occupying an intermediate position (days to decades). Documentation centers, finally, make available and accessible resources that enable the description and interpretation of developments within communication, culture, and society across centuries.

Chapter 1 posed the question of what is the meaning of *media*. The meaning of *media and communication research* is to describe, interpret, explain, and sometimes transform the place of media and communication in society. Research seeks to fulfill this mission with primary inspiration from social-scientific and humanistic traditions, complemented by input from computer science and technical sciences. To an extent, the field is 'assigned' certain tasks by the society of which it is a part – the assignments follow from the interaction of the research institution with other social institutions. At any given time, a wide variety of local and global studies are in progress, for commercial media about media users as consumers and their uptake of advertising campaigns, and for government agencies concerning the public's awareness of road traffic safety or precautions in times of Covid-19 and other infectious diseases. And, from time to time, countries and international organizations set up commissions and large-scale projects to produce an accounting of how media currently perform in and for society, which later informs public and policy debate, as well as preparing legislation.

Media and communication research addresses and assesses the difference media make in and to society – for better or worse. Most generally, studies contribute to the administration of cultural heritages and human legacies with special reference to the media – new and old – that carry and communicate these across generations. The media interpret reality; media and communication research interprets the role of media and communication in society. Having interpreted this book, readers are in a better position to describe, interpret, explain, and, perhaps, transform the media.

Box 7.6 Theories at issue

Administrative and critical research

The distinction between **administrative** and **critical** media and communication research goes back to the origins of the field around the middle of the twentieth century (Lazarsfeld, 1941). At the time, press and radio, in addition to magazines and books, had become key components of the public sphere (Chapter 4, p. 100), just as more or less formalized and specialized communicative practices had come to serve as necessary conditions of many everyday endeavors as well as the administration of public and private organizations. These developments had generated a need for more knowledge about media and communication as institutions and practices, and for more professionally educated practitioners and scholars to attend to these social sectors. But, because the period witnessed deep-seated conflicts both *within* societies and *between* societies (the economic depression of the 1930s and the world war of the 1940s), theories and early studies *of* media and society were similarly conflicted.

Paul F. Lazarsfeld, who articulated the distinction between administrative and critical approaches in a famous article (Lazarsfeld, 1941), was among the founders of media and communication research in the United States, particularly user and effects studies (see, for instance, some of his publications cited in Chapter 5). Lazarsfeld was, moreover, an intellectual entrepreneur, who realized the potential of studying the flows of communication throughout society on behalf of (and with financing from) the media, in addition to other social institutions. To this end, he established the influential Bureau of Applied Social Research at Columbia University in New York, which, among other initiatives, hired social scientists who had fled Nazi Germany (Delia, 1987). And *their* grounding in Marxist social theory provided part of the background to Lazarsfeld's understanding of administrative and critical research.

To one side, research can be **administrative**, when it supports the development, planning, and delivery of various forms of communication, typically in commercial settings. These studies are goal oriented and designed to "solve little problems, generally of a business character" (Lazarsfeld, 1941: 8).

To the other side, **critical** research considers media in wider and longer social, cultural, and historical perspectives, often from the perspective of users and with an understanding of communication as a public good. Here, studies propose to address "the general role of our media of communication in the present social system" (p. 9).

Lazarsfeld's own position was that both forms of research are relevant and legitimate, and that they may supplement and complement one another. For example, critical research might identify issues and articulate concepts in ways that more instrumental, administrative studies do not allow for. But subsequent scholarship and publications have frequently painted the two approaches as contrasts and in conflict, in line with the social theories that the German refugee scholars had imported to the United States as representatives of the so-called **Frankfurt School**. Habermas is commonly considered part of a second generation of the Frankfurt School, and his idea of knowledge interests reflects this heritage: Whereas administrative media and communication research is governed by a technical knowledge interest, critical research serves an emancipatory knowledge interest. In James Carey's (1989b/1975) terminology (Chapter 1, p. 17): Either the aim is to produce, maintain, and repair the media as part of a social status quo – or the aim is to transform the media and their place in society.

Part of the background to ongoing conflicts in this area has been the ambiguity of the concept of critical research or critique. 'Critique' may mean distancing oneself from and evaluating something negatively; critique can also mean taking a stand, negative or positive, in relation to something, following careful reflection. For some research traditions (and research projects and individual researchers), reflection and publication mark the end points of critique; for others, scholarly critiques are only the beginning of other social processes that translate knowledge into engagement with and transformation of media and society as we find and know them.

References

Alasuutari, P. (Ed.). (1999). *Rethinking the Media Audience: The New Agenda*. Sage.

Alvesson, M., & Sköldberg, K. (2009). *Reflexive Methodology: New Vistas for Qualitative Research* (2nd ed.). Sage.

Alvesson, M., & Sköldberg, K. (2018). *Reflexive Methodology: New Vistas for Qualitative Research* (3rd ed.). Sage.

Ancu, M., & Cozma, R. (2009). MySpace Politics: Uses and Gratifications of Befriending Candidates. *Journal of Broadcasting and Electronic Media, 53*(4), 567–583.

Anderson, B. (1991). *Imagined Communities: Reflections on the Origin and Spread of Nationalism* (2nd ed.). Verso.

Anderson, J. (1996). *Communication Theory: Epistemological Foundations*. The Guilford Press.

Araujo, T., Ausloos, J., Atteveldt, W., Loecherbach, F., Mueller, J., Ohme, J., Trilling, D., Velde, B., Vreese, C., & Welbers, K. (2022). OSD2F: An Open-Source Data Donation Framework. *Computational Communication Research, 4*, 372–387.

Atkinson, R., & Flint, J. (2001). Accessing Hidden and Hard-to-Reach Populations: Snowball Research Strategies. *Social Research Update, 33*(1), 1–4.

Austin, J. L. (1962). *How to Do Things with Words*. Oxford University Press.

Bakhtin, M. M. (1981). *The Dialogic Imagination*. University of Texas Press.

Bakshy, E., Marlow, C., Rosenn, I., & Adamic, L. (2012). The Role of Social Networks in Information Diffusion. Proceedings of the 21st international conference on World Wide Web, Lyon, France.

Bakshy, E., Messing, S., & Adamic, L. (2015). Exposure to Ideologically Diverse News and Opinion on Facebook. *Science, 348*(6239), 1130–1132.

Ball, M. (2022). *The Metaverse: And How It Will Revolutionze Everything*. Liveright.

Bandura, A., Ross, D., & Ross, S. A. (1963). Imitation of Film-mediated Aggressive Models. *Journal of Abnormal and Social Psychology, 67*, 601–607.

Barbour, R. S. (2007). *Doing Focus Groups*. Sage.

Barnhurst, K. G., & Wartella, E. (1998). Young Citizens, American TV Newscasts, and the Collective Memory. *Critical Studies in Mass Communication, 15*(3), 279–305.

Baron, N. S. (2008). *Always On: Language in an Online and Mobile World*. Oxford University Press.

Barthes, R. (1973). *Mythologies*. Paladin. (1957)

Bateson, G. (1972). *Steps to an Ecology of Mind*. Granada.

Bawarshi, A. (2000). The Genre Function. *College English, 62*(3), 335–356.

Baym, N. K. (2000). *Tune In, Log On: Soaps, Fandom, and Online Community*. Sage.

Bechtel, R. B., Achelpohl, C., & Akers, R. (1972). Correlates between Observed Behavior and Questionnaire Responses on Television Viewing. In E. A. Rubinstein, G. A. Comstock, & J. P. Murray (Eds.), *Television in Day-to-Day Life: Patterns of Use* (Vol. 4). Government Printing Office.

Beck, U., Giddens, A., & Lash, S. (1994). *Reflexive Modernization: Politics, Tradition, and Aesthetics in the Modern Social Order*. Polity.

Bell, D., & Kennedy, B. M. (Eds.). (2000). *The Cybercultures Reader*. Routledge.

Bell, M. M., & Gardiner, M. (Eds.). (1998). *Bakhtin and the Human Sciences: No Last Words*. Sage.

Ben-David, A. (2020). Counter-archiving Facebook. *European Journal of Communication*, *35*(3), 249–264.

Benedikt, M. (Ed.). (1991). *Cyberspace: First Steps*. MIT Press.

Benjamin, W. (1977). The Work of Art in the Age of Mechanical Reproduction. In J. Curran, M. Gurevitch, & J. Woollacott (Eds.), *Mass Communication and Society* (pp. 384–408). Edward Arnold. (1936)

Benkler, Y. (2006). *The Wealth of Networks: How Social Production Transforms Markets and Freedom*. Yale University Press.

Bennett, T., & Woollacott, J. (1987). *Bond and Beyond*. Methuen.

Berelson, B. (1949). What 'Missing the Newspaper' Means. In P. F. Lazarsfeld & F. M. Stanton (Eds.), *Communications Research 1948–9* (pp. 111–129). Duell, Sloan, and Pearce.

Berger, C. R., Roloff, M. E., & Roskos-Ewoldsen, D. E. (Eds.). (2009). *The Handbook of Communication Science* (2nd ed.). Sage.

Berlin, I. (Composer). (1946). *There's no business like show business (song)*. BERLIN IRVING MUSIC CORP.

Berlin, I. (1969). Two Concepts of Liberty. In I. Berlin (Ed.), *Four Essays on Liberty* (pp. 118–172). Oxford University Press. (1958).

Biagioli, M. (Ed.). (1999). *The Science Studies Reader*. Routledge.

Bijker, W. E., Hughes, T. P., & Pinch, T. J. (Eds.). (1987). *The Social Construction of Technological Systems*. MIT Press.

Blumer, H. (1954). What Is Wrong with Social Theory? *American Sociological Review*, *19*, 3–10.

Blumler, J. G., & Katz, E. (Eds.). (1974). *The Uses of Mass Communications*. Sage.

Boeschoten, L., Mendrik, A., Veen, E., Vloothuis, J., Hu, H., Voorvaart, R., & Oberski, D. (2022). Privacy-preserving Local Analysis of Digital Trace Data: A Proof-of-Concept. *Patterns*, *3*, 100444.

Bolter, J. D. (1991). *Writing Space: The Computer, Hypertext, and the History of Writing*. Lawrence Erlbaum.

Bolter, J. D., & Grusin, R. (1999). *Remediation: Understanding New Media*. MIT Press.

Boorstin, D. (1961). *The Image: A Guide to Pseudo-Events in America*. Atheneum.

Borah, P. (2011). Conceptual Issues in Framing Theory: A Systematic Examination of a Decade's Literature. *Journal of Communication*, *61*(2), 246–263.

Bordwell, D., Thompson, K., & Smith, J. (2024). *Film Art: An Introduction* (13th ed.). McGraw-Hill.

Borzekowski, D. L. G., & Robinson, T. N. (1999). Viewing the Viewers: Ten Video Cases of Children's Television Viewing Behaviors. *Journal of Broadcasting and Electronic Media*, *43*(4), 506–528.

Bower, R. T. (1973). *Television and the Public*. Holt, Rinehart & Winston.

Bradbury, H. (Ed.). (2015). *The SAGE Handbook of Action Research*. Sage.

Brügger, N., Nielsen, J., & Laursen, D. (2020). Big Data Experiments with the Archived Web: Methodological Reflections on Studying the Development of a Nation's Web. *First Monday, 25*(3).

Bruns, A. (2008). *Blogs, Wikipedia, Second Life, and Beyond: From Production to Produsage*. Peter Lang.

Bruns, A. (2019a). After the 'APIcalypse': Social Media Platforms and Their Fight against Critical Scholarly Research. *Information, Communication, & Society, 22*(11), 1544–1566.

Bruns, A. (2019b). *Are Filter Bubbles Real?* Polity.

Bull, M. (2000). *Sounding Out the City: Personal Stereos and the Management of Everyday Life*. Berg.

Bunz, M., & Meikle, G. (2018). *The Internet of Things*. Polity.

Burgess, J. (2008). 'All Your Chocolate Rain Are Belong to Us'?: Viral Video, YouTube, and the Dynamics of Participatory Culture. In G. Lovink & S. Niederer (Eds.), *Video Vortex Reader: Responses to YouTube* (pp. 101–109). Institute of Network Cultures.

Burgess, R. G. (1982a). Keeping Field Notes. In R. G. Burgess (Ed.), *Field Research: A Sourcebook and Field Manual* (pp. 191–194). Unwin Hyman.

Burgess, R. G. (1982b). The Unstructured Interview as a Conversation. In R. G. Burgess (Ed.), *Field Research: A Sourcebook and Field Manual* (pp. 107–110). Unwin Hyman.

Cantril, H. (1940). *The Invasion from Mars*. Princeton University Press.

Carey, J. W. (1989a). *Communication as Culture*. Unwin Hyman.

Carey, J. W. (1989b). A Cultural Approach to Communication. In J. W. Carey (Ed.), *Communication as Culture* (pp. 13–36). Unwin Hyman. (1975)

Castells, M. (1996). *The Rise of the Network Society*. Blackwell.

Castells, M. (2009). *Communication Power*. Oxford University Press.

Chatman, S. (1989). *Story and Discourse: Narrative Structure in Fiction and Film* (5th ed.). Cornell University Press.

Christians, C. G., Glasser, T. L., McQuail, D., Nordenstreng, K., & White, R. A. (2009). *Normative Theories of the Media: Journalism in Democratic Societies*. University of Illinois Press.

Clark, T., Foster, L., Sloan, L., & Bryman, A. (2021). *Bryman's Social Research Methods* (6th ed.). Oxford University Press.

Cohen, B. (1963). *The Press and Foreign Policy*. Princeton University Press.

Courtois, C., & Nelissen, S. (2018). Family Television Viewing and Its Alternatives: Associations with Closeness within and between Generations. *Journal of Broadcasting and Electronic Media, 62*(4), 673–691.

D'Angelo, P., Lule, J., Neuman, W. R., Rodriguez, L., Dimitrova, D. V., & Carragee, K. M. (2019). Beyond Framing: A Forum for Framing Researchers. *Journalism and Mass Communication Quarterly, 96*(1), 12–30.

Dayan, D., & Katz, E. (1992). *Media Events: The Live Broadcasting of History*. Harvard University Press.

de Dijn, A. (2020). *Freedom: An Unruly History*. Harvard University Press.

Deacon, D., Murdock, G., Pickering, M., & Golding, P. (2021). *Researching Communications: A Practical Guide to Methods in Media and Cultural Analysis* (3rd ed.). Bloomsbury.

Dearing, J., & Rogers, E. M. (1996). *Agenda-Setting*. Sage.

Delia, J. (1987). Communication Research: A History. In C. R. Berger & S. H. Chaffee (Eds.), *Handbook of Communication Science* (pp. 20–98). Sage.

Dinesen, N. J., & Kau, E. (2006). The Sound of Nordisk. In L. R. Larsen & D. Nissen (Eds.), *100 Years of Nordisk Film* (pp. 125–143). Danish FIlm Institute.

Divers, J. (2002). *Possible Worlds*. Routledge.

Downing, J. D. H. (2000). *Radical Media: Rebellious Communication and Social Movements*. Sage.

Driel, I., Giachanou, A., Pouwels, J. L., Boeschoten, L., Beyens, I., & Valkenburg, P. (2022). Promises and Pitfalls of Social Media Data Donations. *Communication Methods and Measures*, *16*, 1–17. https://doi.org/10.1080/19312458.2022.2109608

Drotner, K. (1992). Modernity and Media Panics. In M. Skovmand & K. C. Schrøder (Eds.), *Media Cultures: Reappraising Transnational Media* (pp. 42–62). Routledge.

Drotner, K., Jensen, K. B., Poulsen, I., & Schrøder, K. C. (1996). *Medier og kultur [Media and culture]*. Borgen.

Durkheim, É. (1982). *The Rules of Sociological Method*. Free Press. (1901)

Easton, D. (1953). *The Political System: An Inquiry into the State of Political Science*. Alfred A. Knopf.

Eco, U. (1976). *A Theory of Semiotics*. Indiana University Press.

Eco, U. (1987). *The Role of the Reader*. Hutchinson.

Eisenstein, E. L. (1979). *The Printing Press as an Agent of Change: Communication and Cultural Transformation in Early-Modern Europe*. Cambridge University Press.

Ellis, J. (1982). *Visible Fictions*. Routledge Kegan Paul.

Enzensberger, H. M. (1972). Constituents of a Theory of the Media. In D. McQuail (Ed.), *Sociology of Mass Communications* (pp. 99–116). Penguin. (1970)

Ericson, R. V., Baranak, P. M., & Chan, J. B. L. (1987). *Visualizing Deviance: A Study of News Organization*. University of Toronto Press.

Ettema, J. S., & Whitney, D. C. (Eds.). (1994). *Audiencemaking: How the Media Create the Audience*. Sage.

Fairclough, N. (1995). *Media Discourse*. Edward Arnold.

Finnegan, R. (1989). *The Hidden Musicians: Music-Making in an English Town*. Cambridge University Press.

Fish, S. (1979). *Is There a Text in This Class? The Authority of Interpretive Communities*. Harvard University Press.

Fiske, J. (1987). *Television Culture*. Methuen.

Fletcher, R., & Nielsen, R. K. (2017). Are News Audiences Increasingly Fragmented? A Cross-National Comparative Analysis of Cross-Platform News Audience Fragmentation and Duplication. *Journal of Communication*, *67*(4), 476–498.

Flew, T. (2021). *Regulating Platforms*. Polity.

Fosse, B. (Director). (1972). *Cabaret*. ABC Pictures Corp.; Allied Artists.

Foucault, M. (1972). *The Archaeology of Knowledge*. Tavistock. (1969)

Freeman, L. C. (2004). *The Development of Social Network Analysis: A Study in the Sociology of Science*. Empirical Press.

Gadamer, H.-G. (1975). *Truth and Method*. The Seabury Press. (1960)

Gamson, W. A. (1992). *Talking Politics*. Cambridge University Press.

Gans, H. J. (1957). The Creator-Audience Relationship in the Mass Media: An Analysis of Movie Making. In B. Rosenberg & D. White (Eds.), *Mass Culture: The Popular Arts in America* (pp. 315-324). The Free Press.

Gans, H. J. (1979). *Deciding What's News*. Vintage.

Gauntlett, D., & Hill, A. (1999). *TV Living: Television, Culture, and Everyday Life*. Routledge.

Gay, P. d., Hall, S., Janes, L., Mackay, H., & Negus, K. (1997). *Doing Cultural Studies: The Story of the Sony Walkman*. Sage.

Geertz, C. (1973). Thick Description. In C. Geertz (Ed.), *The Interpretation of Cultures*. Basic Books.

Genette, G. (1997). *Palimpsests: Literature in the Second Degree*. University of Nebraska Press.

Gerbner, G., & Gross, L. (1976). Living with Television: The Violence Profile. *Journal of Communication, 26*(2), 173–199.

Gibson, J. J. (1979). *The Ecological Approach to Visual Perception*. Houghton-Mifflin.

Gibson, W. (1984). *Neuromancer*. Ace.

Giddens, A. (1979). *Central Problems in Social Theory*. Macmillan.

Giddens, A. (1984). *The Constitution of Society*. University of California Press.

Gillespie, M. (1995). *Television, Ethnicity, and Cultural Change*. Routledge.

Gitlin, T. (1978). Media Sociology: The Dominant Paradigm. *Theory and Society, 6*(2), 205–253.

Gleick, J. (1987). *Chaos: Making a New Science*. Penguin.

Glessing, R. J. (1970). *The Underground Press in America*. Indiana University Press.

Goehr, L. (1992). *The Imaginary Museum of Musical Works: An Essay in the Philosophy of Music*. Clarendon.

Golding, P., & Elliott, P. (1979). *Making the News*. Longman.

Gomery, D. (1992). *Shared Pleasures: A History of Movie Presentation in the United States*. University of Wisconsin Press.

Goody, J., & Watt, I. (1963). The Consequences of Literacy. *Comparative Studies in Society and History, 5*, 304–345.

Gow, G. A., & Smith, R. K. (2006). *Mobile and Wireless Communications: An Introduction*. Open University Press.

Graber, D. (1984). *Processing the News: How People Tame the Information Tide*. Longman.

Granovetter, M. S. (1973). The Strength of Weak Ties. *The American Journal of Sociology, 78*(6), 1360–1380.

Gray, A. (1992). *Video Playtime: The Gendering of a Leisure Technology*. Routledge.

Greenacre, M. J. (2016). *Correspondence Analysis in Practice* (3rd ed.). Chapman & Hall.

Greenberg, B. S. (1964). Person-to-Person Communication in the Diffusion of a News Event. *Journalism Quarterly, 41*, 489–494.

Greenfield, A. (2006). *Everyware: The Dawning Age of Ubiquitous Computing*. New Riders.

Greenwood, D. J., & Levin, M. (2007). *Introduction to Action Research: Social Research for Social Change* (2nd ed.). Sage.

Gripsrud, J. (1995). *The Dynasty Years: Hollywood Television and Critical Media Studies*. Routledge.

Gunkel, D. J. (2020). *An Introduction to Communication and Artificial Intelligence*. Polity.

Gunter, B. (1987). *Television and the Fear of Crime*. John Libbey.

Guzman, A. L., McEwen, R., & Jones, S. (Eds.). (2023). *The SAGE Handbook of Human–Machine Communication*. Sage.

Habermas, J. (1971). *Knowledge and Human Interests*. Beacon Press. (1968)

Habermas, J. (1989). *The Structural Transformation of the Public Sphere*. MIT Press. (1962)

Habermas, J. (2006). Political Communication in Media Society: Does Democracy Still Enjoy an Epistemic Dimension? The Impact of Normative Theory on Empirical Research. *Communication Theory, 16*(4), 411–426.

Habermas, J. (2022). Reflections and Hypotheses on a Further Structural Transformation of the Political Public Sphere. *Theory, Culture & Society*, *39*(4), 145–171.

Haddon, L. (2004). *Information and Communication Technologies: A Concise Introduction and Research Guide*. Berg.

Hall, S. (1973). *Encoding and Decoding in the Television Discourse*. Centre for Contemporary Cultural Studies. Stencilled Occasional Paper no. 7.

Hall, S. (1983). The Problem of Ideology – Marxism without Guarantees. In B. Matthews (Ed.), *Marx: A Hundred Years On* (pp. 57–85). Lawrence & Wishart.

Hall, W., & O'Hara, K. (2021). *Four Internets: Data, Geopolitics, and the Governance of Cyberspace*. Oxford University Press.

Hallin, D. C. (2020). Comparative Research, System Change, and the Complexity of Media Systems. *International Journal of Communication, 14*, 5775–5786. https://doi.org/1932–8036/2020FEA0002

Hallin, D. C., & Mancini, P. (2004). *Comparing Media Systems: Three Models of Media and Politics*. Cambridge University Press.

Hallin, D. C., & Mancini, P. (Eds.). (2012). *Comparing Media Systems Beyond the Western World*. Cambridge University Press.

Hallin, D. C., & Mancini, P. (2017). Ten Years After Comparing Media Systems: What Have We Learned? *Political Communication*, *34*(2), 155–171.

Hammersley, M., & Atkinson, P. (2019). *Ethnography: Principles in Practice* (4th ed.). Routledge.

Hasebrink, U., & Domeyer, H. (2012). Media Repertoires as Patterns of Behaviour and as Meaningful Practices: A Multimethod Approach to Media Use in Converging Media Environments. *Participations: Journal of Audience and Reception Studies*, *9*(2), 757–779.

Havelock, E. A. (1963). *Preface to Plato*. Blackwell.

Headland, T., Pike, K., & Harris, M. (Eds.). (1990). *Emics and Etics: The Insider/Outsider Debate*. Sage.

Hektner, J. M., Schmidt, J. A., & Csikszentmihalyi, M. (Eds.). (2007). *Experience Sampling Method: Measuring the Quality of Everyday Life*. Sage.

Hendy, D. (2022). *The BBC: A Century on Air*. Public Affairs.

Hermann, E., Morgan, M., & Shanahan, J. (2021). Television, Continuity, and Change: A Meta-Analysis of Five Decades of Cultivation Research. *Journal of Communication*, *71*(4), 515–544.

Hermann, E., Morgan, M., & Shanahan, J. (2023). Cultivation and Social Media: A Meta-Analysis. *New Media & Society*, *25*(9), 2492–2511.

Herzog, H. (1944). What Do We Really Know about Daytime Serial Listeners? In P. F. Lazarsfeld & F. N. Stanton (Eds.), *Radio Research 1942–3* (pp. 3–33). Duell, Sloan, and Pearce.

Hesmondhalgh, D. (2022). Streaming's Effects on Music Culture: Old Anxieties and New Simplifications. *Cultural Sociology*, *16*(1), 3–24.

Hill, A. (2005). *Reality TV: Audiences and Popular Factual Television*. Routledge.

Himmelweit, H. T., Vince, P., & Oppenheim, A. N. (1958). *Television and the Child*. Oxford University Press.

Hirsch, P. (1980). The 'Scary World' of the Non-Viewer and Other Anomalies: A Reanalysis of Gerbner et al.'s Findings in Cultivation Analysis, Part I. *Communication Research*, *7*(4), 403–456.

Hirsch, P. (1981). On Not Learning from One's Mistakes, Part II. *Communication Research*, *8*(1), 3–38.

Hjelmslev, L. (1963). *Prolegomena to a Theory of Language*. University of Wisconsin Press. (1943)

Holtzhausen, D. (2008). Strategic Communication. In W. Donsbach (Ed.), *International Encyclopedia of Communication* (Vol. 10, pp. 4848–4855). Blackwell.

Holub, R. C. (1984). *Reception Theory: A Critical Introduction*. Methuen.

Hosseinmardi, H., Ghasemian, A., Clauset, A., Mobius, M., Rothschild, D. M., & Watts, D. J. (2021). Examining the Consumption of Radical Content on YouTube. *PNAS – Proceedings of the National Academy of Sciences*, *118*(32), e2101967118.

Hovland, C. I., Janis, I. L., & Kelley, H. H. (1953). *Communication and Persuasion*. Yale University Press.

Howard, P. N. (2010). *The Digital Origins of Dictatorship and Democracy: Information Technology and Political Islam*. Oxford University Press.

Hsieh, Y. P. (2012). Online Social Networking Skills: The Social Affordances Approach to Digital Inequality. *First Monday*, *17*(4).

Hughes, T. P. (1983). *Networks of Power: Electrification in Western Society 1880–1930*. The Johns Hopkins University Press.

Hughes, T. P. (1994). Technological Momentum. In M. R. Smith & L. Marx (Eds.), *Does Technology Drive History? The Dilemma of Technological Determinism* (pp. 101–113). MIT Press.

Humphreys, L. (2005). Cellphones in Public: Social Interactions in a Wireless Era. *New Media & Society*, *7*(6), 810–833.

Humphreys, L., & Hardeman, H. (2021). Mobiles in Public: Social Interaction in a Smartphone Era. *Mobile Media & Communication*, *9*(1), 103–127.

Hutchby, I. (2001). *Conversation and Technology: From the Telephone to the Internet*. Polity.

Innis, H. A. (1951). *The Bias of Communication*. University of Toronto Press.

Innis, H. A. (1972). *Empire and Communications*. University of Toronto Press. (1950)

Internet Society. (2023). *Internet Exchange Points (IXPs)*. www.internetsociety.org/issues/ixps/

Iser, W. (1978). *The Act of Reading: A Theory of Aesthetic Response*. Johns Hopkins University Press.

ITU. (2018). *Measuring the Information Society Report*. International Telecommunication Union. Retrieved from www.itu.int/en/ITU-D/Statistics/Documents/publications/misr2017/MISR2017_Volume1.pdf

Jacko, J. A. (Ed.). (2012). *The Human–Computer Interaction Handbook: Fundamentals, Evolving Technologies, and Emerging Applications* (3rd ed.). CRC Press.

Jakobson, R. (1960). Closing Statement: Linguistics and Poetics. In T. A. Sebeok (Ed.), *Style in Language* (pp. 350–377). MIT Press.

Jauss, H. R. (1982). *Toward an Aesthetic of Reception*. Harvester Press.

Jenkins, H. (1992). *Textual Poachers: Television Fans and Participatory Culture*. Routledge.

Jenkins, H. (2006). *Convergence Culture: Where Old and New Media Collide*. New York University Press.

Jensen, J. F. (1999). Interactivity: Tracking a New Concept in Media and Communication Studies. In P. A. Mayer (Ed.), *Computer Media and Communication: A Reader* (pp. 160–187). Oxford University Press.

Jensen, K. B. (1986). *Making Sense of the News: Towards a Theory and an Empirical Model of Reception for the Study of Mass Communication*. University of Aarhus Press.

Jensen, K. B. (1991). When Is Meaning? Communication Theory, Pragmatism, and Mass Media Reception. In J. Anderson (Ed.), *Communication Yearbook* (Vol. 14, pp. 3–32). Sage.

Jensen, K. B. (1993). One Person, One Computer: The Social Construction of the Personal Computer. In P. B. Andersen, B. Holmqvist, & J. F. Jensen (Eds.), *The Computer as Medium* (pp. 337–360). Cambridge University Press.

Jensen, K. B. (1994). Reception as Flow: The "New Television Viewer" Revisited. *Cultural Studies, 8*(2), 293–305.

Jensen, K. B. (1995). *The Social Semiotics of Mass Communication*. Sage.

Jensen, K. B. (Ed.). (1998). *News of the World: World Cultures Look at Television News*. Routledge.

Jensen, K. B. (2006). Sounding the Media: An Interdisciplinary Review and a Research Agenda for Digital Sound Studies. *Nordicom Review, 27*(2), 7–33.

Jensen, K. B. (2009). Three-step Flow. *Journalism – Theory, Practice, and Criticism, 10*(3), 335–337.

Jensen, K. B. (2012). Lost, Found, and Made: Qualitative Data in the Study of Three-Step Flows of Communication. In I. Volkmer (Ed.), *Handbook of Global Media Research* (pp. 435–450). Wiley-Blackwell.

Jensen, K. B. (2013). What's Mobile in Mobile Communication?. *Mobile Media & Communication, 1*(1), 26–31.

Jensen, K. B. (Ed.). (2016). *Dansk mediehistorie [Danish media history]* (Vol. 4). Samfundslitteratur.

Jensen, K. B. (2021a). The Complementarity of Qualitative and Quantitative Methodologies in Media and Communication Research. In K. B. Jensen (Ed.), *A Handbook of Media and Communication Research: Qualitative and Quantitative Methodologies* (pp. 328–348). Routledge.

Jensen, K. B. (Ed.). (2021b). *A Handbook of Media and Communication Research: Qualitative and Quantitative Methodologies* (3rd ed.). Routledge.

Jensen, K. B. (2021c). Introduction: The State of Convergence in Media and Communication Research. In K. B. Jensen (Ed.), *A Handbook of Media and Communication Research: Qualitative and Quantitative Methodologies* (pp. 1–21). Routledge.

Jensen, K. B. (2021d). The Qualitative Research Process. In K. B. Jensen (Ed.), *A Handbook of Media and Communication Research: Qualitative and Quantitative Methodologies* (pp. 286–306). Routledge.

Jensen, K. B. (2021e). *A Theory of Communication and Justice*. Routledge.

Jensen, K. B. (2022). *Media Convergence: The Three Degrees of Network, Mass, and Interpersonal Communication* (2nd ed.). Routledge.

Jensen, K. B., & Helles, R. (2011). The Internet as a Cultural Forum: Implications for Research. *New Media & Society, 13*(4), 517–533.

Jensen, K. B., & Helles, R. (2017). Speaking into the System: Social Media and Many-to-One Communication. *European Journal of Communication, 32*(1), 16–25.

Jensen, K. B., & Helles, R. (Eds.). (2023). *Comparing Communication Systems: The Internets of China, Europe, and the United States*. Routledge.

Jensen, K. B., & Jankowski, N. W. (Eds.). (1991). *A Handbook of Qualitative Methodologies for Mass Communication Research*. Routledge.

Jones, S. G. (Ed.). (1998). *Cybersociety 2.0*. Sage.

Jowett, G. S., Jarvie, I. C., & Fuller, K. H. (1996). *Children and the Movies: Media Influence and the Payne Fund Controversy*. Cambridge University Press.

Kakihara, M., & Sørensen, C. (2002). Mobility: An Extended Perspective. Hawai'i International Conference on System Sciences, Big Island, Hawai'i.

Kapantai, E., Christopoulou, A., Berberidis, C., & Peristeras, V. (2021). A Systematic Literature Review on Disinformation: Toward a Unified Taxonomical Framework. *New Media & Society*, *23*(5), 1301–1326.

Katz, E. (1959). Mass Communication Research and the Study of Popular Culture: An Editorial Note on a Possible Future for this Journal. *Studies in Public Communication*, *2*(1), 1–6.

Katz, E. (2001). Media Effects. In N. J. Smelser & P. B. Baltes (Eds.), *International Encyclopedia of the Social & Behavioral Sciences* (pp. 9472–9479). Elsevier.

Katz, E., Gurevitch, M., & Haas, H. (1973). On the Use of Mass Media for Important Things. *American Sociological Review*, *38*(2), 164–181.

Katz, E., & Lazarsfeld, P. F. (1955). *Personal Influence*. The Free Press.

Katz, E., & Liebes, T. (2007). 'No More Peace!' How Disaster, Terror, and War Have Upstaged Media Events. *International Journal of Communication*, *1*, 157–166.

Kay, A., & Goldberg, A. (1999). Personal Dynamic Media. In P. A. Mayer (Ed.), *Computer Media and Communication: A Reader* (pp. 111–119). Oxford University Press. (1977)

Kim, Y. Y. (Ed.). (2018). *The International Encyclopedia of Intercultural Communication*. Wiley-Blackwell.

King, G., Schneer, B., & White, A. (2017). How the News Media Activate Public Expression and Influence National Agendas. *Science*, *358*(776–780), 1–5.

Kiousis, S. (2002). Interactivity: A Concept Explication. *New Media & Society*, *4*(3), 355–383.

Kjørup, S. (2001). *Humanities, Geisteswissenschaften, Sciences humaines: Eine Einführung [The Human Sciences: An Introduction]*. J.B. Metzler.

Klapper, J. (1960). *The Effects of Mass Communication*. The Free Press.

Kramer, L. (2002). *Musical Meaning: Toward a Critical History*. University of California Press.

Krippendorff, K. (2018). *Content Analysis: An Introduction to Its Methodology* (4th ed.). Sage.

Kristeva, J. (1984). *Revolution in Poetic Language*. Columbia University Press. (1974)

Kroeber, A. L., & Kluckhohn, C. (1952). *Culture: A Critical Review of Concepts and Definitions*. Peabody Museum of American Archaeology and Ethnology.

Kubey, R., & Csikszentmihalyi, M. (1990). *Television and the Quality of Life: How Viewing Shapes Everyday Experience*. Lawrence Erlbaum.

Kvale, S., & Brinkmann, S. (2015). *InterViews: Learning the Craft of Qualitative Research Interviewing* (3rd ed.). Sage.

Lai, S., & Flensburg, S. (2020). Appscapes in Everyday Life: Studying the Implications of Mobile Datafication from an Infrastructural User Perspective. *MedieKultur: Journal of media and communication research*, *36*(69), 29–51.

Lai, S. S., & Flensburg, S. (2023). *Gateways: Comparing Digital Communication Systems in Nordic Welfare States*. Nordicom.

Lai, S. S. (2021). "She's the Communication Expert": Digital Labor and the Implications of Datafied Relational Communication. *Feminist Media Studies*, *23* (4), 1857–1871.

Lang, K., & Lang, G. E. (1953). The Unique Perspective of Television and Its Effects: A Pilot Study. *American Sociological Review*, *18*, 3–12.

Lang, W. (Director). (1954). *There's No Business like Show Business (film)*. 20th Century Fox.

Lasswell, H. D. (1938). *Propaganda Technique in the World War*. Alfred Knopf.

Lasswell, H. D. (1948). The Structure and Function of Communication in Society. In L. Bryson (Ed.), *The Communication of Ideas* (pp. 32–51). Harper.

Lazarsfeld, P. F. (1941). Remarks on Administrative and Critical Communications Research. *Studies in Philosophy and Social Science, 9*(1), 2–16.

Lazarsfeld, P. F., Berelson, B., & Gaudet, H. (1944). *The People's Choice*. Duell, Sloan, and Pearce.

Lazer, D. M. J., Baum, M. A., Benkler, Y., Berinsky, A. J., Greenhill, K. M., Menczer, F., Metzger, M. J., Nyhan, B., Pennycook, G., Rothschild, D., Schudson, M., Sloman, S. A., Sunstein, C. R., Thorson, E. A., Watts, D. J., & Zittrain, J. L. (2018). The Science of Fake News: Addressing Fake News Requires a Multidisciplinary Effort. *Science, 359*(6380), 1094–1096.

Lee, M. (2011). Google Ads and the Blindspot Debate. *Media, Culture & Society, 33*(3), 433–447.

Lemish, D. (1982). The Rules of Viewing Television in Public Places. *Journal of Broadcasting and Electronic Media, 26*, 757–791.

Lévi-Strauss, C. (1991). *Totemism*. Merlin Press. (1962)

Lewin, K. (1945). The Research Center for Group Dynamics at Massachusetts Institute of Technology. *Sociometry, 8*(2), 126–136.

Li, W., & Cho, H. (2023). The Knowledge Gap on Social Media: Examining Roles of Engagement and Networks. *New Media & Society, 25*(5), 1023–1042.

Liebes, T., & Katz, E. (1990). *The Export of Meaning*. Oxford University Press.

Lievrouw, L. A. (2023). *Alternative and Activist New Media* (2nd ed.). Polity.

Light, B., Burgess, J., & Duguay, S. (2018). The Walkthrough Method: An Approach to the Study of Apps. *New Media & Society, 20*(3), 881–900.

Lind, F., & Boomgaarden, H. (2019). What We Do and Don't Know: a Meta-analysis of the Knowledge Gap Hypothesis. *Annals of the International Communication Association, 43*(3), 210–224.

Lindlof, T. R., & Taylor, B. C. (2019). *Qualitative Communication Research Methods* (4th ed.). Sage.

Ling, R. (2004). *The Mobile Connection: The Cell Phone's Impact on Society*. Elsevier.

Ling, R. (2012). *Taken For Grantedness: The Embedding of Mobile Communication into Society*. MIT Press.

Ling, R., Goggin, G., Fortunati, L., Lim, S. S., & Li, Y. (Eds.). (2020). *The Oxford Handbook of Mobile Communication and Society*. Oxford University Press.

Ling, R., & Yttri, B. (2002). Hyper-coordination via Mobile Phones in Norway. In J. E. Katz & M. Aakhus (Eds.), *Perpetual Contact: Mobile Communication, Private Talk, Public Performance* (pp. 139–169). Cambridge University Press.

Livingstone, S. (1990). *Making Sense of Television: The Psychology of Audience Appreciation*. Pergamon Press.

Livingstone, S. (1998). *Making Sense of Television: The Psychology of Audience Interpretation* (2nd ed.). Routledge.

Livingstone, S., & Haddon, L. (2009). *EU Kids Online: Final report*. EU Kids Online.

Lomborg, S. (2011). *Social Media: A Genre Perspective*. University of Aarhus.

Lorenz-Spreen, P., Oswald, L., Lewandowsky, S., & Hertwig, R. (2023). A Systematic Review of Worldwide Causal and Correlational Evidence on Digital Media and Democracy. *Nature Human Behaviour, 7*(1), 74–101.

Lotz, A. D., & Newcomb, H. (2021). The Production of Entertainment Media. In K. B. Jensen (Ed.), *A Handbook of Media and Communication Research: Qualitative and Quantitative Methodologies* (3rd ed., pp. 75–92). Routledge.

Löwenthal, L. (Ed.). (1961). The Triumph of Mass Idols. In *Literature, Popular Culture, and Society.* (pp. 109–140) Prentice-Hall. (1941)

Lull, J. (1980). The Social Uses of Television. *Human Communication Research, 6,* 197–209.

Lull, J. (1988). Critical Response: The Audience as Nuisance. *Critical Studies in Mass Communication, 5,* 239–243.

Lull, J. (2020). *Evolutionary Communication: An Introduction.* Routledge.

Maarek, P. J. (Ed.). (2022). *Manufacturing Government Communication on Covid-19: A Comparative Perspective.* Springer.

MacBride, S. (Ed.). (1980). *Many Voices, One World.* UNESCO.

Mancini, P. (2020). *Comparing Media Systems* and the Digital Age. *International Journal of Communication, 14,* 5761–5774.

Manovich, L. (2001). *The Language of New Media.* MIT Press.

Marres, N. (2017). *Digital Sociology: The Reinvention of Social Research.* Polity.

Mayer-Schönberger, V., & Cukier, K. (2013). *Big Data: A Revolution That Will Transform How We Live, Work, and Think.* Houghton Mifflin Harcourt.

McClary, S. (1991). *Feminine Endings: Music, Gender, and Sexuality.* University of Minnesota Press.

McCombs, M. E., & Shaw, D. L. (1972). The Agenda-Setting Function of Mass Media. *Public Opinion Quarterly, 36,* 176–187.

McDowell, Z. J., & Vetter, M. A. (2022). *Wikipedia and the Representation of Reality.* Routledge.

McKay, A., & Messick, K. [Executive producers]. (2021). *Don't Look Up [Feature film].* Los Angeles, CA.

McLuhan, M. (1962). *The Gutenberg Galaxy.* University of Toronto Press.

McLuhan, M. (1964). *Understanding Media: The Extensions of Man.* McGraw-Hill.

McMillan, S. J. (2002). Exploring Models of Interactivity from Multiple Research Traditions: Users, Documents, and Systems. In L. Llevrouw & S. Livingstone (Eds.), *Handbook of New Media: Social Shaping and Consequences of ICTs* (pp. 163–182). Sage.

McQuail, D. (1983). *Mass Communication Theory: An Introduction.* Sage.

McQuail, D., & Deuze, M. (2020). *McQuail's Media and Mass Communication Theory* (7th ed.). Sage.

Merton, R. K. (1987). The Focussed Interview and Focus Groups: Continuities and Discontinuities. *Public Opinion Quarterly, 51*(4), 550–566.

Merton, R. K., & Kendall, P. L. (1955). The Focused Interview. In P. F. Lazarsfeld & B. Rosenberg (Eds.), *The Language of Social Research* (pp. 477–491). The Free Press.

Meyrowitz, J. (1985). *No Sense of Place: The Impact of Electronic Media on Social Behavior.* Oxford University Press.

Meyrowitz, J. (1994). Medium Theory. In D. Crowley & D. Mitchell (Eds.), *Communication Theory Today* (pp. 50–77). Polity Press.

Mickes, L., Darby, R. S., Hwe, V., Bajics, D., Warker, J. A., Harris et al. (2013). Major Memory for Microblogs. *Memory & Cognition, 41*(4), 481–489.

Miller, C. R. (1984). Genre as Social Action. *Quarterly Journal of Speech, 70*(2), 151–167.

Miller, C. R. (1994). Rhetorical Community: The Cultural Basis of Genre. In A. Freedman & P. Medway (Eds.), *Genre and the New Rhetoric* (pp. 67–78). Taylor & Francis.

Mitu, B., & Poulakidakos, S. (Eds.). (2016). *Media Events: A Critical Contemporary Approach.* Palgrave Macmillan.

Moores, S. (1988). 'The Box on the Dresser': Memories of Early Radio and Everyday Life. *Media, Culture & Society, 10*(1), 23–40.

Morgan, M. (2008). Cultivation Theory. In W. Donsbach (Ed.), *International Encyclopedia of Communication* (Vol. 3, pp. 1091–1095). Blackwell.

Morley, D. (1980). *The 'Nationwide' Audience*. British Film Institute.

Morley, D. (1981). 'The Nationwide Audience': A Critical Postscript. *Screen Education, 39*, 3–14.

Morley, D. (1986). *Family Television*. Comedia.

Morrison, D. E. (1998). *The Search for a Method: Focus Groups and the Development of Mass Communication Research*. University of Luton Press.

Munakata, T. (2007). Beyond Silicon: New Computing Paradigms. *Communications of the ACM, 50*(9), 30–72.

Napoli, P. M. (2003). *Audience Economics: Media Institutions and the Audience Marketplace*. Columbia University Press.

Negroponte, N. (1995). *Being Digital*. Alfred A. Knopf.

Neuman, W. R., & Guggenheim, L. (2011). The Evolution of Media Effects Theory: A Six-Stage Model of Cumulative Research. *Communication Theory, 21*(2), 169–196.

Neuman, W. R., Just, M., & Crigler, A. N. (1992). *Common Knowledge: News and the Construction of Political Meaning*. University of Chicago Press.

Newcomb, H. (1978). Assessing the Violence Profile of Gerbner and Gross: A Humanistic Critique and Suggestion. *Communication Research, 5*(3), 264–282.

Nieborg, D. B., & Helmond, A. (2019). The Political Economy of Facebook's Platformization in the Mobile Ecosystem: Facebook Messenger as a Platform Instance. *Media, Culture & Society, 41*(2), 196–218.

O'Reilly, T. (2005). *What Is Web 2.0? Design Patterns and Business Models for the Next Generation of Software*. Retrieved from http://oreilly.com/pub/a/web2/archive/what-is-web-20.html?page=1

Ohme, J., & Araujo, T. (2022). Digital Data Donations: A Quest for Best Practices. *Patterns, 3*(4), 1–2.

Ørmen, J. (2021). Quantitative Approaches to Media and Communication Research. In K. B. Jensen (Ed.), *A Handbook of Media and Communication Research: Qualitative and Quantitative Methodologies* (3rd ed., pp. 255–285). Routledge.

Palmgreen, P., & Rayburn, J. D. I. (1985). An Expectancy-Value Approach to Media Gratifications. In K. E. Rosengren, L. Wenner, & P. Palmgreen (Eds.), *Media Gratifications Research: Current Perspectives* (pp. 61-72). Sage.

Parameswaran, R. (1999). Western Romance Fiction as English-Language Media in Postcolonial India. *Journal of Communication, 49*(3), 84–105.

Pariser, E. (2011). *The Filter Bubble: What The Internet Is Hiding From You*. Penguin.

Park, D. W., & Pooley, J. (Eds.). (2008). *The History of Media and Communication Research: Contested Memories*. Peter Lang.

Park, J. H., Gabbadon, N. G., & Chernin, A. R. (2006). Naturalizing Racial Differences through Comedy: Asian, Black, and White Views on Racial Stereotypes in *Rush Hour 2*. *Journal of Communication, 56*(1), 157–177.

Parkin, F. (1971). *Class Inequality and Political Order*. MacGibbon and Kee.

Peters, J. D. (1999). *Speaking into the Air: A History of the Idea of Communication*. University of Chicago Press.

Peters, J. D. (2005). *Courting the Abyss: Free Speech and the Liberal Tradition*. University of Chicago Press.

Pike, K. L. (1967). *Language in Relation to a Unified Theory of the Structure of Human Behavior* (2nd ed.). Mouton.

Pink, S., Horst, H., Postill, J., Hjorth, L., Lewis, T., & Tacchi, J. (2016). *Digital Ethnography: Principles and Practice*. Sage.

Popper, K. R. (1972). *Objective Knowledge: An Evolutionary Approach*. Oxford University Press.

Porat, M. (1977). *The Information Economy: Definition and Measurement*. Government Printing Office.

Potter, J., & Wetherell, M. (1987). *Discourse and Social Psychology*. Sage.

Prainsack, B. (2019). Data Donation: How to Resist the iLeviathan. In J. Krutzinna & L. Floridi (Eds.), *The Ethics of Medical Data Donation* (pp. 9–22). Springer.

Press, A. (1991). *Women Watching Television: Gender, Class, and Generation in the American Television Experience*. University of Pennsylvania Press.

Pybus, J., & Coté, M. (2021). Did You Give Permission? Datafication in the Mobile Ecosystem. *Information, Communication & Society, 25*(11), 1650–1668.

Radway, J. (1984). *Reading the Romance: Women, Patriarchy, and Popular Literature*. University of North Carolina Press.

Radway, J. (1988). Reception Study: Ethnography and the Problem of Dispersed Audiences and Nomadic Subjects. *Cultural Studies, 2*(3), 359–376.

Rheingold, H. (1994). *The Virtual Community*. Minerva.

Rheingold, H. (2002). *Smart Mobs: The Next Social Revolution*. Perseus.

Richards, J., & Sheridan, D. (Eds.). (1987). *Mass Observation at the Movies*. Routledge Kegan Paul.

Ricoeur, P. (1981). *Hermeneutics and the Human Sciences: Essays on Language, Action and Interpretation*. Cambridge University Press.

Rogers, E. M. (2003). *Diffusion of Innovations* (5th ed.). Free Press. (1962)

Rogers, R. (2013). *Digital Methods*. MIT Press.

Roose, H., van Eijck, K., & Lievens, J. (2012). Culture of Distinction or Culture of Openness? Using a Social Space Approach to Analyze the Social Structuring of Lifestyles. *Poetics, 40*(6), 491–513.

Rosengren, K. E., Wenner, L., & Palmgreen, P. (Eds.). (1985). *Media Gratifications Research: Current Perspectives*. Sage.

Ross, K., & Nightingale, V. (2003). *Media and Audiences: New Perspectives*. Open University Press.

Rossi, R., & Ahmed, N. (2015). The Network Data Repository with Interactive Graph Analytics and Visualization. *Proceedings of the AAAI Conference on Artificial Intelligence, 29*(1), 4292–4293. https://doi.org/10.1609/aaai.v29i1.9277

Ryle, G. (1971). *Collected Papers* (Vol. 2). Hutchinson.

Salganik, M. J. (2018). *Bit by Bit: Social Research in the Digital Age*. Princeton University Press.

Samuelson, P. A. (1954). The Pure Theory of Public Expenditure. *The Review of Economics and Statistics, 36*(4), 387–389.

Saussure, F. d. (1959). *Course in General Linguistics*. Peter Owen. (1916)

Savage, N. (2022). Virtual Duplicates. *Communications of the ACM, 65*(2), 14–16.

Scannell, P. (2000). For-Anyone-as-Someone Structures. *Media, Culture & Society, 22*(1), 5–24.

Schafer, R. M. (1977). *The Tuning of the World*. Alfred A. Knopf.

Scheerder, A., van Deursen, A., & van Dijk, J. (2017). Determinants of Internet Skills, Uses, and Outcomes: A Systematic Review of the Second- and Third-Level Digital Divide. *Telematics and Informatics, 34*, 1607–1624.

Schensul, J. J., & LeCompte, M. D. (Eds.). (1999). *The Ethnographer's Toolkit*. Alta Mira Press.

Scheufele, D. (1999). Agenda-Setting, Priming, and Framing Revisited: Another Look at Cognitive Effects of Political Communication. International Communication Association, San Francisco, CA.

Schiappa, E. (2016). Rhetoric. In K. B. Jensen & R. T. Craig (Eds.), *The International Encyclopedia of Communication Theory and Philosophy*. Wiley-Blackwell.

Schlesinger, P., Dobash, R. E., Dobash, R. P., & Weaver, C. (1992). *Women Viewing Violence*. British Film Institute.

Schmitt, K. L., Woolf, K. D., & Anderson, D. R. (2003). Viewing the Viewers: Viewing Behaviors by Children and Adults During Television Programs and Commercials. *Journal of Communication, 53*(2), 265–281.

Schramm, W., Lyle, J., & Parker, E. (1961). *Television in the Lives of Our Children*. Stanford University Press.

Schrøder, K. C., Drotner, K., Kline, S., & Murray, C. (2003). *Researching Audiences: A Practical Guide to Methods in Media Audience Analysis*. Hodder Arnold.

Scott, C., & Lewis, L. (Eds.). (2017). *The International Encyclopedia of Organizational Communication*. Wiley-Blackwell.

Searle, J. R. (1969). *Speech Acts*. Cambridge University Press.

Sebeok, T. A., & Umiker-Sebeok, J. (1980). *You Know My Method: A Juxtaposition of Charles S. Peirce and Sherlock Holmes*. Gaslight Publications.

Seidl, D., & Schoeneborn, D. (2016). System Theory. In K. B. Jensen & R. T. Craig (Eds.), *The International Encyclopedia of Communication Theory and Philosophy*. Wiley-Blackwell.

Shapiro, M. A. (2008). Memory, Message. In W. Donsbach (Ed.), *International Encyclopedia of Communication* (Vol. 7, pp. 3072–3076). Wiley-Blackwell.

Shuker, R. (2016). *Understanding Popular Music Culture* (5th ed.). Routledge.

Siebert, F., Peterson, T., & Schramm, W. (1956). *Four Theories of the Press*. University of Illinois Press.

Silverstone, R. (1999). *Why Study the Media?* Sage.

Simonson, P., Peck, J., Craig, R. T., & Jackson, J. P. (Eds.). (2013). *The Handbook of Communication History*. Routledge.

Skey, M. (2021). W(h)ither Media Events? Building a Typology for Theorizing Exceptional Events that Break with the Norm in a Complex Media Landscape. *Communication Theory, 31*(2), 151–168.

Smythe, D. W. (1977). Communications: Blindspot of Western Marxism. *Canadian Journal of Political and Social Theory, 1*(3), 1–27.

Sonnevend, J. (2018). Special Section: Media Events. *Media, Culture & Society, 40*(1), 110–157.

Spigel, L. (1992). *Make Room for TV: Television and the Family Ideal in Postwar America*. University of Chicago Press.

Stacey, J. (1994). *Star Gazing: Hollywood Cinema and Female Spectatorship*. Routledge.

Statista. (2023). *Number of New Film Releases in India from 2017 to 2022*. www.statista.com/statistics/1346845/india-number-of-film-releases/#:~:text=2022%20saw%20a%20rise%20in,number%20of%20productions%20that%20year

Steimle, J. (2022). On-Skin Computing. *Communications of the ACM, 65*(4), 38–39.

Stephenson, N. (1992). *Snow Crash*. Bantam.

Sterne, J. (Ed.). (2012). *The Sound Studies Reader*. Routledge.

Stewart, D. W., & Shamdasani, P. N. (2015). *Focus Groups: Theory and Practice* (3rd ed.). Sage.

Stokes, M., & Maltby, R. (Eds.). (1999). *Identifying Hollywood's Audiences: Cultural Identity and the Movies*. British Film Institute.

Stone, A. R. (1991). Will the Real Body Please Stand Up? Boundary Stories about Virtual Cultures. In M. Benedikt (Ed.), *Cyberspace: First Steps* (pp. 81–118). MIT Press.

Strate, L. (2016). Media Ecology. In K. B. Jensen & R. T. Craig (Eds.), *International Encyclopedia of Communication Theory and Philosophy* (Vol. 3, pp. 1159–1167). Wiley-Blackwell.

Strömbäck, J., & Kiousis, S. (2010). A New Look at Agenda-Setting Effects: Comparing the Predictive Power of Overall Political News Consumption and Specific News Media Consumption Across Different Media Channels and Media Types. *Journal of Communication, 60*(2), 271–292.

Sunstein, C. R. (2007). *Republic.com 2.0*. Princeton University Press.

Tannen, D., Hamilton, H. E., & Schiffrin, D. (Eds.) (2015). *The Handbook of Discourse Analysis*. John Wiley & Sons.

Tewksbury, D., & Rittenberg, J. (2012). *News on the Internet: Information and Citizenship in the 21st Century*. Oxford University Press.

Thompson, J. B. (1995). *The Media and Modernity*. Polity.

Thompson, J. B. (2000). *Political Scandal: Power and Visibility in the Media Age*. Polity.

Thompson, K., & Bordwell, D. (2018). *Film History: An Introduction* (4th ed.). McGraw-Hill.

Thorhauge, A. M. (2007). *Computerspillet som kommunikationsform: Spil og spillere i medievidenskabeligt perspektiv [Computer gaming as communication: Games and gamers in a media studies perspective]*. University of Copenhagen.

Thorson, E. (1994). Using Eyes on Screen as a Measure of Attention to Television. In A. Lang (Ed.), *Measuring Psychological Response to Media* (pp. 65-84). Lawrence Erlbaum.

Tichenor, P., Olien, C., & Donohue, G. (1970). Mass Media Flow and Differential Growth in Knowledge. *Public Opinion Quarterly, 34*(2), 159–170.

Toffler, A. (1980). *The Third Wave*. Bantam.

Trenaman, J. S. M., & McQuail, D. (1961). *Television and the Political Image*. Methuen.

Tuchman, G. (1978). *Making News: A Study in the Construction of Reality*. Free Press.

Turing, A. (1965). On Computable Numbers, with an Application to the Entscheidungsproblem. In M. Davis (Ed.), *The Undecidable* (pp. 116–151). Raven Press. (1936)

UK Parliament. (2023). *The Chairman of Ways and Means/Deputy Speakers*. The Chairman of Ways and Means/Deputy Speakers.

van Dijck, J., Poell, T., & de Waal, M. (Eds.). (2018). *The Platform Society: Public Values in a Connective World*. Oxford University Press.

Venturini, T., & Latour, B. (2010). The Social Fabric: Digital Traces and Quali-quantitative Methods. In *Proceedings of Future En Seine 2009* (pp. 87–101). Editions Future en Seine.

Venturini, T., & Munk, A. K. (2021). *Controversy Mapping: A Field Guide*. Wiley-Blackwell.

Wachowski, L., & Wachowski, L. (Directors). (1999). *The Matrix*. Warner Bros; Silver Pictures

Walter, N., Cody, M. J., & Ball-Rokeach, S. J. (2018). The Ebb and Flow of Communication Research: Seven Decades of Publication Trends and Research Priorities. *Journal of Communication, 68*, 424–440.

Wasko, J. (2020). *Understanding Disney: The Manufacture of Fantasy* (2nd ed.). Polity.

Ways & Means. (2023). *United States House Committee on Ways & Means*. https://waysandmeans.house.gov

Webb, E. J., Campbell, D. T., Schwartz, R. D., & Sechrest, L. (2000). *Unobtrusive Measures* (Revised ed.). Sage.

Webster, J. G. (2014). *The Marketplace of Attention: How Audiences Take Shape in a Digital Age*. MIT Press.

Webster, J. G., & Phalen, P. F. (1997). *The Mass Audience: Rediscovering the Dominant Model*. Lawrence Erlbaum.

Weiser, M. (1991). The Computer for the Twenty-First Century. *Scientific American*, *265*(3), 94–104.

Welles, O. (Director). (1941). *Citizen Cane*. RKO Radio Pictures; Mercury Productions.

Wikipedia. (2023). *List of Hollywood-inspired Nicknames*. https://en.wikipedia.org/wiki/List_of_Hollywood-inspired_nicknames#:~:text=Kollywood%20is%20the%20informal%20name,nickname%2C%20dating%20back%20to%201932

Williams, D. (2006). Virtual Cultivation: Online Worlds, Offline Perceptions. *Journal of Communication*, *56*(1), 69–87.

Williams, R. (1974). *Television: Technology and Cultural Form*. Fontana.

Williams, R. (1975). *Culture and Society 1780–1950*. Penguin. (1958)

Williams, R. (1977). *Marxism and Literature*. Oxford University Press.

Winston, B. (1998). *Media, Technology, and Society – A History: From the Telegraph to the Internet*. Routledge.

Wittgenstein, L. (1953). *Philosophical Investigations*. Macmillan.

Yates, J., & Orlikowski, W. J. (1992). Genres of Organizational Communication: A Structurational Approach to Studying Communication and Media. *Academy of Management Review*, *17*(2), 299–326.

Ytreberg, E. (2022). *Media and Events in History*. Polity.

Zhao, Y. (2012). Understanding China's Media System in a World Historical Context. In D. C. Hallin & P. Mancini (Eds.), *Comparing Media Systems Beyond the Western World* (pp. 143–174). Cambridge University Press.

Zimmermann, J. (2015). *Hermeneutics: A Very Short Introduction*. Oxford University Press.

Zuboff, S. (2019). *The Age of Surveillance Capitalism: The Fight for a Human Future at the New Frontier of Power*. Public Affairs.

Index

For Product Safety Concerns and Information please contact our EU
representative GPSR@taylorandfrancis.com
Taylor & Francis Verlag GmbH, Kaufingerstraße 24, 80331 München, Germany

www.ingramcontent.com/pod-product-compliance
Lightning Source LLC
Chambersburg PA
CBHW050347270326
41926CB00016B/3640

* 9 7 8 1 0 3 2 6 5 5 0 4 8 *